mylène rémy and
jean-claude klotchkoff

ghana
today

translated by j.s. kundra

**84 color photograph pages
by olivier blaise
except when mentioned
9 maps and circuits**

LES EDITIONS DU
JAGUAR

summary   # panorama

town by town site by site

the ghanaian journey

panorama

the land and its people

■ Accra, the capital city of Ghana, is progressively emerging as a centre for international encounters such as the Conference of Non-Aligned Nations, held in September 1991. For a while foreign visitors were notably absent in Accra's streets, but since 1985-86 a steady stream of foreigners has given business to new hotels like Novotel, North Ridge, Sunrise and Shangri-La.

It would be erroneous to conclude that "broni," — the Ghanaians' affectionate nickname for Westerners — are unwelcome. Ghana's hospitality is legendary, and whatever their race, religion, nationality or the colour of their skin, visitors can be certain of being received with both warmth and sincerity.

Until very recently, tourism has simply lacked the possibilities for real development. An old proverb states that before building a guest room, it is first necessary to construct the house. In this case, the house in question covers an area of 239,460 square kilometres and comprises 15 million inhabitants.

Ghana's first president, Dr. Kwame Nkrumah, was determined that it should be built without reliance on foreign aid.

From the Gold Coast to Ghana

The desire for national autonomy and the determination to become a leader among West Africa's developing nations was clearly manifested on March 6, 1957, when Ghana celebrated the simultaneous birth of its freedom and that of its new national identity.

The Gold Coast originally received its name from Europeans lured to its shores by the country's fabulous wealth. In choosing to call itself Ghana, the fledgling nation consciously associated its identity with that of a fabled empire which had left an indelible imprint upon the history and peoples of sub-Saharan Africa.

The choice further reflected the new nation's refusal of immobility in favour of dynamic action and the right to self-determination rather than a passive acceptance of the status quo. This policy also implied taking the risks and responsibilities of error as well as success.

Geographically, the regions comprising the present-day state of Ghana were never part of the ancient empire, even if some of its original ethnic groups are believed to have migrated to Ghana's territory following the empire's disintegration. This is suggested by several of the traditions of the Akans, Ghana's largest ethnic group. One interesting coincidence concerns the mystical relationship that the Akans maintain with gold. Similarly, the power and prestige of the ancient emperors was essentially based upon their possession of large quantities of the precious metal, to the point that a contemporary Arab historian wrote that « their horses were tethered to posts of solid gold. » This coincidence is perhaps the distant echo of the quasi-supernatural qualities accorded by the ancient emperors to the metal, as embodied in the legends that the emigrants brought to their new homeland.

The fact remains that for better and occasionally for worse, an unbroken thread of gold traverses Ghana's entire history, from the ancient empire that was her namesake to the present-day modern state. The symbol of the traditional chiefs who used it in the insignia and objects that constituted their environment (beginning with the sacred ancestor stools representing their ongoing presence), gold is also present in the streams and soil of the so-aptly named "Gold Coast".

Nevertheless, when Kwame Nkrumah decided to restore the ancestral link, gold had lost much of its primordial economic role. The new president thus counted much more on the revenues generated by massive exportations of cocoa, timber and the huge Akosombo hydroelectric complex on the Volta River to develop Ghana's economy and achieve his objective of transforming the country into a leader of the African continent, totally liberated from colonialism. Unfortunately, this would take longer than he had foreseen...

With the passage of time and ideological currents, Ghana has successfully confronted innumerable challenges to its ongoing stability and immense potential as a developing nation. But in the space of ten short years, the government has nevertheless succeeded in overcoming many of the largest obstacles to development and progress. At present, the nation is well on the way to becoming one of West Africa's major powers. However, like the empire whose name Ghana bears, an empire whose diplomatic, commercial and cultural exchanges extended to its surrounding neighbours, Asia and even Europe, the leaders of present-day Ghana are committed to a policy of peace and fruitful cooperation both with the world at large and the sister-nations of the African subcontinent.

Overleaf:
These massive and colourfully decorated ocean-going canoes of Abandze near Cape Coast are skilfully manned by local fishermen who maneuver them safely through the turbulent surf of the bar.

In this respect, it is no coincidence that Ghana's highway system links Accra to Ouagadougou, the capital of Burkina-Faso, as well as to Lome, Togo's capital city. And with the recent construction of a modern freeway from Accra to Abidjan, the capital of the Ivory Coast, it can be said that the cause of inter-African unity has never had a more dynamic champion than Ghana. Even if present-day Ghana appears to foreign observers as the modern West African state that Kwame Nkrumah had dreamed of, this transformation is due to the ten full years of analysis and hard work accomplished by the team led by Flight-Lieutenant Rawlings. And once again, almost as if predestined, gold — the symbol of the traditional chiefs both past and present, upon whose prestige the state continues to draw much of its authority — has regained its ancestral position in the country's economy. Far from having disappeared, the precious metal is once again becoming Ghana's leading source of mineral wealth, thanks to dynamic policies of prospection and extraction.

Ghanaian pragmatism

The historical link has thus been re-established in all of its former significance, emphasising one of the most attaching qualities of the Ghanaian population : pride and fidelity to their past, customs and traditions that no visitor desirous of understanding the people and their country can afford to ignore.

But this fidelity to the past should not be considered as being all-encompassing. It is true that a great number of traditional ceremonies ranging from the dances performed at funeral celebrations to the golden pomp accompanying the coronation of a new king continue to attract admiring visitors from all over the world. At the same time, Accra lawyers and Kumasi and Tema businessmen are as likely to appear in the halls of an ultra-modern hotel or pursuing their occupations in a Western-tailored suit as with the traditional toga-like garment draped across their shoulder.

This flexible, pragmatic attitude, capable of harmonizing immemorial tradition with modern imperatives can be seen in all aspects of contemporary life in Ghana. If the coastal fortifications constructed by the successive waves of European colonial governments represent a reminder of an era blighted by slavery, the memories of this bitter legacy have nevertheless been definitively relegated to the distant past. On a lighter note, the same spirit can be seen in the unique *posuban* altars constructed by the warriors of the Fanti area in the southwest upon which the ancestors of the present-day inhabitants used to pray for victory before a battle. The statues adorning these altars are inspired by local religious traditions as well as Biblical characters and even the European colonials themselves, right down to their warships and Victorian clock-towers !

The Ghanaians, with their highly-developed commercial instincts, have always known how to observe the essential and make the most of it.

And if it has been argued that a close relationship often exists between the land and its inhabitants, then this is particularly true of Ghana, whose unlimited horizons and often breathtaking vistas perfectly reflect the open, outward-looking spirit of her people.

According to geography manuals, the topography of Ghana is a fairly straight-forward affair. A series of broad coastal plains run from Sekondi on the west to the Togolese border on the east, narrowing as they approach Accra. Dominating the seacoast of western Ghana, the plains gradually descend to the Volta River Delta, where they transform into a series of jagged, rocky eminences called "inselbergs" because of their resemblance to islands jutting out of the sea.

Above these plains, the eastern half of the country is almost entirely formed by the Voltaian Basin. The land is comprised of sandstone and other varieties of friable rock, with altitudes rarely exceeding one hundred metres. The basin is dominated by the Gambaga Escarpment to the north, on the southwest by the Kwahu Plateau, whose southern edge is ringed by sheer cliffs, and from south to east, the arc of the hills of Akwapim and Togo.

With altitudes ranging from 200 to 300 metres, the plains of the savanna are dotted by occasional inselbergs and rounded hills. The savanna occupies the entire northwest of the region and culminates along the border of Burkina-Faso and the Ivory Coast. On the west, the savanna gives way to a pre-Cambrian plateau of roughly the same elevation, covered by forests and pierced with deep gorges. The plateau widens as it slopes down to the coast to join the Kwahu Plateau on the east.

Geographers also claim that Ghana's average altitude is less than a few

Future skippers... Children playing in
the surf of Kpone Beach near Tema...
The handmade boats are miniature versions
of their fathers' canoes
which they will one day be sailing themselves.

hundred metres, and that its highest peaks rarely attain one hundred metres. The visitor, however, will quickly see things quite differently.

From Accra, the plain seems to roll eastward like an ocean. Nevertheless, just outside of Accra, stand a number of the celebrated inselbergs in all of their stunning height and despite their relatively modest elevation. Whether isolated — and hence all the more impressive — or grouped together as in the Shai Hills (which are in themselves steep enough to satisfy would-be alpinists), the inselbergs are an unforgettable sight.

The horizons to the north of Accra are dominated by the crests of the Akwapim Hills. A glance at a roadmap reveals that the highway begins to twist into a series of hairpin curves, and that the relief is definitely becoming what can be qualified as mountainous.

In the west of Ghana, however, kilometre upon kilometre unwind before one encounters the merest ripple or rise in the flat landscape.

From one end of Ghana to the other, the situation is similarly unpredictable. The briefest itinerary will include its unexpected hill or even range of hills, rugged or rounded to varying degrees, and whose appearances change in relation to the stone itself. This ranges from the most friable to the most resistant, and includes light-beige limestone to black granite shot through with reds.

If what some maps indicate were absolutely true, there would be little difference in the relief between Ghana's escarpments and her mountain ranges. Here again, the maps are wrong, since the horizon of these regions constantly changes its outlines, and just when one least expects it, an indented crown of varying widths, its slopes more or less wooded, rings a town, lake or valley. Sometimes the highway appears to follow the plain, and then unexpectedly begins to rise to the edge of a prominence offering a plunging view over vast, apparently endless expanses. Once again, the mountains assert their presence by capriciously-shaped boulders recalling human or animal forms that confer a startling appearance to the landscape. In many places, the combination of rocky forms and wind-swept trees produce stunning natural sculptures that might well have been created by a particularly inspired surrealist artist. Elsewhere, the rocky landscape winds upward like a strange stairway to the heavens, or forms hollows where the oblique rays of the sun produce constantly-shifting zones of shadow and light.

It's as if a talented set designer has made an all-out effort to captivate the visitor's attention, with each individual scene bringing its own perfect climax, preceded and followed by periods of calm, since such protracted intensity would otherwise soon become unbearable.

An ever-changing coastline

For 560 kilometres along Ghana's coastline, sandy beaches and rocky bluffs alternately follow and meet along the Gulf of Guinea, but nowhere is their contrast more striking than at Accra. To the west of the capital, in the mist and spray produced by the breakers dashing relentlessly against the shore, the visitor is confronted by sandy expanses surrounded by dunes. If one leaves the shoreline and then returns two or three kilometres further up, one comes upon new landscapes of staggering wilderness whose rocky, rugged coastline stands proudly aloof above the seething waves.

All along the route to the Ivory Coast, sand and stone alternate in endless combinations, with no two landscapes alike.

On the east, the cliffs give way to a horizontal shoreline. But their rough outlines seem to spread across the landscape like great shadows. The very land seems to be bursting under the pressure of both fresh and salt water, as it subsides into lagoons, and lets the arms of the Volta infiltrate at will. And now we come to the most impressive spot of all, despite its total lack of relief... or rather because of its relief in reverse.

Here the ground, lower than sea level, is protected only by a sand bank that is being increasingly threatened by the sea as the years pass. At Keta, a city martyrized by the sea, the waves have already destroyed the fields and habitations.

All along the Gulf of Guinea, at varying distances from the shore, the ocean rises and forms enormous breakers that dash violently against the sandy bottom, sucking it in and dragging it along. Depending on the direction of the current, this suction, which exerts considerable force, is destructive to differing degrees. At Keta the sandy, friable soil is attacked head-on. Elsewhere, it puts up a stiffer resistance to the waves that sidle in on the bias, or is protected by rocky cliffs sturdy enough to hold out against the strength of the currents.

However, wherever a river empties into the ocean, the ocean cuts into the cliff, and behind the foaming line of the bar, forms a vast mouth whose motionless surface contrasts with the agitation of the sea. On the west, the steep coast is indented with bays, entirely protected from the bar by a shield of rocks upon which the sea harmlessly crashes.

In the heart of the Ashanti homeland, the strange lake of Bosumtwi receives the waters of the surrounding streams without ever relinquishing them, and thus keeps inexorably filling up. With this single exception, all the Ghana's major rivers cast themselves into the ocean, carving out channels along the way that occasionally blossom out into veritable gorges. Although this is the case for the permanent streams, many of the northern waterways are fed only by rains. These fall hard throughout a single season lasting from July to October, which is sometimes delayed or ends too soon. Consequently, the impetuous torrents that submerge the roadways for a few weeks vanish as fast as they appeared. In the south, the rains are spaced from May through November, with an extremely variable let-up in July or August. Not only do the rivers have a fairly steady volume of water throughout the year, but particularly in the southwest, where humidity and rain are permanent features, they form a relatively dense network. There are permanent rivers even in the north. One of them is the Volta, the uncontested but three-headed sovereign, since it springs from three points and takes the name of Black, White or Red Volta before merging into a single waterway and shedding its adjectives.

The three Voltas

The Black Volta used to be completely independent and flowed blithely on its way after serving — as it still does today — as a western border between Ghana and Burkina-Faso. Prior to the construction of the Akosombo hydroelectric complex, the Black Volta emptied straight into the ocean near the Tano River. On the other side, i.e., the northeast, the White Volta has always flowed obliquely into Ghana, almost immediately joining forces with the Red Volta and after a sizable loop, flowing back eastward to finish its course at Ada. One of its tributaries, which flowed from west to east, gradually captured the waters of the Black Volta and carried them off with its own, to feed the course of the White Volta; the latter proceeded to do the same thing with the little Tain River, a tributary of the Tano. The question which then arose was, which was the tributary of which? So as not vex either of them, their combined flow was dubbed the Volta. This "kidnapping" explains why the Black Volta, when it is about halfway through Ghana, seems to change its course and veer sharply east.

Ghost streams and gangster rivers

The forest region does not lack for streams merely because two of them happen to have been spirited away.

The Tano, whose source is south of Techiman, forms a border between Ghana and the Ivory Coast, from where it flows into the sea. Although much shorter, the Ankobra River has the time to become majestic and to divide up into two arms before emptying into the sea west of Axim. The Pra winds its way down from the Kwahu Plateau, sets off in a westernly direction and preens itself to admiring gazes from the ramparts of Fort Shama, a few kilometres east of Sekondi.

All three of these rivers receive multiple tributaries. But it is pointless to try to decide which flows into which, because the Tano and the Ankobra wage a close contest to see which can capture the greatest number of tributaries, and no one can predict how this war of attrition will finally end.

Farther east, the two main rivers are the Ayensu, navigable along almost its full length as far as Winneba, and the Densu, which supplies Accra with drinking water.

Whatever their volume of water, these rivers are virtually inaccessible to ship traffic, since they are cut by rapids at various places. However, they have always been plied regionally by pirogues, whose owners use them to traverse impenetrable forest areas or for fishing.

Motorists catch only fleeting glimpses of them because the roads — which are still rare in the southwest — almost never follow the stream beds. They can only dream of trips on silent boats that would be the sole means of really viewing the near-virgin forest and the life that goes on there, since the smallest roadway would bring about irreversible changes in no time.

However, navigation along considerable distances is not unheard of in the interior of Ghana, especially since a gigantic dam at Akosombo has spawned a huge lake constituted by the mingled waters of the three Voltas.

The original purpose of this lake was not to link several regions of the country but rather, through the dam and its hydroelectric power plant, to double the national energy output. Whatever the reasons may have been, the upshot is the same: a lake 400 kilometres long, representing almost two-thirds of the country, since 672 kilometres separate the northern border from the coast, has metamorphosed the entire eastern central part of Ghana. Navigable throughout, it offers the visitor a different approach from the one he usually gets, if only by an infinitely more restful pace than that of driving.

It takes over two days to complete the entire distance, and this lets you glide gently from the forest area to the savanna region as soon as you reach the port of Keta-Krachi, the halfway mark. Be sure to stand back far enough to see the shapes of the hills of Togo and the Kwahu Plateau looming up behind you.

Diversity of plant life

With regard to plant life, Ghana is divided into regions as clearly defined as those of its relief. The forest, which coincides with the pre-Cambrian Plateau, is divided into two parts.

On the southwest stands the tropical forest, the real one, the one that children dream of because they imagine it as impenetrable and mysterious, with its gigantic, age-old trees bound with lianas and countless parasitical plants, and the thick, never-shedding foliage that gives it an air of immutability.

A short distance farther east, toward the plains and Lake Volta, there is a forest of slightly smaller, less densely packed trees, some of them deciduous during the dry season.

Actually, in both cases one factor has triggered a significant change in the plant life, i.e., the introduction and the subsequent large scale cultivation of cocoa. What was spared by the cocoa plantations has been worked by the timber industry. When the felling isn't too concentrated, the trees have a chance to grow back to almost normal height. Near the towns and main highways, on the other hand, the rotation is fast, and the forest stands less tall, while the number of clearings devoted to crops increase.

The wooded savanna represents practically all the rest of the country, with three exceptions: the largely bare coastal plains, which will increasingly be planted with various crops as irrigation is extended; the Volta Delta, with a rim of mangroves intermingled with coconut palms and inland, fields and pasturelands ; lastly, the rectangle stretching eastward between Lake Volta and the border from Ho and the hills of Togo, comprising a semi-deciduous forest zone.

The savanna and its metamorphoses

According to certain textbooks, the characteristic of the savanna is that it is sparsely wooded, except along the banks of streams and near the forest zone.

The above statement proves that certain geographers don't know how to observe. In Ghana, these vast expanses of land shaded by sparse trees give an impression of amazing diversity. Like Japanese gardens whose every element is necessary and sufficient, the savanna landscapes, forever uncluttered, never empty, enhance the outlines of every tree, hill, rock and the balanced mass of dwellings, consistently on a human scale, whose shapes and colours offer a profound correspondence with those of the surrounding countryside.

This is true even in the least favourable season, when the leaves have dried or fallen and when, in these stark compositions, you can rely only on the outlandish shape of a baobab trunk or the sheer lines of branches etched sharply against the deep blue sky.

During the rainy season and immediately after it, for approximately six months of the year, the savanna is one unbroken stretch of fairyland. With their foliage restored, the trees regain their distinctive appearance. Even people whose knowledge of botany is non-existent note the extraordinary numbers of different species. In the acacia family alone there are dozens of closely related species with differing sizes, blossoms, and even fragrances, all of whose nuances stand out with particular clarity, since each specimen is distinctly separate from the others.

The houses, whose ochre and black tones have been receding into the landscape, now begin making the most of the contrasts, and emerge against backgrounds of tall grasses and variegated plants, each of which contributes its par-

*If certain stretches of Lake Volta
in eastern Ghana appear to be infinite,
other portions resemble a labyrinth
dotted with an endless number
of islands and inlets.*

ticular note to this green symphony. The savanna is the triumph of individualism, since although certain trees of similar species do sometimes grow in clusters, they seldom mingle with others, thereby obliging the beholder to become aware of their personality. And since the forest undergrowth is never dense, and the sun — seldom absent for long — penetrates every nook and cranny, the savanna is also the triumph of ubiquitous light and skies with a kaleidoscope of clouds.

A magic universe

If the savanna in Ghana is exceptionally lovely, tribute must also be paid to the forest. Despite logging activities, in most places it is still so dense that when one drives through rapidly, the various species seem to merge into an anonymous mass. The scene changes the minute the driver agrees to become a pedestrian and to discover things on foot.

In this continuously rugged relief, the top of a hill or a deep valley allow you to catch your breath, occasionally taken away by humidity that can easily become oppressive. By following the trails through this tangle of vegetation, you can easily distinguish the countless riches concealed in its midst, which it reveals only gradually. The forest can be a source of concern: under the ferns, grasses, lianas and the occasionally gigantic flowers lurks a whole world of insects and animals about which one knows nothing. For a stranger, coming face to face with this world and moving through it can require a physical effort and no small amount of courage. But this is the price to be paid. Otherwise the forest yields up nothing, or next to nothing.

You can go back twenty times to the same place and, twenty times, come across some new plant or insect whose existence you hadn't even suspected. In the Kibi Hills northwest of Accra, naturalists could live out a whole career without discovering all the local riches: some of these naturalists are smitten with the enchanted forest in the same way that they might be with an indifferent mistress, impossible to dominate.

On his very first venture into this or any other Ghanaian forest, the visitor will experience a fascination that intensifies with time. The forest is a melting pot whence emerge all the myths — or are they truths? — relating to the supernatural world, and if the savanna suggests a single God, the forest imposes the idea that this single God is surrounded by multiple, autonomous forces. The savanna is an artistic success, a beckoning toward, and link with, all the unknowns that lurk in every human being.

Unfortunately, like animals that gradually become extinct, the forest, reduced by the spread of plantations, cities, and the development of highway networks, disappears if nothing is done to protect it. In Ghana, as in most countries, awareness of the dangers represented by man's lack of respect of nature has long existed.

The Game and Wildlife Department, under the Ministry of Lands and Natural Resources, was set up to combat this danger. It is headed by an official available for interviews in Accra, although the Department's headquarters are at Damongo, in the Northern Region, at the gateway to Mole National Park.

The conservation of wildlife

However, the Department's approach differs somewhat from the one generally adopted in other countries, in that although it does its utmost to protect endangered species and encourage the multiplication of wildlife, there are also certain natural laws which are respected.

In the wild, the laws of hunting are universal between animals, including the family of the carnivorae, who cannot subsist without slaying other beasts. Man is not wholly carnivorous, but meat is part of his diet.

Consequently, Ghana's authorities allow the country's inhabitants — under certain conditions designed to preserve a vital equilibrium and when the animals have sufficiently multiplied — to supplement their frequently inadequate meat supply by killing wild game. In any event, what has depleted wildlife is not so much hunting for food as it is hunting for sport — if the word sport can be applied to the activity of people who use vehicles to pursue animals, as has often been the case.

Another contributing factor in the disappearance of fauna has been the transformation or elimination of natural habitats. For this reason, the Department began by delineating huge areas with intact flora, or areas whose ecological balance could be rapidly restored, so as to preserve or restore this habitat.

But the Department's plan is also to

develop animal life in these parks and reserves for tourist purposes. It is common knowledge that Westerners are drawn to Africa by the prospect of viewing wildlife unknown in their own countries.

National parks and wildlife reserves

At present, the only animal reserve that is organized for tourism is Mole National Park, located in northwest Ghana. Featuring a comfortable motel, a road system and Land Rover rental, Mole Park's ideally-located viewing shelter offers visitors the opportunity of observing antelope, monkeys, lions, elephants, buffalo and leopards at close range both day and night.

Mole Park currently consists of 519,000 hectares and was created in 1971, as was the Shai Hills Game Production Reserve. Situated northeast of Accra and covering some 5,180 hectares, the Shai Hills Reserve offers few possibilities for visitor accommodation. Camping is nevertheless permitted, and horses may be rented for excursions.

The 312,600-hectare Digya National Park was also created in 1971. Bordered on the north, east and south by Lake Volta, the park can only be accessed by boat. Wildlife is somewhat scarce, but spectacular, and includes elephants, buffalo, panthers and various species of antelope. In the same region, and also created in 1971, the Kogyae District Nature Reserve comprises 32,400 hectares essentially destined for agricultural and botanical research.

Located near Wenchi, between the northern provinces and the Brong-Ahafo Region, the 207,360 hectares of Bui National Park run parallel to the Ivory Coast. Although the roads are far from satisfactory, Bui offers visitors the opportunity of viewing the largest hippo population in Ghana. Water sports and improved visitor accommodation are expected to be available soon.

Accessible from Kumasi, Bia National Park was enlarged to 7,780 hectares in 1977. Largely comprised of secondary-growth forest after intensive farming destroyed much of the original vegetation, Bia is a haven for elephants, monkeys, leopards and birds. Visitor accommodation is non-existent, as are roads, and the only way of exploring the park is by foot.

Located near Tumu in the savanna of northwestern Ghana, Gbele Game Production Reserve occupies 54,690 hectares and contains a limited wildlife population.

With a comparable range of wildlife as Bia, Ankasa Game Production Reserve (30,740 hectares) and Nini-Suhien National Park (10,630 hectares) were created in 1976. Located in the tropical forests of western Ghana, both reserves can be accessed by Mpabata.

Kalakpa Game Production Reserve (32,440 hectares), located in the Volta Region and a few kilometres from the Accra-Ho highway, offers a dense forest inhabited by almost the same animal population as Mole Park, with the exception of elephants and lions.

The Bomfobiri and Owabi Wildlife Sanctuaries (5,180 and 7,260 hectares respectively) are both located in Ashanti territory, in a transitional, lightly-wooded region lying between the savannas and the tropical forest. Although totally lacking roads and visitor accommodations, both sanctuaries offer a wide variety of bird life, monkeys and small antelope.

Although Wli Falls, located on the Togolese border can be reached by car, its 1,200 hectares are limited to visitors on foot, and the gathering of wildflowers or fruits is prohibited.

Boabeng-Fiemi Sanctuary, situated to the east of the Kintampo-Nkoranza axis in the Brong-Ahafo Region, is celebrated for its black and white-furred colobus monkeys, considered by the local inhabitants as being protective spirits and allowed free run of their homes during the day.

Innumerable animal species

The recently-created Kakum and Assin-Attandanso Reserves, located between Cape Coast and Elmina in central Ghana, offer 420 square kilometres of semi-deforestated tropical heartland. Long the site of logging operations, a recent study revealed the presence of innumerable animal species, certain of which were on the verge of extinction. These include the forest elephant and buffalo, the bongo (a rare variety of antelope), panthers, colobus monkeys, a wide variety of birds and reptiles, including Nile crocodiles and a wide range of tropical flora. Both reserves have been given a highly-protected status with hunting and logging completely prohibited. These measures are also expected to protect the Kakum River, which is the region's main source of potable water.

The funds allocated for the creation of these nature reserves will be obtained in part from foreign debtors who have agreed to donate debts owed them by Ghana toward these nature conservation efforts.

In the southeast Volta Region, another wildlife sanctuary is being planned for the Hohoe area.

Hiking is both authorized and even recommended in all of the above-mentioned parks and reserves, despite the presence of potentially dangerous wildlife. The only prerequisite is the presence of an armed guide to ensure visitors' safety, and to prevent them from inadvertently provoking attacks. The Wildlife Department officials deserve praise for having adopted this policy, which provides the opportunity of a direct and non-destructive contact with wildlife which is unique in Africa.

The development of tourism

For many years, tourism was not a major government priority in Ghana. The first official policies were outlined by the Ghana Tourist Corporation, created in 1968. In November 1973, a decree led to the transformation of the Tourist Corporation into the Ghana Tourist Control Board and the subsequent creation of the Tourist Development Company. The first agency was responsible for defining overall goals and solutions, as well as for the promotion of Ghanaian tourism abroad, while the second served as a financing structure.

Tourist accommodation was managed by the State Hotels Corporation, which ran seven luxury hotels in the Accra-Tema area (572 rooms), plus three hotels in Kumasi (70 rooms), Takoradi (70 rooms) and Akosombo (40 rooms). The State Hotels Corporation also controlled a number of rest houses located outside the capital, for a total of 82 rooms.

Government policies concerning tourism and tourist accommodation have radically changed since. The promotion of tourism, which became a top-priority objective following the creation of a ten-year development plan in 1985, is currently the responsibility of the Ministry of Trade and Tourism. The government is privatizing many state-owned hotels, including the Star, Continental, and Ambassador in Accra, the Atlantic in Takoradi, the City Hotel of Kumasi and the rest houses of Kumasi, Cape Coast, Sunyani and Bolgatanga. The first three

*Environmental concern in Ghana has led
the governement to create a number of nature reserves
across the country. In many of them,
African wildlife such as antelope, crocodiles, elephants
and lions may be approached at close range.*

hotels, currently undergoing renovation, have already been acquired by private owners. The Continental, located on the Accra airport highway and renamed the Golden Tulip, has already opened. The two remaining hotels should be open for business in early 1992, while the rest houses are still in operation and awaiting purchasers. The State Hotels Corporation itself will be dissolved following the sale of its remaining property.

Private initiative and investment

It is obvious that concerning tourism, the Ghanaian government is following the same policy of private initiative and investment that it is applying to almost every other sector. The laxity of public officials that led to the closing of Accra's largest hotels has convinced the government of the necessity of conferring management and upkeep to the private rather than to the public sector.

The encouragement of privately-owned tourist infrastructures has led to the creation of the Ghana Hotels Association, comprised of 420 establishments nationally. Similar professional associations are being created to defend the collective interests of night-clubs, bars, restaurants, travel and tour agencies and even the local artisans.

In 1988, a Novotel was built in the centre of Accra and was consisting of 200 rooms, plus a swimming pool and a business support centre. The hotel was financed by a combination of foreign loans and private investment, including that of Ghana Tourist Development Company. In the same year, the smaller (36-room) but luxurious Shangri-La hotel also opened. Offering a swimming pool, polo grounds, a health centre and sauna facilities, the hotel is located near the Accra airport. Both the Novotel and Shangri-La are rated three-star, while the Golden Tulip, also located near the airport but closer to the centre city, is in the four-star category following its renovation. Other four or five-stars establishments include the Star, Ambassador and Labadi Beach Hotels, with the latter offering 100 rooms, four suites, a pool, a health club, squash and tennis courts and a business centre.

Located on Labadi Beach to the east of Accra, facing the International Trade Fair grounds and the Tema Port highway, the Labadi Beach Hotel will un-doubtedly attract a privileged clientele of international businessmen.

Accra currently offers more than a dozen two - and three-star hotels totalling 491 rooms, as well as numerous smaller one-star establishments. The greater Accra area, including the Tema Port and industrial complex, has a total capacity of 1,674 rooms. Outside of Accra, hotel categories rarely exceed two-star levels in the regional capitals, with the exception of Akosombo, where the Volta Hotel is scheduled to achieve three-star status following its renovation. A project for the construction of a four-star Pullman Hotel located on Lake Volta and featuring a French restaurant, conference and water sports facilities is also underway in Akosombo.

Another important project concerns the development of the Brenu Akyinm beachfront, ten kilometres to the east of Elmina. Shaded by coconut trees and protected by a low reef offering ideal swimming conditions, the development of the three-kilometre beach is part of a regional programme which includes the renovation of the Elmina and Cape Coast fortresses and the construction of guest houses and hotel complexes.

The twenty-six fortresses constructed on Ghana's coast from the fourteenth to the eighteenth centuries also possess immense potential for development as hotels. Some, in fact, have long served as rest-houses offering varying degrees of comfort, but always marvellously situated.

Living in the villages

For visitors attracted to Ghana by the beauty of its landscapes, the authenticity of its traditions and the hospitality of its inhabitants, the ideal solution is the rest-house. Providing contact on a human scale while preserving the integrity of the surrounding villages, it can only be hoped that certain minor improvements for increasing visitor comfort will be undertaken in the near future, and in particular, the addition of restaurants and food shops.

Since the regional capitals serve as the base for numerous excursions towards the interior, a massive effort is underway to develop an expanded hotel infrastructure offering 5,500 international-class rooms and 4,300 more modestly-appointed lodgings. The number of visitors to Ghana is expected to rise from 145,000 in 1990 (of which 60,000 were non-African) to 334,000 by the middle of the decade.

The availability of luxury hotels will never replace the unique experience of lodging in the villages themselves, an experience which provides an unforgettable contact with the richness and cultural diversity of Ghana's numerous ethnic groups. To get to know the people, and to understand the Ghanaian's justifiable pride in his nation and traditions, there is no substitute for a chat with a village chief, a local artisan or one of the outgoing and hospitable inhabitants.

The ethnic families

The diversity of Ghana's ethnic groups is actually less than it seems, for numerous groups have gradually emerged from a single ethnic family which generally made its appearance in the country via small successive migrations and infraethnic transformations.

The circumstances — different forms of environment, contacts with the autochthonous population who fled from or mingled with the new-comers — ultimately resulted in "relative" divergencies that were accentuated to varying degrees in languages and customs. But the similarities persisting amid certain differences permit the identification of common origins.

The Accra Region — before the capital had attracted so many people from all the other regions — was largely occupied by the Ga. The Ga share the same origin as the Adangbe, who arrived in Ghana with them and who split up into the Ada — on the Volta Delta — the Shai, and the Krobo. The Shai, after long occupying the hills of the same name northeast of Accra, gradually fanned out over the coastal plain. The Krobo live on the eastern rim of the Kwahu Plateau, reaching to the west bank of the Volta.

But the Ga also found on site a people of a different origin who were fairly mysterious — the Kpesi, belonging to the Guan group. Despite almost total assimilation, they nevertheless have had a marked influence on the Ga group.

The Guan are found scattered far and wide over the land. Are they autochthons belonging, as certain scholars claim, to the Akan group, which they may have preceded? It's a moot question. The fact remains that they speak a language that is all their own and that juxtaposes itself in many places to the language of the majority.

This is the case in the western region, occupied by Akan communities such as the Nzima, in the far west, the Ahanta, and the Fanti, who dwell between the Pra River and the limits of Greater Accra. In towns like Winneba and Senya Beraku, the language and certain customs of the Guan coexist with those of the Fanti.

The Akan family includes many other groups in addition to those along the coast, since it has spread to the edges of the northern region and has consequently peopled the entire forest, from north to south and from the western border to the limits of the eastern region, where they cohabit with the Krobo.

Among these groups, mention should be made of the Ashanti, whose name has been given to one of the nine administrative regions; of the Adanse; the Denkyera, farther south; the Akwamu; the Akim, on the east; and the Brong, on the north.

On the other side of the Volta, the Delta as well as a major part of the Togo Hills are occupied by the Ewe. But north of the Volta Region there are numerous small groups whose members fled from the wars waged by the more powerful ethnic groups in Ghana and Togo.

In the midst of the Ewe territory live the Avatime, probably of Guan origin, who fled from the Ahanta on the west coast and followed the ocean shore to Prampram, eventually settling in the mountains north of Ho.

The Northern and Upper Regions also have a wide variety of populations, some of which share a common origin that harks back to more or less ancient times.

A wide variety of population

From south to north, there are first of all the Gonja. These are Mande people from the Sahel who probably belonged to the Mali empire. They made their way into the territory by repulsing the Guan and the Dagomba, who settled in the east, as well as the Nanumba, to whom they are closely related. The Mamprusi group, whose ancestors are the same as those of the Dagomba and Nanumba, are found up to northern and northeastern borders, where its members cohabit with several minorities: east of the White Volta are the Konkomba, on the Togolese border, considered as autochthons, or in any event as having taken up residence prior to the Mamprusi; the Kusala, at Bawku; and the Nateba, the Koma, and the Chamba. West of the river, the

*Rising proudly above the ghanaian
costline, the fortress of Elmina
is one of the most
impressive vestiges
of Ghana's colonial era.*

Frafra occupy the Bolgatanga Region, while the Talensi have taken refuge in the Tongo Mountains, a few kilometres southeast of this town. Farther to the west, the Sissala include a small Dagati nucleus. But the bulk of the Dagati settled a little farther south, along the western border despite the presence of a few Lobi enclaves.

This ethnic diversity represents what seems to be a wide variety of religious beliefs. However, analysis of the divergencies yields deeper analogies.

From animism to monotheism

By and large, the coastal regions, which for centuries were in contact with the Westerners and their missionaries, have been almost entirely converted to Christianity. Since these missionaries belonged to different confessions, the result is that virtually all Protestant sects are represented, as well as the Catholics.

Conversely, the north was almost totally won over to Islam, initially through the influence of caravaneers from the banks of the Niger, who had long had contacts with the Arabs, and later subsequent to the settling of Mande groups in the area.

In the central region, Christian and Islamic faiths coexit with animism. But does the latter ever entirely vanish from the soul of a Ghanaian? Besides, why should it disappear if it is not incompatible with monotheistic religions?

It is a widespread opinion that animism is often associated with the worship of numerous gods.

It would be more accurate to say that the Ghanaian believes in a single supreme being, the creator of the world, but that this God seems to him a power too important to be importuned by the petty concerns of human beings. Ghanaians hence pray to deities who are either subordinate to this supreme God or who simply represent Him in His multiple aspects. For a Ghanaian, God is everywhere and present in all things.

But although the concept of God can vary from one Ghanaian to the next, there is total unanimity concerning the attitude toward ancestors, whose invisi-

THE SPIRIT OF TRADITIONAL CELEBRATIONS

■ *Whatever the region, and excepting family celebrations such as baptisms, marriages or burial services, all other celebrations held by the inhabitants of a given locality or even an entire ethnic group are generally based on three common beliefs. The first concerns the homage paid to the distant ancestors who founded the clan, as for example, King Osei Tutu of the Ashantis, whose golden stool which originally served as the altar for ritual sacrifices has since become a symbol of the continuity of the clan itself. The annual celebration serves to reaffirm the historical links between the past and present, while at the same time reminding the ancestors of their duty to guide and protect their present-day descendants.*

The celebration is always accompanied by rites of purification which enable the clan to face the future with confidence, particularly since part of the ritual includes a collective discussion in which the year's conflicts and quarrels are aired and pardoned. The social importance of such customs are obvious, since they represent an institutionalized yet informal means of resolving the pent-up tensions and misunderstandings among the individuals and families of the clan. The possibility of being able to speak one's mind often results in the person's seeing either that the grievances are unjustified or of receiving an explanation on the

ble but constant presence ensures vital protection.

The true owners of the land

However, one must perform rites enabling ancestors to enjoy a proper existence in a Great Beyond that is so near (in every sense of the word) to daily life. The ancestors remain the true owners of the land which the living enjoy. This means that the latter conserve inalienable rights to their ancestors' property, but that they cannot sell it under risk of incurring the anger and resentment of the spirit to whom it belongs.

Independently from the ancestors whom their descendants have known personally, there are the other more or less mythical forebears responsible for the origin of the clans. The clan is also a concept shared by all the ethnic groups.

A clan includes all the individuals who hark back to a common founding ancestor. Members of different clans may coexist in a given town or village. All the individuals who represent the same clan in a given settlement form a lineage, headed by the eldest male member. Every official representative of a lineage, or elder, is a member of a council that elects a chief from among the men of a particular lineage. As in European royal families, power is thus handed down within a favoured group. But in contrast with the Salic law and succession by primogeniture, the eldest sons sometimes enjoy no specific hereditary rights. In every lineage there are several possible candidates, while a chief convicted of a serious offense can be stripped of his powers by a council of elders and replaced by another member of the lineage.

Patrilineal or matrilineal filiation

One basic difference prevails between the Akan and the other ethnic groups: with the Akans, filiation within the lineage and the clan is via the women, whereas with the other groups, filiation is patrilineal. Every Akan belongs to the lineage and clan of his mother, or *abusua*, and a man's legacy is inherited

part of the "guilty" party which clears up the source of conflict, especially since the person or party addressed is expected to offer a justification for the acts in question.
Although the official pretext can be a celebration related to agricultural activities such as harvests or the anniversary of a given event, all are based on a common system of characteristics. An analysis of these ceremonies reveals similarities with certain elements found in Christian religion, such as a sense of communion, the worship of sanctified founders, confession, forgiveness and even a ritual sacrifice and communal partaking. Given such similarities, the ease by which it is possible to adopt the tenets of Christianity while still maintaining one's native religion is understandable. Although in past, the all-white Catholic and Protestant clergy formerly disapproved of such traditional celebrations, today the Ghanaian ecclesiatics see things quite differently. At present, it is common to actively participate in a traditional festival on Saturday and attend mass or a Protestant service on Sunday. It is just such cultural paradoxes which give Ghanaian life its inimitable charm.
Adapted from A.A. Opoku
Festivals of Ghana

not by his own children but by the children of his clan wherever they may be.

In the election of a new chief, the candidates are chosen not from among the sons of the deceased or outgoing chief but from among his uncles, his cousins on his mother's side, his brothers by the same mother, or his nephews who are the sons of his sisters.

This system of matrilineal filiation has resulted in a particular consideration for women, and the queen mothers have always enjoyed and retained a great influence in the choice of the successor to the stool (the sacred insignia of power) and even in the carrying out of everyday affairs.

This by no means implies that children have no ties with their fathers. In the view of the Akans, every living being obtains his material substance from his mother, and his spirit from his father. Alongside the *abusua*, or the clan founded on blood ties, the *ntoro* establishes filiation via the spirit, i.e., through the father, going all the way back to the initial — and usually supernatural founder.

The names designating the various geographically scattered Akan groups refer neither to clans nor to *ntoros*, but to classifications by states, meaning confederations of localities whose chiefs, for political reasons, have accepted a bond of vassalage with a paramount chief. They recognize his authority, but, like the elders of their own towns, they form a council of subchiefs, elect the paramount chief, and assist him with attending to the business of the confederation.

In consequence, and independently of the name of the state to which they belong, all the Akan people belong to one of the eight recognized clans, or *abusua* as well as to one of the eight recognized *ntoro*.

The role of chiefs in Ghana today

Far from seeking to eliminate these chiefs, the Ghanaian government recognizes their moral, social and political authority.

Since the creation of the State of Ghana, there have been various acts of parliament and decrees aimed at defining and guaranteeing the chief's functions. Thus, a 1972 decree ratified the previously approved creation of a national parliament of chiefs, which heads the regional associations. In consequence, the chiefs in all the regions hold responsibilities at various levels: in

*All the splendour of the ancient kingdoms, with their royal courts,
ceremonial orchestras and traditional art can still be seen
in Ghana, where chiefs and local sovereigns continue to play
an important role. (Upper and lower left: the Asantehene, or
supreme chief of the Ashanti and the King of the Walas).*

the traditional local councils in even the smallest settlements, in the regional associations and even in the national parliament. They also serve as government consultants, notably on matters concerning revisions of customary law. In his community, a chief enjoys the rank of importance corresponding to his personal worth. Ideally, he remains the social and political leader and is responsible for organizing the development of his town or region, in agreement, of course, with the national planning scheme.

In some cases he occupies an eminent position in the major state agencies, thereby forming an efficient link between the government and the populations. Last but not least, every chief organizes the various traditional festivals in his region. These are an opportunity for reunions between all the members of a community, especially when certain of them have had to leave it in order to take jobs elsewhere, and often an occasion for the reconciliation of disputes which have occurred during the year.

From the traditional to the modern world

Although the government has retained much of the past, and is having the traditional chiefs participate in daily political life, il also intends for these chiefs to assist it with modernizing certain outmoded customs. Immobilism is unheard of in Ghana!

After coming to power in 1981, the PNDC (Provisional National Defence Council, headed by the Ghanaian Air Force Lieutenant Jerry John Rawlings), was confronted by an extremely difficult economic and political context. Ghana's commercial, social and political infrastructures required almost total reorganization. The reconstruction of Ghanaian society was guided by the radical application of measures destined to eliminate the rampant social injustice and economic exploitation then prevailing.

These high ideals were translated into positive action, resulting in a spectacular economic comeback whose full impact began to be felt in 1983. The reasons contributing to the success of Ghana's programme for economic recovery can be summarized as follows: the abolition of abuses of power, the elimination of graft and corruption at all levels of society, strict government budgeting procedures and trimming of public service to achieve greater efficiency, divestiture of state enterprises and increased opportunities for

private investment. Other measures include the improvement of the living conditions and salaries of mine workers (particularly at Obuasi, the principal gold mining centre) and cocoa farmers.

Women had also suffered from various types of discriminatory or sexist practices under the precedent regimes, despite the fact that in general (and particularly among the Akans), tribal "queen mothers" had traditionally played an essential role in the nomination of local chieftains from members of the royal family. In 1982, Nana Konadu Agyeman-Rawlings, the wife of Ghana's Head of State, founded the 31 st December Women's Movement to provide a new dynamic to the mobilization of Ghanaian Women.

In Ghana, as in most other African countries, the considerable and often unacknowledged contributions made by women at all levels of society represent a prime force for progress, especially in the domain of national reconstruction. The official encouragement of feminist movements by the charismatic wife of Ghana's Head of State adds inestimable momentum and prestige to the task of raising the social and political consciousness of the nation's women.

In a more general fashion, and affecting all of Ghana's population, a number of sweeping reforms have been carried out, while others are in the planning stages. Among specific reforms already carried out are the guarantee of inheritance rights to widows and children even in the matrilineal systems, and the registration of customary marriages to ensure recognition of the rights of a spouse. The ancestral traditions governing inheritances are being reexamined, and the local chiefs have been requested to facilitate the abolition of those judged reactionary, such as the dowry that men are traditionally expected to pay to the family of their future bride.

Broad-based educational policies

Ghana has always been proud of the number and quality of its secondary schools, its three universities (Accra-Legon, Kumasi and Cape Coast) and the progress accomplished in the 1960s, when an estimated 70 percent of the population achieved functional literacy.

Unfortunately, the disruption caused by a decade of economic decline has since considerably reduced literacy levels. In addition, the necessary imposition of economy measures and the overall dilapidation of school buildings and classrooms has resulted in the streamlining of the educational cycle from seventeen years (six years of elementary school followed by four years of intermediary education, plus seven years of pre-university classes) to a total of nine years of primary school and three years of secondary education.

This reduction has also resulted in the improved distribution and training of teaching personnel as well as permitting the renovation of the schools themselves. A particularly delicate problem was posed by the restructuring of Ghana's universities, whose upkeep had become prohibitive. After proposing to suppress the boarding facilities, which would have resulted in a *de facto* geographical segregation of students from the outlying regions, the government decided to have them paid for by students.

The offer of loans for higher education was received with a notable lack of enthusiasm by Ghana's student population, which had long been accustomed to being treated as the nation's most precious natural resource. Caught between the obligation to facilitate higher education and the necessity of balancing a national budget particularly vulnerable to fluctuations in the international market prices of its exported products, the government has once again placed the accent upon individual initiative. Thus, even the most brilliant students are expected to assume the financial burden of their education. This attitude has not prevented the government from considering education as an all-important national priority.

Ghana's educational system

Among other objectives, the restructuring of Ghana's educational system in 1987 was an attempt to increase the number of students receiving primary schooling, whereas the government had previously placed greater emphasis upon secondary and university-level studies.

The modifications of secondary and higher education have since resulted in improved technical and professional training and the multiplication of differ-

THE UNIVERSITY OF GHANA AT LEGON

The University of Ghana was founded by an act of parliament on the first October 1961, but the institution had already been in operation since 1948, under the name of University College of the Gold Coast. In the beginning it cooperated closely with the University of London, preparing students for admission to the latter, until it eventually became a university in its own right.

The premises include residence buildings that, from October through June, accommodate virtually the entire student body in five main buildings and six annexes.

Legon University boasts seven faculties, as follows: Agriculture, Medicine, Arts, Law, Social Studies, Business Administration, and Sciences; these have a total of forty-four subdivisions. In addition the following are attached to the University: the Institute for African Studies, the Adult Training Institute, the Institute for Statistics and Social and Economic Reseach, and the Institute for Journalism and Media Research. Last but not least, the University also sponsors research institutes such as the Linguistic Centre and the Volta Basin Research Project, concerned with the repercussions on the environment caused by Lake Volta.

*Located in a magnificent region
of green, rolling hills
and suspended gardens, the University
of Legon near Accra
educates Ghana's intellectual youth.*

ent categories of secondary schools in all of Ghana's ten administrative regions. In addition, a study is currently underway to determine the feasibility of constructing a fourth state university in northern Ghana.

Birth control

As in most developing countries, population growth has become an alarming problem in Ghana, which was one of the first African nations to adopt an energetic policy of birth control. Since the government's efforts to stabilize population growth have as yet not yielded the results expected, the massive literacy campaign scheduled for 1992 will be combined with birth control information targeted to special population segments (including men, rather than just women, as was previously the case) having the highest birth rates.

By tackling the complex problem of over-population, which could eventually jeopardize even the most energetic development efforts, the Ghanaian government has once again demonstrated that it is capable of combining realism with idealism.

art and culture

In Ghana, traditionally, art for art's sake does not exist. Nothing is created exclusively for the purpose of adorning or embellishing, but primarily to fulfil a function, and the slightest object invariably has a link with a religious belief.

Since, for the animist, God is omnipresent, this object already establishes a relationship with the supernatural world at the level of its material form, and in particular, wood taken from trees in which spirits have lived. These spirits must be appeased with prayers, while at the same time it is important to choose especially appropriate colours, shapes and designs for sculpture and carving.

What for a Westerner would be mere decoration is for a Ghanaian a language addressed to a divinity or to other members of the community, all of them able to perceive the symbolism.

In Ghana, all things are fraught with symbolism: the expression of an idea, a desire, or a fear enables them to come to life or be repressed, and only a symbol can bring abstract concepts into a clearly stated form. It hence seems rational and economical to use whatever comprises the daily environment both as tools and vehicles for expression.

Carvings on metal

The weights used on the Akan gold-weighing scales are a perfect example of this dual-purpose utilization. These small copper rectangles, produced by the lost-wax process, are always decorated. In most cases their designs illustrate a proverb. Thus the person who uses them accomplishes the act of weighing gold, and at the same time sends a message to the spirit-world... or to himself, much in the same way as when we "cross our fingers" or "knock on wood."

The message sometimes has two levels of meaning. Thus, one widely-used pattern represents two crocodiles with their two heads and two tails, but sharing a single body. This can be interpreted as meaning that within a single people, conflicts may arise even when senseless, just like the two crocodiles who are ready to fight over a meal, even though they both share the same stomach. The deep meaning of this proverb is the unity in diversity that characterizes mankind.

These weights are often adorned with geometric designs, and even the specialists themselves are not absolutely sure of their meaning.

The decorative treatment of the scales, spoons and containers used for gold dust is practically the same as for the weights.

The *kuduo* are copper receptacles in which the Akans place offerings designed for gods or ancestors. They serve simultaneously as religious objects and as an occasion for their owners to express their beliefs and concerns. The lid of one of these receptacles, of Akwamu origin and displayed at the National Museum of Accra, bears the representation of a leopard attacking a porcupine. The leopard is the emblem of the Akwamu, the porcupine is that of the Ashanti : these two peoples waged merciless war on each other in the nineteenth century. In addition, a scene engraved on the same lid represents a war council. The purpose of the ceremony in which the *kuduo* was used was therefore in all probability a request for victory, with the language of the object strengthening the language of prayer.

The *forowa* is another type of Akan receptacle designed for domestic or religious use. It differs from the above by the absence of added figurines, but the metal is always engraved with symbolic images.

The various Akan royal insignia, such as the chiefs' sceptres, the pendants, the sandal straps, the linked rectangles forming crowns, chiseled out of gold or carved from wood and gold-plated, also invariably display designs either engraved or carved in relief.

This applies to the handles of royal swords, whose blades, occasionally double, are of openwork iron, representing animals or geometrical or abstract figures.

In northern Ghana, the knives, daggers and dirks have chiseled blades with decorated metal or wooden handles and sheaths which are often made of leather, a typical northern material.

A rich and varied pottery

The millenary art of the potter, practised by the women, has been developed to a high level in all the regions of Ghana. Numerous shards of all types have been found in the archaeological sites, some of which are 3,000 years old.

Clay was used to make many categories of objects — oil lamps, vases, bowls, miscellaneous receptacles with or without lids, decorated with figures in relief or designs traced on the clay prior to firing. The firing was usually done over a naked flame and the pottery was polished by friction with sand rubbed with extremely dry leather.

The Accra Museum displays a water jug from the Kpandu region on Lake Volta: two birds form the handles, while a third bird provides a grip for the cover. Another receptacle from the same region, designed for keeping water cool, is in the shape of a rhinoceros.

A large-sized container was found along the seashore in Labadi, one of the quarters of Accra. Its round-shaped body is covered with reliefs depicting snakes, lizards and turtles. Its origin is unknown, but in all likelihood it was used for religious rituals.

The Akan region is rich in variegated ceramics: bowls, sometimes with scant ornamentation; slender-necked decanters with carved stoppers and receptacles for funeral rites. One of the latter has a cover formed by a human figure, possibly a portrait of the deceased.

Ghana is an outstanding exception among its neighbouring countries, whose inhabitants have developed to a high level the use of masks in their religious ceremonies. Naturally, this does not imply that Ghanaians ignore magic, i.e., the practical methods of entering into contact, through objects, with invisible powers, either to ask them to reveal the future or to request their intervention.

Wooden carvings

In Ghana, this aim is achieved through the intermediary of clay or wooden statuettes. These statuettes are placed on altars in special rooms in the fetish houses, which are a kind of animist temple and often the dwelling-place of the juju priests who officiate in them. They are also displayed on the inside or outside of ordinary dwellings, in niches and on small platforms.

They are sometimes male or female dolls whose purpose is three-fold. They can be mere playthings devoid of magical significance. But a sterile woman may carry one or two dolls on her back, depending on whether she wants to have children of only one sex or of both. Her desire will gradually be transmitted to the doll, which will become infused with a

GHANAIAN SYMBOLISM

■ *In Ghana, both colours and forms have symbolic value and form a kind of unspoken language which appears on garments, gold weights, and, by and large, everything that can be adorned with carved or painted motifs.*

Gold and yellow colours represent the presence of God, royalty, eternal life, prosperity, and warmth. White stands for purity, virtue, joy and victory, while green is a sign of newness, fertility and vitality. Red is used for mournful occasions like the death of a friend, wars or a national crisis. Blue is the colour of love and symbolizes the power of the queen mother among the Akans. A combination of yellow and red signifies the power of life and its superiority over illness.

As for the principal geometrical figures, their meanings differ depending upon whether they appear alone or in a combination with other figures. An isolated circle is a symbol of the presence and all-mightiness of God. Rectangles and squares indicate holiness and virility, while the triangle stands for feminity, and also the focal point toward which one's regard naturally converges. Its first level of meaning signifies charm, friendship, and even love. The triangular rod presented by a young man to his future wife on the occasion of her initiation into womanhood represents his pledge to cherish her for as long as she lives. In its second meaning, it symbolizes the chief's prospective situation. In the Northern Region, it is invariably found on court ornaments.

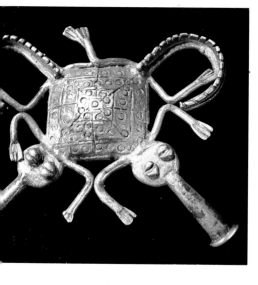

Ghana's century-old artistic
traditions are expressed in
the sculptured wood of elegant
royal stools, clay statues, stone carvings,
and bronze weights.

strength able to capture divine influences and bestow fertility upon the person with whom it remains in permanent contact. Dolls placed at the entrances to villages keep watch over them and ward off evil spirits.

The sculptor endeavours to adorn these statues with all the features that for him and the people of his culture represent human beauty such as a certain plumpness or an oval-shaped face for a woman, or a slightly rectangular head for a man. The scarifications indicate the ethnic origin or explain what is being requested of a god in the event of illness.

The treatment of the nose, mouth or ears of female dolls often reveals the attitude of a society toward women: they can mean, for example, that women must neither hear what a man says nor — above all — answer back, even if he has insulted them!

The sacred stools

A very special place is assigned to ancestor stools, objects of vital necessity, a veritable extension of the individual among all the peoples in central and southern Ghana, and more especially among the Akans.

This is the first gift bestowed by a father on his child and by a fiance on his future bride. Every individual owns his preferred stool, which he never relinquishes, and on which, after his death, his body will be cleansed in a sitting position prior to burial. A close association is formed between the person and the object, which becomes steeped in its owner's spirit and remains impregnated therewith subsequent to the latter's disappearance. This is why the stools belonging to certain prominent persons are conserved after their deaths. The stool of a deceased person is given a special blackening finish and is placed in the room reserved for ancestor worship, where it will be honoured on the occasion of numerous ceremonies. This practice parallels the custom of considering the stool as the supreme insignia of a chief, to such an extent that the dethroning of a king is sometimes signified by the word "destoolment."

A stool consists of three parts: the base, which is rectangular; the seat, in the shape of an incurved rectangle; and an intermediate zone that gives it its height and above all confers its personality, since this zone is always adorned with carvings. The number of themes are infinite, and all of them have a symbolic meaning. Some are reserved for special categories of individuals, such as the king, who enjoys the privilege of choosing whatever model he prefers. Certain stools are specially designed for women or men, while others are "unisex."

In very rare instances, and only for important people like the queen mother, they are silver-plated. But only a king is entitled to a gold stool and actually only a single gold stool exists — the one that descended from the skies in the days of King Osei Tutu, the founder of the Ashanti kingdom. During the ceremonies participated in by the Ashanti confederation chiefs, who had just won a victory over the Akans, their spirits were communicated to the stool, which thenceforth contained the real presence of the founding ancestors of the nation and became the latter's sacred symbol. No one, not even the supreme Ashanti king, or *Asantehene*, is allowed to sit on this stool, which is kept away from all contact with the outside world except on extremely rare occasions, and itself stands on a special stool or on an animal skin.

The stools are left unfinished, meaning that they are neither painted nor waxed, but simply washed from time to time. The blackening process is applied to a stool only after its owner's death, and provided that the latter was not only important but also virtuous. The product used is a blend of soot, egg yolk and sheep's blood. Naturally, these ingredients correspond to symbols: the sheep evokes peace, like the paschal lamb. The egg, which must be handled gently, is a sign of caution, patience, perseverance and calm.

Stool carvers enjoy an important rank in Ghanaian society. Their function is also religious, since certain ritual ceremonies must be performed at the time the tree supplying the wood is felled, and also before use is made of the tools that will be employed to carve it.

The drum, a messenger

Similar precautions must be taken with the drum, a multipurpose object used as an instrument for sacred or profane music, a messenger announcing news to be spread afar, or the distinctive sign of a ceremony or an important individual.

During the *Durbars* — the ceremonies in which the paramount chiefs receive homage from their vassals — the chiefs are borne on palanquins partly or entirely made of carved wood, with woven seats and a decoration of engraved copper plates.

The role of painting

Painting plays a preponderant role with regard to the traditional pirogues. The boats are constructed from scratch right in the forest, from a special tree called the *wawa*, whose trunk is hollowed out in a single piece, after ritual ceremonies similar to those performed for stools. They are then manually transported to the place at which they are to be launched into the sea. There they are decorated with geometrical designs painted in vivid colours, which bear a symbolic significance, sometimes echoed by the name of the pirogue, which may also take the form of a proverb or aphorism.

It is interesting to note that these inscriptions are also found adorning the vehicles used for public transportation called "mammy trucks" or "tro-tros." Which category influenced the other? It's a moot question, because the pirogues, clearly anterior to the "mammy trucks", did not always bear such inscriptions. Painted decorations were formerly the rule, especially back in the times when no written language was used. Be as it may, decorative motifs have not completely abandoned their place to language, and among the Fanti people they add considerable enhancement to the splendour of the procession of boats moving out to sea on their fishing expeditions.

Painting plays an important role in many other aspects of life. In the south, painting is applied in solid pastel colours to adorn habitations. Traditional Ashanti buildings display only one colour — ochre — which covers the exterior walls up to about one-third of their height, the upper part always remaining white. The northern villages, mainly between Bawku and Navrongo, are distinguished by geometric frescoes done in a blend of brown tones, from straw yellow to a near-black brown, covering the outer walls and, less often, those facing the inner courtyards.

At the present time in Ghana painting has a place everywhere in daily life. Aside from the easel paintings displayed at the Accra Museum in its modern art collection, along every street in the popular quarters your gaze is attracted by highly coloured scenes painted on the walls and serving as shop signs for artisans and traders. The accompanying slogans display the same humour and poetic fantasy as those on the "tro-tros,"and the personages represented often show a sharp sense of caricature. Here again, the artists are less concerned with harmony than with a message at several levels: naturally, the main thing is to attract the customer, but this is no obstacle to translating into visual form the way in which one views the world. In fact, the Ghanaian, who possesses a highly developed religious sense, is also a realist who instantly grasps the inherent flaws and absurdities in a given person or a situation. To express his deepest thoughts, to belittle annoyances, to humanize a frequently hard life, to reinvent an improved reality — without however letting himself be duped — he resorts to all possible means of expression, including carving, painting, and even tattooing. One memorable example of this attitude is the woman who not owning a watch, had the delightful idea of getting one tattooed onto her wrist. This is indeed a very different conception of art, which can be said to be simply the art of living.

Architecture on the human scale

If there is a realm in which this art of living best reveals itself, it is surely in architecture.

Unfortunately, in the south, traditions in this respect are less and less evident, except in a few coastal villages of woven-palm-leaf huts. All the towns have been modernized, and only the extraordinary Fanti *posuban* , which are temples erected by their warriors in honour of the gods that brought them victory, still express the genius of the race. And even these are more sculptural than architectural, insofar as the main interest of the *posuban* lies in the statuary that completely fills the verandahs and balconies surrounding the temples from their ground floor to the upper storeys. It borrows its themes from African traditions, the Bible, modern history, and Western techniques with a freedom, an imagination, a sense of synthesis and an elliptical approach that are positively breathtaking to the foreign observer.

Naturally, in addition to the above, the many castles and forts that dot the coast, particularly between Accra and the border of the Ivory Coast, attract visitors by their highly interesting architecture. But the latter is exclusively European, and hence bears no connection with Gha-

An intimate glimpse of family life
in one of northern Ghana's
traditional "kraals", where the eldest
sister often serves as a "second mamma"
for the younger children of the family.

naian art, even though it played a role in the country's history.

But architecture was once a genuine art for the Ashanti : this fact emerges from prints depicting Kumasi prior to its destruction by the British, a reconstructed royal pavilion at the Cultural Centre in the modern city, and from certain still-intact fetish houses in the region.

The Ashanti house consisted of four buildings around an inner courtyard onto which gave facades of various degrees of openness, while the walls giving onto the street were blind, except for the central loggia that served as an entrance to private dwellings. This loggia was supported by carved columns, while access was provided by a few steps or occasionally by a double stairway. In both palaces and fetish houses, the loggia was replaced by a vestibule that ran along one end of one of the four buildings, extending from the street to the inner courtyard.

Around the courtyard, carved symbols completely covered the walls, doors and shutters, the wood of which was sometimes enhanced with chased gold or silver.

With the exception of a few fetish houses, all this has completely vanished. However, the most modern houses often conserve the central loggia used for receiving guests. It still confers a stamp of distinction on buildings that are otherwise utterly banal.

In the north, the towns, both large and small, have also been modernized. But the *kraals* , or compounds, in the rural areas are largely intact. The word *kraal* applies to a series of grouped dwellings inhabited by an "enlarged" family comprising the descendants of two or three generations of a common ancestor who has the role of chief.

Starting from Tamale, in order to best appreciate the traditional style of living of which these *kraals* provide an image, the traveler should proceed along a great east-to-west loop along the northern border. Visitors will note the gradual transformation of the shapes, if not the spirit, of these compounds, consistently set off amid fields and enclosing one or several courtyards. The roofs, more or less pointed and covered with thatch in the east, gradually give way to a terrace-roof, a kind of living room in which cereals are put to dry and where the family sleeps at night during periods of particularly hot weather.

Each ethnic group has left the stamp of its individual personality by altering the sizes and interior layout of the habitations, the ways in which they are artic-ulated and the amount of wooden structure left exposed, to which are applied clay walls or unfired flat or curved tiles. The decoration, whether plain, painted or incised, changes ceaselessly, as do the accessories of daily living, reflecting slightly different customs. From one *kraal* to the next, the visitor will come upon some new detail, some feature of the collective system that has been either accentuated or minimized, or an improvement brought about for some type of activity. Provided your visit isn't too unexpected, the inhabitants are wonderfully eager to do you the honours of their dwellings, and when language fails, they staunchly resort to gestures to explain their methods. Thanks to them and to an architecture that has remained alive, your journey through the north will be fascinating.

The complex "kente" designs

When an important visitor leaves Ghana, the custom is to give him a *kente*. This is an immense piece of cotton that men wear draped like a Roman toga, one part thrown back over the left shoulder. A *kente* is always multi-coloured, and its designs, woven with one woof, represent such a wealth of hues and patterns that this simple garment is considered as one the crowning achievements of the country's artistic patrimony.

The *kente* is worn throughout the south, from west to east, and weaving it is a job reserved for males although nowadays there are a few girls working alongside the boys in the workrooms at the Kumasi Cultural Centre who seem to be holding their own quite successfully. Usually, working a weaving loom requires considerable effort on the part of the legs, which must continuously bear down on the pedals. But the painstaking work involved in producing a *kente* takes more patience and imagination than muscle. The patterns are so intricate that the artist, amid a welter of balls of cotton thread of every colour, must sometimes snip off tiny bits to be applied over a width of about one centimetre, or even one millimetre, while carefully counting the woof threads.

The Ashanti kings and queen mothers all had their private weavers, commissioned to create original patterns reserved exclusively for royal clients. Naturally, every design had a meaning. At the Accra Museum there is a *kente* of unsurpassable complexity, created exclusively for an *Asantehene* and whose symbolic meaning suggests that "ideas come to an end." Humour never relinquishes its rights in Ghana!

The motifs used are strictly geometric. Only the manner in which they are combined, their variations and the mix of colours, create their diversity.

The *adinkra*, which women are entitled to wear, are also made of natural white or vividly coloured cotton, printed with extremely varied black or dark-brown symbolic motifs. This garment is worn more on solemn occasions, unlike the *kente*, which is reserved for more joyous moments.

Music, singing and dancing

At any ordinary or religious event, and with or without musical accompaniment, singing and dancing are engaged in by all Ghanaians, children and adults alike, both men and women, peasants and city dwellers, and ordinary citizens as well as chiefs.

To the foreign observer, their chants may sound monotonous, but instead of trying to understand the meaning of the words, if you watch the audience, you soon realize that these lyrics express a wide range of feelings, that they tell a story, and comment on events — in short, they fill the role of the antique Greek chorus on many occasions. Very often, in between the choruses in which everyone joins, a soloist will launch into a complete improvisation, to the great delight of the members of the audience, who clap and laugh uproariously when these impromptu performances are especially witty and exactly match the beat and the refrain.

Religious ceremonies, however, are closely governed by a protocol that requires the immutable performance of rites, songs and music. The instruments, which vary depending on circumstances and sometimes depending on the type of audience, fall into different categories: the idiophones are made of materials that vibrate under percussion, and include xylophones, gongs, bells, rattles, cattle bells, clappers, and the prempensua, a kind of piano with five wooden keys, tuned to produce different pitches. The

KOO NIMO : AMBASSADOR OF THE GHANAIAN CULTURE

Daniel Amponsah, a chemical laboratory technician at the University of Kumasi, is none other than the celebrated Koo Nimo, one of Ghana's most popular musicians.
Amponsah is also well known in Ghana's neighbouring West African countries as well as in Great Britain, where he and Glasgow University professor Joe Latham have largely contributed to making Ashanti culture known through the publication of Ashanti Ballads, *consisting of collected songs from his repertoire in English translation. These veritable poems set to music represent the fruit of twenty years of patient research in which Amponsah has recorded more than eighty traditional chants in* Twi, *the language of the Ashantis. These recordings serve both as an imperishable archive of the collective memory and a means of providing particularly rich examples of Ashanti culture to a public extending far beyond the national territory. Amponsah is devoted to this task, and makes a special effort to perform before those who are particularly disfavored.*
Born in 1934 in the Ashanti village of Foase, Daniel Amponsah comes from a family of musicians : his father played the guitar and trumpet, and his mother sang in the local Methodist Church choir. Amponsah's sister is married to the brother of the Asantehene (the Ashanti king), which, in the words of the musician, has resulted in his "total immersion" in the traditions of his people.

*In the Aburi Botanical Gardens
north of Accra, traditional
musicians and dancers often
give impromptu performances on weekends
to the delight of visitors.*

membranophones include all the varieties of drums, made of wood or hollowed out of gourds. Their extremities are bound with the hide of various animals (elephants, sheep, goats, monkeys). They are struck with curved sticks or batons, or simply pounded with the hands. Some of them are reserved for particular circumstances, such as war, or for important personages like the *Asantehene* .

The drum frequently is the sole accompaniment for singing, dancing, marching, and certain kinds of work. It is also used for sounding alarms and transmitting messages. For this purpose an extremely sophisticated language has been developed, requiring the use of two drums of different pitches. By making use of these pitches, the rhythm of the beats, the pauses, and the intensity of his pounding, the messenger has a veritable alphabet enabling him to convey all the elements of the news to be communicated.

Last but not least are the wind instruments, including horns, trumpets, and flutes. They are used less frequently, although all the regions of Ghana possess them in some form or other. It is mainly in the north that one finds carved wooden trumpets and flutes, which can also be made of carved bamboo- or millet stems. It is likewise the northern regions that make the widest use of stringed instruments, such as lutes, harps, lyres and zithers.

No one is anxious to lose this intensely rich cultural patrimony, least of all the government.

The University of Legon and its Institute for African Studies is a particularly active centre for the study and dissemination of Ghanaian music, dance, chants and orally-transmitted traditions. A number of local Ghanaian dialects, including Twi, Ewe, Ga, Dagbani, Fanti, Haoussa, Nzima, Mamprusi, Wala, Frafra and Kassena, have been codified and are currently employed in the writings of contemporary Ghanaian authors. At present, nearly fifty Ghanaian writers are producing novels, plays, poetry and critical essays. Atukwei Okai, a polyglot poet and secretary-general of the Pan-African Writers' Association, has written a series of nursery rhymes in English, but the main problem confronting visi-

THE PAN-AFRICAN WRITERS' ASSOCIATION

African writers are often confronted by a thorny paradox: although conscious of the importance of their national roots and language, the commercial imperatives of book publishing require that they write either in French or English to be read by the intra-African populations who use one or the other of these two languages — the heritage of centuries of colonial rule — as a common means of communication.

In an effort to resolve this dilemma and the numerous other difficulties encountered by African authors from one end of the Continent to the other, the Pan-African Writers' Association (PAWA) was founded by the Ghanaian poet Atukwei Okai. The Association's first meeting took place in November 1989, and was attended by representatives from thirty-five African nations. Currently headquartered in the Roman Ridge district of Accra, the Association's members includes both international and African writers, such as Wole Soyinka, a Nobel Prize-winning Nigerian author. Conscious of the vital role that literature plays in the discovery and affirmation of African identity, Atukwei Okai is currently planning the creation of a pan-African publishing house.

tors desirous of reading Ghanaian literature is simply finding it. At the offices of the Ghana Publishing Company, Accra's largest publishing house, it is nearly impossible to find any example of contemporary Ghanaian literature whatsoever.

Luckily for Ghana's playwrights, the Accra National Theatre, the Drama Studio, the Art Centre and the Kumasi Cultural Centre regularly produce a wide variety of theatre and dance representations, ranging from traditional to modern. The Tamale Arts Council is also active in the arts, as are other regional cultural centres such as that of Bolgatanga. Ghanaian television also provides national exposure for a number of dance and theatre companies, with plays often being given in one of the local dialects.

The vitality of Ghanaian art

Ghanaian orchestras, theatre and dance companies are given maximum encouragement by the government, which provides opportunities to perform during national holidays, official receptions and at prize-giving ceremonies in schools.

Koo Nimo, a native of Kumasi, chemical laboratory technician by profession and storyteller by love for Ghana's heritage of orally-transmitted literature, is known nation-wide for his radio and television performances, as well as for his frequent appearances at traditional ceremonies and cultural centres. His art consists in the recasting of traditional Ghanaian stories and riddles into contemporary contexts while preserving their essentially pedagogical character. Playing the guitar and tamborine and accompanied by his musicians, Koo Nimo also sings traditional Ashanti ballads.

Nimo has worked closely with Professor Manwere Opoku, of the School of Dance, as well as Professor Kwabena Nketia, the director of Legon's Institute of African Studies and professor of ethno-musicology at the University of Pittsburgh. A pianist and composer, Professor Nketia is also the author of numerous books on Ghanaian music and has recorded the traditional chants of the countryside.

For visitors interested in dance, the Academy of African Music and Arts directed by Mustapha Tetty Addy and located in the seaside Krokobite Motel thirty kilometres from Accra, offers three-week courses in traditional Ghanaian dance, chant, percussion instruments, painting and wood sculpture, while every Sunday, visitors are treated to a festival of African music and dance.

Ghana is equipping itself with up-to-date film and recording facilities, such as those of the Ghana Film Industry Corporation. The country's musicians have also organized a union which, among its other activities, is addressing the growing problem of pirate recordings. Ghana's film-makers, such as King Ampaw, Ata Yarney, Joe Daniels, Kofi Yirenkyi and Kwaw Ansah, are turning out high-quality productions which are receiving increasing critical acclaim at international film festivals. This was the case for *Heritage Africa*, Kwaw Ansah's first feature-length film, which won the Best Film prize by the jury of the Ouagadougou Film Festival in 1989. His triumph was perceived as an important victory for all of Ghana's film-makers; at present, Kwaw Ansah is shooting *Harvest at Seventeen*, a film dealing with prostitution and the problem of abortion.

Running parallel to the emergence of Ghanaian cinema is an interesting current of modern art, which began appearing shortly after the nation achieved independence. Adapting Western techniques to deal with traditional subjects and everyday life, artists such as Glover, Victor Butler, Ato Delaquis and Wiz are regularly represented at international exhibitions and particularly appreciated by collectors. Glover's style runs from figurative to abstract and mirrors the artist's strong personality, while Delaquis paints in a charmingly naive style; the works of other Ghanaian artists such as Sika, Christopher Yarney, Betty Acquab, Victor Odoi — appreciated for his bold swathes of colour — Ankuh Golloh and the batik and silk painter Tsatsu Doku can be seen at the Accra Art Centre.

Another recent development is the emergence of a first wave of Ghanaian fashion designers, such as the talented Ricci Osei. After opening a boutique to showcase his fashions, Osei is currently collaborating with a group of Accra-based designers to offer an entire range of high-fashion clothing and accessories, including jewellery, footwear and handbags. All of the merchandise, even to the wrapping paper, will be designed and manufactured locally and available in boutiques both in Accra and Paris.

*Besides sculpture, music and dance,
the talent of Ghanaian artists
expresses itself in painting:
examples of theatrical advertisements
announcing a forthcoming production.*

history of ghana

■ Before it could adopt its motto of "One people, one nation, one destiny," Ghana experienced almost as many metamorphoses as man himself, witnessing, if not his birth, at least his adolescence.

The oldest traces of sedentary habitation in Ghana date back 30,000 or 40,000 years along the coast, notably near Tema. Although little is known about the human beings who lived there, the very fact of their existence upsets the theories that only a few years ago maintained that West Africa had at the earliest begun to be inhabited only from the beginning of the Christian era.

Not only does it appear that Ghana was already inhabited more than two hundred centuries ago, but, in the Brong-Ahafo Region, close to the Black Volta, vestiges have now emerged of a civilization dating from 1700 to 1500 B.C., referred to as the Kintampo culture.

The latter probably lay between the Ivory Coast border, on the west, Lake Volta on the east, and between Kintampo on the south up to Ntereso on the north.

The representatives of this culture were tillers of the soil, livestock breeders, and fishermen, and by the end of the second millenium they had developed a naturalistic art. Who were they? Nobody knows, but the Akan people in the modern village of Hani and its environs speak of an interesting legend: they claim that their ancestors surged forth out of the earth through a hole located some six kilometres outside the village, i.e., in the immediate vicinity of the sites belonging to the Kintampo culture.

There is a certain temptation to interpret this legend as the proof that the Akans' ancestors belonged to this ancient civilization. But hasty conclusions must be avoided. In addition, one kilometre from one of these twenty-five-century-old sites, a veritable city — Begho — is gradually emerging from the excavations. This is a much later settlement: carbon 14-dating has pinpointed the buildings as having been constructed between 1350 and 1750 A.D.

At what period did the Hani villagers' ancestors "come out of the ground?" Did this occur in the first or the second period? Is it possible that they have never left the region for 2,500 years? Or is this a legend designed to justify *a posteriori* the occupancy of a conquered territory?

Be as it may, it seems unlikely that life came to a standstill between the period in which Kintampo flourished and the era when Begho was a marketplace frequented by northern caravans. In fact, it was during that period that the mighty empire of Ghana had the time to be born — and to vanish.

The empire of Ghana

Although the southern borders of this empire, which existed from the fourth to the eleventh century, were modified several times over, they never touched Ghana's present borders. At the most, trade relations existed between the two regions. It is also possible that from time to time, following a rebellion or unrest over a succession, groups of dissidents may have migrated southward to escape retaliation and either intermarried with the autochthons or settled in nearby sites.

When the empire of Ghana collapsed under the attacks of the Almoravid Arabs, it had already been known for two centuries to Eastern and Spanish traders with whom it carried on commercial transactions. What happened to the populations who belonged to the empire? According to one of the Akan traditions, their ancestors fled from Almoravid domination and after years of wanderings finally settled at the confluence of the Pra and the Ofin, in the Adanse, where their true civilization was presumably created.

There is one coincidence that can give cause for wonder. Around 1077, the Arab writer El Bakri described the fabulous wealth of the kings of Ghana who "hitched their horses to blocks of solid gold!" The Akan group's links with gold are of a mystical nature. Is this a reflection of the era in which this gold rendered their ancestors all powerful?

The mysterious Akans

It is largely impossible to find out where the Akans came from, so contradictory are their descendants' traditions: some of them claim to be autochthonous, while others state that their various groups gradually emerged from the northern regions of the forest. According to members of the Denkyira group living along the Ofin River, "During two centuries our ancestors made their way from the sources of the Nile, crossed through Moslem countries and settled in Nkyiraa, in Brong-Ahafo." As for the Adanse at Fomena, north of the confluence of the Pra and the Ofin, not only do they claim to have sprung from the soil that they presently occupy, but they further maintain that Adanse was the site at which the Creator caused the eight Akan clans to come into existence.

The historians' versions are scarcely more concordant. According to some observers, the Akans were already settled around the Ofin 2,000 years ago. They set about absorbing the inhabitants of the coastal plains and forests on the west, developed their customs, social organizations, and language, and founded the states of Twifo, Adanse and Denkyira.

Other sources are more cautious and confine themselves to noting that between the years 1000 and 1400, a number of communities were already in existence, most of them on the coast.

In the fifteenth century, the kingdom of Acames (Acanni) was established on the site of Elmina and, farther west, that of Ahanta. When the first European travelers to these shores encountered their chiefs, they left descriptions of the royal insignia (stools, special drums, trumpets, etc.) that have remained in use.

The destruction of the Ghana empire seems to have been the signal for migrations that gradually peopled the regions south of the Niger. A number of ethnic groups had already settled in the north by then, including the Vagala, the Sissala, the Kassena, the Dagati, the Tampylensi, the Talensi, the Guan, the Konkomba, the Nafaba, the Koma and the Chamba.

There is no reliable evidence as to whether these ethnic groups were actually autochthonous and, as concerns the Guan, the mystery is complete. Some observers claim that they were the vanguard of the Akan. In any case their ancestors proliferated, and were found from north to south and from east to west. In addition, their language had adopted a different pattern from that of the Akan, and has since remained distinct from despite all the conquests. The Guan are also quite different from the other ethnic groups in the north who speak a language based on the same pattern and who live in a similar manner, i.e., in small, independent communities under the authority of the eldest males of the individual families. Alongside these family chiefs, in the strongest sense of the word, there coexists the *Tindana*, the custodian of the earth, who distributes land

THE CULTURE OF KINTAMPO

■ *Not until 1959, at the Pan-African Congress of Prehistory, held in Leopoldville (present-day Kinshasa), did the archaeologist Davies announce the discovery of this previously unknown culture. Since then, major progress has been made in the discovery of this culture, thanks to the excavations at Mumute and Bonoase (near Begho) in the Brong-Ahafo Region, at Chukuto and Ntereso, southwest of Tamale in the north, as well as near Kintampo.*

Around 1700 B.C., for reasons still unknown, the inhabitants of these regions realized that hunting and gathering wild food were no longer sufficient to provide sufficient nourishment. For the first time they cleared forest land and planted oil palms, peas and celtis. Their tools included stone axes, "mass"-produced in Kintampo and eventually at two other sites near the Buruburo and Wiwi Rivers. Other crops were presumably cultivated, but archaeologists have based their conclusions only on the seeds that have been found. Similarly, if we know that cattle were raised by these people, it is because cattle bones have been discovered at these sites. At Ntereso, near the Volta River, these farmers and livestock breeders also practised fishing, using bone harpoons, hooks and arrow tips. These tools had originated in the southern Sahara and Niger. In all likelihood, it is due to this same influence that the inhabitants of Ntereso adopted flat instead of peaked straw roofs for their buildings. This style was also adopted by Chukuto, as was the rectangular shape, while the round hut remained in favour in the other cities marked by this civilization.

to the farmers, directs the annual festivals and holds forth as a priest.

In the thirteenth century, the ancestors of the Mamprusi and the Dagomba probably set out from Lake Chad and crossed through northern Nigeria. On the way they perpetrated a few raids in the company of a certain king Melle, in Timbuktu and Walata, which were cities of the then-powerful Mali empire. They may have bitten off more than they could chew, because they turned up again at Pusiga, on the northeastern edge of Ghana, under a chief named Gbewa. Skilled in the martial arts, they were led by enterprising chiefs, and outfitted with swords, spears and horses. This was more than sufficient to strike terror into the hearts of the hapless local ethnic groups who had lived in peace with one another, enjoying a sufficient amount of room so as not to interfere with their respective existences.

Gbewa carved out a kingdom in the area between the Gambaga Escarpment and the northern border. Naturally, matters deteriorated with the advent of the generation of his grandsons, who disputed the power. A certain Tohogu, the legitimate heir, fled southeast to Mamprugu, on the other side of the Gambaga Escarpment. His two brothers, Sitobu and Mantambu, failing to find him at Gambaga as they had expected, continued south and founded the kingdoms of Dagomba and Nanumba. Many years later a branch of the royal family of the Dagomba, in the wake of a quarrel over a succession, migrated to a territory near the western border, where it ruled over the Dagati.

But Tohogu, after giving the slip to his enemy brethren, returned to Gambaga, founded the city (which had been existing only as an agricultural settlement) along with the kingdom of Mamprugu, while his subjects became known as Mamprusi. He assumed the title of *Nayiri*, which was retained by his successors.

The descendants of one of his brothers, the Dagomba, continued their migrations, while in the sixteenth century, from the north came the Mande, whose ancestors probably belonged successively to the great empires of Mali and Songhay. Moslems and warriors, after infiltrating the country from the north, west of the White Volta, they settled in the territory of the Dagomba, who proceeded to migrate eastward and founded Yendi, which has remained their capital. The Mande, who took the name of Gonja, thereupon occupied, under the

Mamprusi kingdom, an extremely vast area stretching to the north-west extremity of the present Lake Volta.

Despite their different origins, the Mamprusi-Dagomba and Gonja have similar institutions. All have a king, the equivalent of the Nayiri, who governs with a council of elders. Succession is via the male line, hence only the sons who are brothers born of the same father, and paternal uncles are eligible for appointment by the council of elders. However, the *Tindana* has retained his role as custodian of the earth, and he is even consulted on important occasions, notably in connection with the elections of kings.

Except for the mysterious ancestors who sprang from the earth or descended from the sky, everything of any importance in the history of the country had thus far come from the north. But in the fourteenth century, there occurred an event that at first went almost unnoticed: ships from Dieppe put in at the Bay of Guinea, and their occupants probably founded a trading post at Elmina, which they abandoned early in the fifteenth century.

Even then, news traveled, and the Portuguese undoubtedly got wind of the discoveries made in Africa by the French navigators. In any case, they proceeded to install themselves in Elmina and built San Jorge castle.

Whom did they find inhabiting this coast, where they lost no time building numerous camps west of Cape Coast, then known as Oguaa?

The Akans had not confined themselves to the area around the confluence of the Ofin and the Pra. Its members spread out toward the north as far as Brong-Ahafo, which they eventually occupied entirely. Another group then went back down to the coast: their members were the Fanti, who carved out their territory by pushing back or exterminating the original occupants, including the Efutu and the Asabu, whose origins are lost in history. According to one theory, they belonged to the same ethnic group as the Guan, despite the fact that their language resembles that of the Fanti. In the sixteenth century, Pacheco Pereira noted that the inhabitants of the coastal regions between the Pra and Senya Beraku, near Accra, spoke the same language.

To further complicate matters, despite the legends evoking the circumstances of their journey from Brong-Ahafo — for the accounts vary — both the Fanti and the Efutu claim that their ancestors descended out of the sky or emerged from the bowels of the earth. Whatever the case, they were on the scene when the Portuguese settled in Ghana and decided to maintain the exclusive monopoly over the huge quantities of gold they found at Elmina and its neighbouring regions. The Portuguese were proper Christians, and this was to serve them well. In order to maintain their "rights," they headed off and stopped all the European vessels navigating off the Ghanaian coast, and in 1443, inveigled Pope Eugene IV into issuing a papal bull whereby Portugal was granted all the territories between Cape Bojador and the East Indies. For good measure, his successor Sixtus IV, made it a formal offense, under penalty of excommunication, to penetrate the territories assigned to the Portuguese.

Lastly, to discourage would-be usurpers, in the event that the first two measures proved insufficient, the new "owners" of the Gold Coast threw up fortresses at Axim, Shama, and Fort Duma, now vanished, near the mouth of the Ankobra.

But the Portuguese hadn't been clever enough: by obtaining papal intervention for the title to their lands — which they claimed were not worth the trip — and by exterminating everyone who even attempted to find out more about them, they merely convinced all of Europe that the slices of the pie were indeed hefty. Navigators and crews from other countries gradually grew bolder and provoked bloody wars to which the native coastal populations obligingly lent a hand.

The Europeans and the lure of gold

Shortly after the arrival of the Portuguese, the Ga-Adangbe appeared on the coast. Hailing from the mouth of the Niger, the earliest arrivals, the Ada, settled on the western shore of the Volta Delta, while their brothers — the Adangbe, the Shai, and the Krobo — fanned out over the inland plains and hills and began clearing the land.

Their close relatives the Ga had pushed on farther west and had absorbed the Kpesi, of Guan origin, who were living in the area. In the latter half of the seventeenth century, their capital, Accra, as well as most of the kingdom they had founded in the inland plains up to the Akwapim Hills, fell prey to the Akwamu,

an Akan group. They had no choice but to fall back under the protection of the forts built by the Europeans on the site of modern Accra and to get along peacefully with the foreigners, whoever they might be.

Meanwhile east of the Volta, a new migration had been taking place — that of the Ewe, who came from Dahomey. Expelled from their land by other invaders, they had trekked westward in small groups, first settling in Togo, on the site of Nuatja, where they founded a kingdom. Unfortunately, the heir of the founder, Agokoli, developed into a despot, obliging some of his subjects to take their departure. In the mid-seventeenth century, they reached the Delta of the Volta, settled on the eastern bank, and peopled the coast and the inland territory as far as the hills of Togo, which they gradually penetrated.

The Ewe formed several small independent states, governed by both a chief and an elders' council. By 1900, there were some 120 of these states, including Anlo, Dzodze, Ave, Peki, Ho, Kpandu, Tongu, etc.

The Europeans had been drawn to the coasts of Ghana by the lure of gold. Now a new commodity was keeping them there. The New World had been discovered, conquered, and emptied of its Indian occupants, while cultivation of the vast expanses of America and the Caribbean Islands required cheap labour — better yet, slaves. Where else could they be come by except on the African coast?

Slavery had been in existence at least since the days of the great empires of Ghana, Mali and Songhay. And since, in accordance with custom, after every battle the defeated warriors and their families became the slaves of the winners, migrations occurred that produced new wars... and new slaves.

The Akan group had been continuously expanding since the sixteenth century. In the seventeenth century, a map drawn by the Dutch noted twenty-nine new Akan states from the Wenchi in the north to the Ahanta, Komenda, and Fanti on the coast, including the Ashanti, in the centre, who were by no means standing by idly. In the east, the Akwami were continuing to spread terror, but they would soon be having trouble with the Akim who were other members of the Akan group.

Although they were the territories of related peoples, their occupants had no compunction about warring with one another at the drop of a hat nor about taking prisoners... more and more prisoners as the demand for slaves grew.

The European countries were fighting less and less along the coast, since the slave trade was so flourishing that it provided "work" for everyone: however they did continue to build forts. The Akan, in whatever territory they lived, were excellent warriors, and only too willing to prove their mettle. It was hence wiser to enclose between sturdy walls the human "merchandise" — which was being paid for no longer with baubles but with guns.

In the eighteenth century, thirty more forts were erected, including twelve by the Dutch, who remained more powerful in the area than the English. By the time slavery was abolished in 1848, the total number of forts of various sizes was seventy-six, from the mouth of the Ankobra on the west, to Keta on the east.

The Europeans had gradually realized the horrors of slavery. However, it is odd to note that within a few years after its definitive abolition, the thrust of colonialism made its presence felt in no uncertain terms. It is even stranger to realize that racial segregation, which, for

example, was unknown in Accra, where many English and Dutch traders resided in the native districts, developed only with colonization.

The English gradually bought up the Dutch forts in Ghana, while the Germans gained a firm foothold in Togo. However, up to the mid-nineteenth century, generally speaking, the governments hardly concerned themselves with the presence of the missionaries who founded schools, nor with that of private business.

The British had enjoined the traders to administer their forts themselves but later appointed governors like the famous Governor Mac Lean to supervise the castles and forts. In this role he began to act as a conciliator between the Ashanti and the Fanti and serving in African courts of justice.

Consequently, in 1843 the British Crown took the administration of the Gold Coast back under its jurisdiction and signed a treaty with the Fanti chiefs on March 6, 1844, defining relations between the English and the southern populations.

But not until 1872, when the Dutch

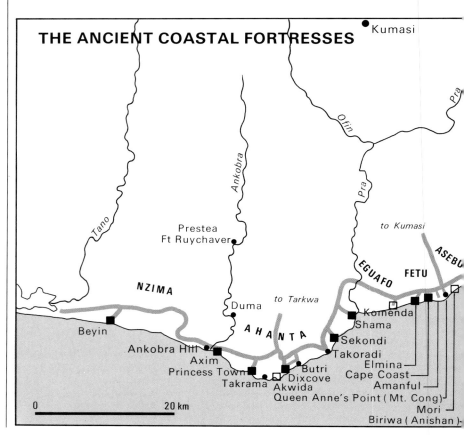

THE ANCIENT COASTAL FORTRESSES

had completely withdrawn from the country — after selling their rights to the British — did Queen Victoria's government undertake to carry on a colonial policy in dead earnest.

It found the opportunity to impose its will thanks to the first of the two wars in which its armies clashed head-on with those of the Ashanti.

To understand how the latter had successfully formed a great confederation, it is necessary to go back to the time when King Osei Tutu, from 1695 to 1711, had sealed the doom of the Akan-Denkyira kingdom by uniting all its neighbours. His clever minister and priest, Okomfo Anokya, had been inspired to create the famous Golden Stool, which he claimed was descended from the skies and contained the spirit of the nation. In a solemn ceremony, a special beverage had been drunk by the chiefs, whereupon drops of it were sprinkled on the stool. The Ashanti union henceforth enjoyed a sacred character that enabled it to exert considerable influence over the other states, of which Kumasi had become the sovereign city. The Ashanti set about pushing back their territorial limits in every direction, and even dispatched an expeditionary force to the Talensi, in the Bolgatanga region, where the local deity put it to flight. Their expansion also extended to the east, at the expense of the Akim, who, since they had earlier inflicted the same treatment on the Akwamu, got a dose of their own medicine. The Ga in their turn became vassals, and it was at this point that the Ashanti began turning toward the coast. Since the Fanti were not about to let themselves be overrun, war broke out between them.

MacLean nevertheless managed to achieve a temporary peace. But after his departure the Ashanti raids along the coast resumed even more fiercely and, in 1872, when the English purchased Elmina castle from the Dutch, the situation was reversed: with the help of the Fanti, their hereditary enemies, they attacked San Jorge. In 1873, England decided to dispatch an expeditionary force against Kumasi. The war lasted two years. Immediately afterward, the British officially founded the Gold Coast colony.

This by no means spelled the end of their troubles with the Ashanti, and

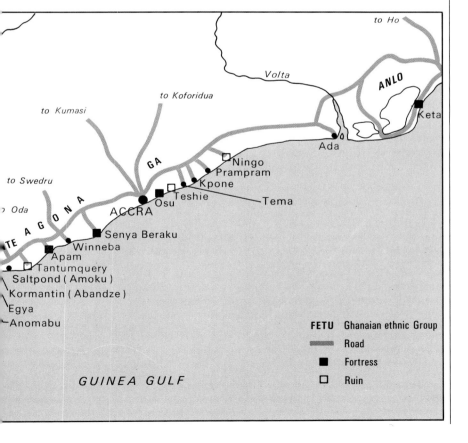

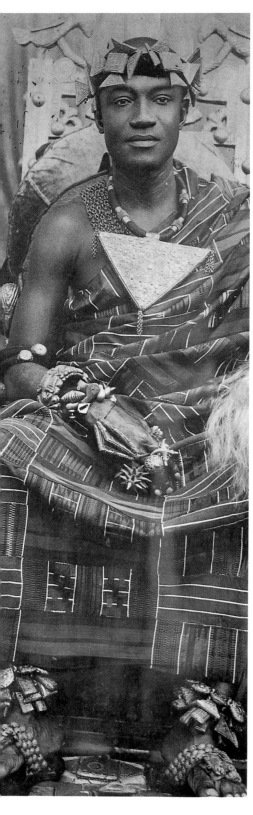

*Now a museum, the former British fortress of Kumasi
offers a rich array of period documents and artifacts
such as these portraits of the Ashanti kings Primpeh I and
Primpeh II with members of their court. Below: the British
garrison during the siege of Kumasi in 1900.*

difficulties suddenly began arising with the Ga, who refused to pay the taxes that the colonists deemed necessary for the upkeep of the city of Accra. These difficulties became so serious that in order to keep a closer watch over the Ga, the authorities decided to transfer their administrative headquarters from Cape Coast to Accra in 1877.

Up to that time, only the coast had been under British domination. But beginning in the 1880s, the need for raw materials became increasingly acute in Europe, where industrial expansion was in full swing. All eyes were fixed on Black Africa, which beckoned promisingly as the source of new resources. In 1884, at the Berlin Conference, which went on for several years, fourteen countries joined forces to take "legal" possession of the African territories. Bismarck's Germany imposed its "might is right" policy and gained recognition of its entitlement to Cameroon, Tanganyika and Togo.

The colonial adventure had now gotten off to a flying start, and with it came the systematic control of everything it could lay its hands on.

In Ghana, it became vital that control no longer be confined to the small southern territory. To this end it was necessary to overcome the Ashanti. In 1886, the *Asantehene* was exiled to the Seychelles, while official representatives were dispatched to the northern regions to sign treaties with the traditional chiefs.

Rather than risk the loss of their Golden Stool, the Ashanti preferred not to oppose the arrest of their King, Prempeh I. And in all likelihood they would never again have resorted to arms if the English governor Frederick Hodgson, in March 1900, had not committed the error of demanding the stool, which he took to be a mere insignia of power. Three days later the Ashanti, for whom this demand was out-and-out sacrilege, attacked the Kumasi fort.

Unfortunately for them, this time the war spelled their undoing, and brought about the almost total destruction of their capital. By 1901, the Ashanti homeland had been placed under a protectorate. The only remaining task was to agree on the borders with the neighbouring colonial powers — the French in the Ivory Coast and the Germans in Togo. In 1902, three decrees established the limits of the colony, of the land conquered from the Ashanti and of the protectorate in the north. Later on in 1919, after the German defeat, Togo was divided up between France and England, and the latter received part of what is now the

nucleus of the Volta Region. A plebiscite in the northern part of the Volta Region in 1956 finally determined which part of the Region was to be integrated into the about-to-be independent ghana.

The riches of the Gold Coast

Since the turn of the century, cocoa-growing had been progressively increasing in the Eastern Region. By 1910, cocoa had become the country's foremost production, even as mining continued to develop. In 1900, gold was still the only ore exported, and it was for the purpose of transporting it that the first railway line had been built, not from the capital but between Sekondi, which was then the sole commercial port, and Tarkwa, the largest mining town. In addition to this line, constructed from 1898 to 1903, another one between Accra and Kumasi was laid from 1909 to 1923. The line runs through the cocoa region and makes stops in other mining towns, where not only gold but also diamonds, manganese, and bauxite are mined.

If trade had continued to be carried on through the intermediary of the Africans, as had been the practice with palm oil and kola nuts, the entire population would have benefited from the cocoa boom that began in the 1920s. Gone were the days when the whites used to deal with the local inhabitants, whose middle class was beginning to emerge. This middle class had been ruined with the advent of Western companies that worked the soil and the mines and shipped the products directly to Europe, purchasing produce from farmers at prices set unilaterally by the companies, as also were the prices of articles imported and sold by them.

Matters worsened in other ways. The Europeans, in the beginning had been rent-paying tenants in the houses they occupied in the native quarters, or had acquired simple concessions, later sought to claim ownership of the lands. This was inadmissible in the eyes of the locals, who considered the land as belonging to their ancestors, and hence untransferable. In 1897, the Aboriginal Rights Protection Society was formed, headed by a lawyer named John Mensah-Sarbah, basically to prevent the land from becoming the property of the British Crown or of the English colonists.

This society proved that despite colonial rule, the schools that mushroomed throughout the country had yielded results. Increasingly greater numbers of Africans were receiving secondary education. But since until 1948, the Gold Coast had no university, the most brilliant among them, like young Kwame Nkrumah, completed their studies in Europe or America. They learned how to fight laws by the law, and by becoming lawyers, they acquired political experience by associating with leaders and reading books condemning colonialism. This was the case of Nkrumah, and also of Joseph Smith and J. Hutton Brew, the secretaries of the Fanti Confederation, and of all those who went on founding nationalist movements.

The system of indirect rule practised in the 1920s and the 1930s was one whereby the English used local chiefs as their instruments for administration thus co-opting them into colonial administration. The British sought to exclude all the members of the younger generation who had been educated abroad and who no longer acknowledged the authority of the chiefs, often because the latter had been appointed not by native councils, but by the colonial government.

In addition, the political status of the Africans had steadily deteriorated since the onset of colonization. Whereas in 1893, out of the 43 principal administrative posts only 9 were held by Africans, by 1908 this figure had fallen to 5 out of 278, further declining in 1919 to 2 out of 278.

To those most prone to rebellion this exclusion from civil government sparked violent indignation against the British, particularly when the Aboriginal Rights Protection Society which had enjoyed considerable prestige up to 1925 and had successfully combated a number of laws between 1925 and 1927, was deliberately destroyed by Governor Guggisberg, the principal architect of the barrier erected between the youthful university graduates and the traditional chiefs.

However, a lawyer named Joseph Casely Hayford, appointed to the Legislative Council in 1916, had inaugurated the West African Congress in 1917. This movement was different from the Aboriginal Rights Protection Society since it represented the middle class, had nothing to do with the chiefs, and was endeavouring to extend its action not only throughout the Gold Coast but also to Britain's other colonies in Africa. In his initial proclamation, Hayford naturally demanded for Africans the right to participate in the governments of their countries, freedom to vote, the

abolition of nominations (instead of elections) to the Legislative Council, the establishment of a West African Court of Appeals and the creation of a university for West Africa. A delegation had been sent to London without success. After its founder's death in 1930, the party swiftly declined. Although youth movements were founded in that same year by Dr. Azikiwe and Dr. Danquah, they only managed to keep the nationalist policy alive, without implicating the country's masses.

The march toward independence

In August 1947, in Sekondi, the United Gold Coast Convention was formed, with the avowed objective of leading the country to self-government in the shortest possible time. Kwame Nkrumah, who had spent several years in the United States and England, was invited to serve as its general secretary. He eventually departed to found the Convention People's Party, which won total support from the workers.

Representing an utterly new direction in the nationalist struggle, which thus far had been led by intellectuals supported by an intelligentsia, the new party enjoyed the backing of the country at large.

The war had triggered a difficult situation: low wages, rising cost of living, and unemployment. Those who had fought alongside the British overseas, occasionally on terms of equality, were in no mood to accept this situation lying down.

The cabinet formed in 1951 contained eight Africans, Kwame Nkrumah among them. The latter became prime minister the following year. In 1954, the British officers who were still high ranking members of the defense, foreign affairs, finance and justice ministries were replaced by Ghanaians. The only non-national was the head of this cabinet, who stayed on until March 6, 1957, the date the proclamation of the national independence of the Gold Coast, rechristened Ghana. On July 1, 1960, the country became a republic with Dr. Nkrumah as its first president.

Until 1966, Nkrumah remained the promoter of Ghana's growth in every field — education, health, social services, industry, and, above all, the colossal achievement of the Akosombo Dam. But he had perhaps also expected too much from a people unprepared for the intensive efforts required to modernize a country only just emerging from years of colonial torpor.

On February 24, 1966, shortly after the inauguration of the Akosombo Dam, Kwame Nkrumah was overthrown by the armed forces. A military government, known as the National Liberation Council, proceeded to administer the affairs of state until Chief Justice Edward Akufo-Addo was elected president of the republic (with Dr. Busia as prime minister) in 1970.

The Second Republic

The adoption of a second constitution appeared to offer the possibility of a healthy balance of power between the presidency and the government's legislative, judiciary and executive branches. Unfortunately the promise of a viable democratic political structure was never fulfilled. On January 13, 1972, Ghana's army again interceded and placed Colonel Acheompong at the head of the government. Colonel Acheompong was in turn overthrown in 1978 by Akuffo, who was in turn overthrown by Flight Lieutenant Rawlings on June 4, 1979.

From the very beginning, the astonishing Rawlings proclaimed his indifference to power, while justifying his intervention for the sake of permitting free parliamentary elections. When these were held in September 1979, Lieutenant Rawlings kept his word and departed from the government, leaving the place to the People's National Party candidate, Dr. Hilla Limann, who had been democratically elected for a two-year term.

The ensuing period of political and economic disorder prompted Lieutenant Rawlings to intervene once again, and on December 31, 1981, he reassumed control of the government. At present, some ten years later, considerable progress has been accomplished, although much still remains to be done.

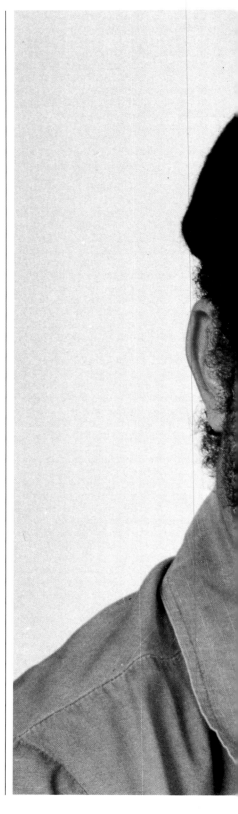

Ghana's Head of State
Flight Lieutenant Jerry John Rawlings
has led the country
into a new era of economic
and social progress.

ghana's economy

■ All of the governments that followed in the wake of Kwame Nkrumah attempted to save the country from imminent bankruptcy. The objective of the 1981 revolution was the same, with the essential difference that this time, the objective is being gradually attained.

After ten years of national austerity during which the rest of the world continued to believe that Ghana's economy was definitively gutted, irrefutable statistics began to reveal the progress that had been accomplished: an average growth-rate of 5 percent annually, constant reduction of the national debt, inflation reduced by a factor of ten and a generally positive foreign trade balance.

Although 1990 was marked by the negative effects of drought conditions on agricultural exports, diminishing world market prices for products such as cocoa (Ghana's leading export) and increasingly expensive oil imports, the 1991 budget estimations project a 4 percent increase in gross domestic product due to fiscal reforms favoring private investment and exports, coupled with reduced government spending in the public sector following the massive privatization of state-owned enterprises and the streamlining of the civil service administration. In all of these areas, the tendency is toward the progressive dismantlement of centralized government planning in favour of individual responsibility and initiative. And even if the present government has taken a hard-line approach to the necessity of imposing vital but often severe economic measures over the last ten years, Lieutenant Rawlings remains committed to the ideal of creating an authentic participatory democracy, exercised by citizens increasingly conscious of their power and responsibilities. In this respect, both the Economic Recovery Programme of 1983 and the Structural Adjustment Programme of 1986 are models of concrete, pragmatic reasoning, grounded in a realistic evaluation of current national priorities in terms of available resources.

Two-thirds of Ghana's 239, 460 square kilometres are suitable for cultivation. The plains of northern Ghana mainly produce cereal crops such as numerous varieties of millet and corn, and to a lesser degree, sorghum, yams, peas, beans and peanuts. On the northern savannas,

THE PORTS OF TAKORADI AND TEMA

■ The port of Takoradi, constructed in 1928 to facilitate shipment of lumber, cocoa and ore, boasts a main entryway 200 metres wide and 12 metres deep. The basin covers a surface area of 82 hectares and is protected by a main jetty 2,500 metres long. Special wharves permit the loading of manganese, bauxite, coal, cocoa and lumber, while the main docking facilities can accommodate six ships simultaneously.

The port of Tema, constructed in 1961, was primarily designed for the trans-shipment of imports and the unloading of material bound for Akosombo and the aluminium foundry. Its entryway is 260 metres wide and 12 metres deep. The main port covers a surface area of 172 hectares, with a 2,000-metre jetty. The total length of the wharves is 2,400 metres, interconnected by rail spurs. The main port also features a fishing harbour with an outer basin for large trawlers and an inner basin for accommodating pirogues, small motor launches and the facilities of the Accra Yacht Club.

the fruit of karite trees provides oil and a flour-base, while in the more humid valleys, rice, sweet potatoes, tomatoes and eggplant are cultivated. Despite their proximity to the sea, Ghana's coastal plains are often arid, and are generally given over to the cultivation of drought-resistant strains of corn and manioc. With irrigation, the dry but fertile soil of these regions would be capable of sustaining many other types of crops.

Industrial crops

Kola nuts and palm oil once formed the time-honoured basis for trade between the northern caravans and the inhabitants of Ghana's forested regions, and later on between the latter and the Europeans on the coast. Kola trees and palm trees grow naturally in the forest — in other words, in the areas where an obtrusive neighbour, the cocoa tree, was increasingly destined to be planted. However, kola has maintained its stability in Brong-Ahafo, in the northern Ashanti region, and in parts of the central and eastern regions. As for palm oil, after representing the major export in 1884, production declined sharply as a result of the introduction of cocoa and began retrieving its position only long afterwards.

Around 1850, coffee was also an export product, basically grown in the hills of Akwapim and Krobo. Like the palm, it suffered from the introduction of the cocoa plant, which required the same type of climate and soil.

Rubber extracted from trees growing naturally in the forest had also become a major export by the end of the nineteenth century. But the plants were stricken by disease, and the quality of their product became inferior to that of Asian products. However, after Ghana achieved its independence, hevea plants were introduced into the southwest, where they are still thriving.

Sugar cane grows in the forest regions and in the valleys that are damp or flooded during the rainy season.

The peasant farmers formerly grew cane only for their own consumption, except in the area near Komenda, on the coast, and Asutsuare, in the eastern region, where there are sugar refineries.

Not until 1951 did tobacco — originally imported by the Portuguese — come into its own, after the creation of the Pioneer Tobacco Company. It is raised in the Brong-Ahafo region, the eastern region, the Volta region, and several northern districts.

Until 1920, no serious attention was given to the cultivation of coconuts except in the region of Keta, on the east coast. From that time on, all along the littoral, encouragement was given to the creation of farmsteads specializing in copra, the pulp of the coconut from which oil is extracted for both export and local consumption.

Last but not least, jute has been cultivated since the accession to independence, especially in the Kumasi region, where it supplies a sack factory.

The cocoa revolution

In 1879, a Ghanaian named Tetteh Quarshie introduced Brazilian cocoa plants and successfully acclimatized them in the region of Akwapim.

The colonial government quickly realized the value of this crop, and in 1890, in the Botanical Garden at Aburi, a few miles from Accra, it set up a cocoa-tree nursery for the purpose of supplying seedlings to growers at low cost. This newcomer embarked on a career that eventually led it to occupy all of the forest zone and to become a foreign major source of revenue, accounting for two-thirds of total exports.

For many years, purchases and sales of cocoa were carried on by private companies that imposed their terms on the local producers. But the year 1947 saw the founding of the Cocoa Marketing Board, responsible for determining the optimum conditions for producers and for distribution to the world market. In normal periods, the purchase price was lower than the selling price, and the difference saved was earmarked for a compensation fund in the event of a price drop. But throughout the period leading up to independence, the cocoa trade was carried on under first-rate conditions and the fund set aside constituted a considerable reserve.

There are virtually no farmsteads in any region on which poultry, sheep or goats are not raised. The non-Moslems also raise pigs. As for cattle, the herds can be seen on the coastal plains and in the northern savannas. Yet Ghana has a meat shortage and is obliged to import 60 percent of its consumption requirements.

Several causes account for this shortage. Up to recently, no importance was assigned to fodder crops. The cattle

*The savannas of Northern Ghana are often
the victim of periods of drought.
But with the first drops of rain comes
the miracle of rebirth, as trees and grasslands
burst into new and verdant life.*

grazed exclusively on the tall grass that sprouts up with the onset of the rains, a determining factor that, when rainfall is insufficient, has catastrophic repercussions on the animals' food and water supply. In the north, many of the streams are intermittent, and drought is a cruel menace hanging over the livestock if the water holes dry up too fast.

Even if the cattle do not perish, the quality and quantity of their meat are affected.

In addition, many areas whose permanent humidity ensures constantly-available pasturelands are infested with the tsetse fly, which is difficult to exterminate in forest areas since often the only solution is the uprooting of the bushes that shelter them.

The protein deficiency caused by the meat shortage could be compensated by the consumption of fish, which contains approximately the same amount of protein. Ghana's permanent rivers and Lake Bosumtwi are rich in various types of freshwater fish, and have been fished since time immemorial. This activity was traditionally non-intensive, since in the south a number of prohibitions restricted the methods of fishing, or even completely outlawed it. In the north, the local inhabitants were traditionally far more interested in cattle raising. In any event, the lack of refrigerated trucks and warehouses rendered the transport and distribution of the catches virtually impossible; in consequence, fishing never represented a significant resource on the national scale.

Although the coastal dwellers had always fished the lagoons and the sea, their activities remained artisanal and were confronted by the same transportation problems for supplying non-local markets.

The Volta River Dam projet

In 1915, several ambitious ideas dawned simultaneously in the imagination of a brilliant, far-sighted engineer named Albert Kitson: he realized that the Kwahu Plateau contained a rich bauxite deposit; that the Volta River at Akosombo would lend itself admirably to the building of a dam that would supply an enormous amount of electricity; that the lake created by the rising waters would enable transporting the bauxite to Akosombo, where a foundry operating with the energy generated by the power plant could convert it into aluminium;

and that the reserve of lake water could irrigate the uncultivated land on the Accra plains. He submitted his report to Governor Guggisberg, who shelved it because he was too busy building the port of Takoradi.

Down through the years this idea was periodically re-examined, modified and once again pigeonholed, while the cost of the project steadily went on increasing. But for the future president Nkrumah this project became a primary goal for ensuring Ghana's modernization and independence.

In addition to the possibilities envisioned by Kitson, it was clear that the considerable size of the lake would make it an ideal means of communication between the regions it encompassed, and that once fish had been released into its waters, it would become a first-rate source of food for the shore dwellers. Thanks to the electricity generated, the problem of refrigerated storage would be solved, and a boost would be given to a metallurgical industry that would lack for nothing, from the ore to the final conversion into the items of all kinds needed by the country. Finally the electrification of the various regions could be achieved.

In addition, long before, other surveys had pointed up the fact that the site of Tema, some 20 kilometres from Accra, was suitable for a deep-water port. And the dam project was supplemented by that of the port that would equilibrate on the east the commercial and industrial power represented since 1928 by Takoradi on the west. The president was convinced that in order to be effective, his country's political independence should be accompanied by economic independence. To this end, it was necessary to industrialize the country, and this meant carrying out the full programme et all costs.

The capital investment involved was considerable, and even if it were possible to obtain loans, it would be necessary to achieve cost-effectiveness early on in order to meet repayment dates. In the long term there was no problem, but it was the first few years that were financially critical.

Careful budgeting was necessary, including an inventory of all the country's financial resources, aside from the

THE AKOSOMBO DAM

■ *With an eye to improved earthquake resistance (Accra has been hit by two serious quakes in the course of its history), Akosombo Dam was not constructed in solid concrete, but has a central vertical nucleus of clay covered on either side by a layer of crushed rock and its outer walls reinforced by great blocks of rocks. On either side of the main dam there is a spillway leading to the power plant, while two conduits carry off overflow in the downstream direction of the river. Another dam of similar design holds the waters of a secondary branch of the river.*
The height of the principal dam is 124.5 metres, its width across the base is 368.4 metres, and the width across the water's surface is 675 metres. The power plant, measuring 171 metres long and 52 metres wide and standing 32 metres high, includes six generators with a total combined power of 912,000 kilowatts.
The lake's surface covers 8.469 square kilometres, contains 147,600 million cubic metres of water, and stretches for 402.5 kilometres, with 4,830 kilometres of shoreline. When the rainy season causes the lake waters to rise, the latter can flood as many as 101,250 additional hectares.

reserves in the funds of the Cocoa Marketing Board.

Mining resources

The gold that had lured so many foreigners was obtained by panning the sands of streams such as the Ankobra and the Birim.

Not until around 1877 did the Frenchman Pierre Bonnat discover a gold mine in Tarkwa that had been worked for fifty years by Africans. By 1882, six European mining companies were already established in the region. Up to 1914, the sole mining product was gold. At that time, just south of Tarkwa, bauxite was discovered.

In 1919 came the discovery of the first diamonds in the Birim River, northwest of Kibi. Several sizable deposits were eventually located in this area, notably at Oda and Akwatia, and were worked by European companies, while the Bonsa Valley, whose diamond deposits were somewhat less abundant, remained the domain of private African prospectors.

Next came the finding of bauxite, discovered near Bakwai and at Awaso. But the extraction of aluminium from bauxite requires cheap electricity; the ore was therefore exported raw.

Shortly before the gaining of independence, annual revenue from gold production was approximately ten million pounds sterling, while that of manganese was 8.7 million pounds sterling, that of bauxite three million pounds, and that of diamonds around four million pounds sterling. Altogether, this accounted for one-fourth of total exports, and the bauxite deposits on the Kwahu Plateau and at Kibi had not yet been touched.

Lumber production

Ghana's forests contain timber of high market value, the exporting of which began in 1891. The initial transportation problem, involving the dispatching of logs by floating them downstream, was solved by the building of a railroad from the timberlands to Takoradi. If the port of Takoradi was chosen over Tema, this was because in 1928 the bulk of the raw materials for export came from the west. Three hundred species of trees were felled, but up to World War II, mahogany was almost the only wood exported, the others going to supply primarily small local industries. At the time Ghana achieved its independence, lumber sales amounted to between seven and eight million pounds sterling per year.

Once the costs had been determined, the risks calculated and the loans obtained, the decision was made to begin the construction of the Volta Dam. However, the plans for extracting bauxite from the Kwahu Plateau had to be shelved, since to supply the foundry that would be using the electricity from the power plant, it would have been necessary to import the raw materials. This sacrifice was imposed by the budget, and despite the savings thus achieved, getting the necessary funds together was nevertheless a major undertaking.

In April 1961, parliament created the Volta River Authority, headed by President Nkrumah.

It was assigned the job of planning, carrying out and administering all the phases of the operation, including the resettlement of the 80.000 people forced out by the forming of the lake. This was a major challenge both in practical and human terms, since it was necessary to build houses, equip villages, and find land that was the equivalent of what the local inhabitants were obliged to abandon.

Building the Akosombo Dam

Work on the dam and hydroelectric plant began in July 1961, at the same time as the building of the city of Akosombo and the Port of Tema — vital for importing the equipment required for achieving the project — with its industrial zone and the foundry. It was considered logical to locate the latter near the port where the aluminium would be unloaded, since in any event Tema would be supplied with electricity from the power plant.

These projects complemented one another with rigorous logic, and it became clear that the results would be on a scale worthy of the political revolution triggered by the country's independence: on the east, Tema would balance Takoradi in terms of activities, jobs, and foreign trade; the relocated rural and urban populations would enjoy the comfort of newly-constructed housing, several fishing ports would be built around the lake, and the latter would supply all the water necessary for irrigating the south plains. Nothing was lacking.

Unfortunately, the total cost was

*The pride of Ghana and
a major source of hydroelectric energy,
Akosombo Dam in the Eastern Region
has immensely contributed to
the country's economic progress.*

steep, due to the secondary expenses involved, which included the necessity of having numerous foreign technicians on the payroll, sending young Ghanaians to Western countries to take crash training courses, relocating the population in what amounted to a veritable city — Keta-Krachi — on the lake's north shore, and for equipping new fishing fleets, not to mention the town of Tema and the transformations that were going on in the region.

In addition, in the wake of independence, the price of cocoa had dropped sharply on several occasions, while numerous diseased trees had had to be destroyed.

The price of progress

Despite the basic soundness of his development programme, President Nkrumah, judged responsible for the government's economic difficulties, was overthrown. Until the intervention of Lieutenant Rawlings, none of the successive governments that followed were able to resolve Ghana's economic crisis. Today, however, the success of the Akosombo project has resulted in the rehabilitation of ex-president Nkrumah's reputation as a visionary leader, a far cry from the accusations of having financially ruined Ghana that were leveled against him in the 1960s. Not only has the electricity generated by the dam stimulated the industrial development of the entire country, but Ghana has also become a major exporter of electrical energy to most of her immediate neighbours, including Togo, Benin, and the Ivory Coast.

Lake Volta is used for the shipment of merchandise at far more reasonable rates than by road transport, and is significantly contributing to the development of intra-African commerce. Oil, for example, will transit from Tema to Burkina-Faso by the lake, even as the local population profits from fishing in its waters. Although for years, little was done to develop Akosombo as a tourist destination, the current renovation of its existing accommodations and the upcoming construction of a four-star Pullman Hotel are likely to result in significantly higher levels of visitor frequentation.

The creation and stocking of Lake Volta resulted in an extensive fish reserve which in turn led — after government encouragement and assistance — to the emergence of a new industry. As this prospered, Ghana's other provinces became conscious of the fact that beyond their obvious contribution to electrification and irrigation, dams also offered direct economic possibilities for the local population, since their lakes could be developed to permit fishing and industrial-scale pisciculture.

The ongoing development of the Lake Volta fisheries led to the creation of a fishing port at Kpandu in the 1970s, whose infrastructure includes a refrigerated processing plant, distribution facilities and a boat-yard for the construction of fishing vessels.

Fishing thus represents a non-negligeable economic factor for Ghana, since the revenues generated by this activity rose from 93 million cedis in 1984 to 112 million in 1990, with an overall revenue of 115 million cedis projected for 1991. Despite the export of products such as shrimp, tuna and the 32,000 tons of frozen or conserved fish shipped overseas in 1990, the Ghanaian fishing industry does not at present represent one of the nation's principal sources of foreign exchange.

The cocoa industry

Despite the fluctuations in its international market price — unilaterally established by foreign buyers — cocoa remains Ghana's leading export.

Unfortunately, this sector suffered a near-total collapse in the troubled years following Ghana's independence. After being the world's leading cocoa producer with a record-breaking output of 500,000 tons in 1965, Ghana's exports dropped to 150,000 tons following the 1983-84 harvest. The cocoa industry was a priority objective of the Economic Recovery Programme launched in 1983, and by 1990-91, output had increased to 250,000 tons with an expected yield of 300,000 tons projected for 1995.

In 1990, cocoa represented 40 percent of Ghana's overall export revenues, 12 percent of which were directly perceived by the state. One-third of Ghana's cultivable land (more than one million hectares) is employed for cocoa production, providing employment for 600,000 families. This preponderance of a profitable monoculture also has its drawbacks, insofar as cocoa production is highly vulnerable to factors such as inevitable international market downturns, droughts, plant disease and the progressive migration of the younger cocoa-workers to Ghana's cities.

While investing in more stable revenue-producing sectors of the economy invulnerable to the above-mentioned vicissitudes, the government has been obliged to make an all-out effort to increase the yield and quality of cocoa. One such approach was to incite growers to produce more by increasing the wholesale price paid to producers from 16 to 50 percent since 1981 of the world market price. Other factors, such as the drought conditions which occured during the 1989-90 growing season are more dificult to master, even though the planting of drought-resistant strains of the cocoa plant is being considered. All of the problems and potential solutions relative to cocoa culture are the responsibility of a central planning agency known as the Ghana Cocoa Board (Cocobod).

The Cocobod empire

Cocobod is a government agency possessing the legal monopoly for the purchase and sale of cocoa. Its scope extends far beyond these two basic functions, since the agency is comprised of numerous divisions including a research institute and laboratories specialized in cultures such as coffee and karite. Cocobod's affiliated Cocoa Services Division offers agricultural training, equipment and seed distribution to growers, runs health checks on their produce, and provides managerial support for some of the larger plantations. Cocobod Plantations Ltd. directly controls twenty-one cocoa and nineteen coffee plantations, while the Produce Inspection Division provides a health inspection service for cocoa, coffee and karite nut growers. The Produce Buying Company is responsible for the purchase, storage and transport of agricultural products which upon arrival at the ports of Tema and Takoradi, are passed on to Cocobod's Cocoa Marketing Company, responsible for overseas sales. Lastly, the Cocoa Processing Company manages three plants which transform raw cocoa into liquor, biscuits, cocoa butter, powder and chocolate.

As may be gathered from the above, Cocobod is an immense organization whose overall efficiency is unfortunately hampered by its very size. Although Cocobod's Research Institute has in the past accomplished valuable research into drought-resistant plant strains, parasite and disease control and natural fertilizers made from cocoa-bean pods (previously considered as a waste product), the operating costs generated by Cocobod's numerous activities progressively became prohibitive. Given the necessity of streamlining the organization, certain of its personnel were made redundant and some plantations privatized. Additional measures included the acceleration of marketing procedures and the encouragement of a competitive, free-market environment and the entry of foreign partnerships.

Diversification of agricultural products

Coffee production, which was formerly one of the Cocobod monopolies, has since been entirely privatized. Companies interested in the purchase, processing and exportation of coffee beans are nevertheless required to obtain trade authorizations issued by Cocobod. It is interesting to observe Ghana's current drive toward the liberalization and privatization of its economy. Formerly similar to the economies of Eastern Europe, particularly that of Czechoslovakia, for the last two years Ghana has displayed a similar determination to reduce government control in favour of free enterprise.

This progressive liberalization is being conducted with measure and prudence by Ghana's governement, in an effort to avoid the exploitation of a workforce potentially vulnerable to labour abuse within the newly-emerging economic context. Foreign aid is contributing to Ghana's overall efforts of modernization: the World Bank has recently financed a one hundred million dollar project to permit the replacement of diseased cocoa plants, obsolete machinery and the general upgrading of the means of production.

If cocoa represents Ghana's principal export and source of foreign exchange, the government accords no less importance to other types of agricultural produce. Their variety and quality contribute to the general health and well-being of the population, reduce the need to import similar items and represent a positive economic factor for Ghana's international trade balance.

In addition, once the national demand is satisfied, this produce will constitute a potentially exportable — and profitable — resource for the country.

In the 1970s, Ghana's Bureau for the Development of Cereals and Vegetables actively encouraged the cultivation of corn, rice, sorghum, peanuts and the newly-introduced soy bean plant, an invaluable source of vegetable protein.

*Cocoa culture, fishing, gold
and bauxite mining as well as
manufacturing, traditional handicrafts
and a growing tourist industry all
contribute to Ghana's burgeoning economy.*

Since that time, corn production — among others — has considerably increased, rising from 173,000 tons in 1975 to 715,000 tons in 1989.

In collaboration with the World Bank, Ghana's government implemented a medium programme to ensure agricultural self-sufficiency for all of the nation's provinces, the creation of rural employment, the reinforcement of agricultural/industrial collaboration and the development of non-traditional (other than cocoa and coffee) produce for exportation.

Among these initiatives was the creation of new agricultural centres such as those implanted in the central provinces and Brong-Ahafo, uniquely specialized in the cultivation of yams. Similar projects for the mono-cultivation of spices, cashew nuts and mushrooms are being planned for Ghana's ten provinces, in an effort to expand the range of primary exports such as pineapples, fresh yams and kola nuts. In 1989, a special agricultural award was accorded to the Combined Farmers Company, which had exported a record-breaking 2,187 tons of pineapples during the year, representing 27.3 percent of Ghana's overall exported tonnage of this product.

Other main agricultural exports appear in the pages of "The Exporter," published by the Ghanaian Council for the Promotion of Exportation, and include several varieties of bananas, cotton seeds, tobacco, rubber tree sap, ginger, medicinal plants and processed products such as palm oil and beer.

Gold: increased exportation

Although the ancient empire of Ghana was geographically situated to the northwest of its present-day namesake, its principal source of wealth was the gold extracted from the mines of upper Senegal.

Gold was an immemorial symbol of the Akans, still one of modern Ghana's largest ethnic groups, and continued to represent a highly profitable resource following Ghana's independence. At present, it is projected that gold exports will represent Ghana's principal source of foreign exchange within the decade, thus forming a symbolic link between the ancient empire and the young state.

In the 1960s, and following independence, the State Gold Mines were created to take over a number of mines which were being closed by foreign private companies. The government acquired a 55 percent stake in the AGC in 1969 with Lonrho as a minority partner responsible for management. The output of Ghana's other mines had diminished to the point that in 1983, the Obuasi fields alone were producing 86 percent of the total national output. In 1984, Ghana's present government decided to massively invest in the development of mining activities. Appropriate legislation was passed and a governmental Minerals Commission created. At the same time, the Ghanaian cedi was successively devalued to a more realistic level, permitting its use in foreign trade and exchange. As Ghana's economic infrastructure improved, exports resumed, and the World Bank accorded funds for the renovation of the SGMC in 1985.

In 1990, total gold production stood at 550,000 ounces, and is expected to rise to 1 million ounces in 1993 and 1.2 million in 1995.

New legislation in 1989 accorded private citizens the right to prospect for gold in Ghana's rivers and streams. This had long been prohibited during the period when any form of gold mining and prospecting was the exclusive privilege of state-owned companies. At present, alone or in groups of two or three, often the urban unemployed or former mine workers armed with little more than a simple shovel, small-scale prospectors are striking out on their own across Ghana's countryside. Small-scale mining has resumed not only in rivers and streams but also a number of areas with a long history of individual workings.

At the same time, the number of privately-owned mines and mining companies has increased. The Ashanti Gold Fields Company operates the Obuasi mines; the government-owned SGMC runs the Prestea, Tarkwa and Dunkwa fields, and in 1988, the Southern Cross Mining Company cast the first gold bar from ore extracted from the new Konongo mine. The Canadian firm Bogosu Resources Ltd. reopened an abandoned mine northeast of Prestea in 1989, while Teberebie Goldfield controls the fields located southwest of Tarkwa. Sixty-eight authorizations for large-scale prospection have been granted since 1985, of which twenty-two were accorded to principally foreign-owned companies. One of the particularly noteworthy features of these licensing agreements is the environmental protecting clause requiring mining companies to totally renovate the site once operations are definitively terminated; in concrete terms, this means that the companies must totally refill the quarry and replant the surrounding land.

Other mineral wealth

Ghana also produces nearly 85 percent of the world's industrial-grade diamonds and is the source of 15 percent of its gemstones. These are initially purchased directly by the government-owned Precious Minerals Marketing Company from producers such as Ghana Consolidated Diamonds, Ltd. Although Ghana Consolidated produces some three million dollars worth of rough diamonds annually, this is exactly one hundred times less than the three hundred million dollars generated by Ghana's gold exports in 1991. The Precious Minerals Marketing Corporation also purchases rough diamonds from private mining companies; after momentarily decreasing, overall production rose to 14 million dollars in 1990, largely due to modernization efforts and the liberalization of the market.

The gold extracted from Ghana's rivers and streams by local prospectors is also purchased by the Precious Minerals Marketing Corporation. One of its more interesting sidelines is the creation of diamond and gold jewellery, patterned after traditional Ghanaian decorative motifs such as Ashanti ancestor stools or native fertility dolls. For centuries, Ghana's skilled goldsmiths turned out splendid pieces of symbolic and ceremonial jewellery, examples of which can still be seen worn by the traditional tribal chieftains. Today, contemporary jewellery-makers exercise their craft in all of the country's regions, and a project is underway to create a trade association affiliated with the Corporation.

Ghana's other mineral resources include manganese (246,869 tons in 1990), and bauxite from the Akosombo region (368,659 tons in 1990; with a projected 1993 output of 500,000 tons). The presence of the latter mineral, whose extraction and transformation into aluminium is particularly energy-intensive, was one of the major reasons behind the construction of the Akosombo hydroelectric project. Since at the present time there are no facilities for transforming bauxite into aluminium oxide, Ghana's bauxite is exported overseas while aluminium oxide is imported and transformed into aluminium at the Tema industrial complex.

Ghana's mineral resources are progressively being privatized; as the government pursues its ongoing policy of developing a free-market economy, negotiations concerning the acquisition of the State Gold Mining Company and Ghana Consolidated Diamonds by foreign investors are currently underway.

At the same time, and with the technical assistance of Germany, the systematic exploration of Ghana's mineral wealth and reserves is being carried out in the southwest, while the government's Minerals Commission is seeking financing from other foreign partners to extend the project to the entire country.

Wood production and petroleum

From 1990 to 1991, the exports of raw timber and wood products constituted Ghana's third-ranking source of foreign exchange. Output in 1990 increased 35 percent over the preceding year, for a total of 370,000 m³ of roughcut logs representing 120 million dollars and 70,000 jobs.

As elsewhere in the world, Ghana's timber resources are seriously endangered by wholesale deforestation, natural enemies such as fires and disease, as well as by intensive domestic consumption in the form of firewood or charcoal.

Although the World Wood Programme recently allocated ten million dollars for replanting, the solution to the problem of deforestation can only occur through the development of substitute forms of domestic combustibles. In this sense, the experiments in electrical generation by solar energy conducted by German technicians at Krokobite (a beach on the outskirts of Accra) are of particular interest. The electricity obtained is being used as a general source of energy rather than simply for the heating of water, as is often the case in such applications. In this connection the Government's efforts to promote the use of liquefied petroleum for domestic use to replace firewood, which occupies such a dominant place in Ghana's energy balance, is of great interest.

The Ghana National Petroleum Corportation (GNPC) was created in 1983 with the objective of supervising the exploration and exploitation of Ghana's oil resources. Among its other activities, the GNPC is also responsible for the importation of crude oil which is refined by the Tema Oil Refinery and sold to distributors such as Shell, Mobil or the Ghana Oil Company (GOIL).

Ghana possesses four major sedimentary basins, including the Tano Basin which extends from western Ghana to the Ivory Coast and contains both offshore and onshore oil and natural gas reserves. Oil and natural gas have been discovered in a number of fields offshore Ghana and oil seepages have been well known in the onshore part of the Tano Basin for almost a century. However, only the Salt-pond field was put on production between 1978 and 1986 when the field was shut in because of a sharp decline in production. A reevaluation of the field is being undertaken by the Ghana National Petroleum Corporation with a view to determining the viability of rehabilitating the field to produce both oil and natural gas. Studies have been undertaken on the possibility of using natural gas reserves in the Saltpond field as well as the North and South Tano fields to generate electricity in order to complement Ghana's existing hydro-electric system.

The Accra-Keta Basin is part of a basin that extends from Ghana to Togo and Benin. An offshore well was drilled in 1990, but the results remain inconclusive. The Voltaian Basin comprises nearly half of Ghana's national territory, and is as yet untapped.

The GNPC is promoting the potential of Ghana's basins to international oil companies with whom it wishes to enter into joint ventures to undertake the substantial investments needed to develop commercial oil and gas reserves in Ghana. For the moment, then, it is difficult to foresee what the country's petroleum and natural gas reserves will represent in terms of output and financial revenues.

Ghana's industrial centres

Ghanaian industry is principally concentrated within three urban areas: Accra-Tema, Kumasi and Sekondi-Takoradi.

Accra's main manufacturing base includes a tile and brick works, distilleries, breweries, furniture manufacturers and light industries. Tema industrial zone includes steelworks, drydock and fabrication facilities ; the Tema Food Complex, which packages fresh and smoked fish, as well as produces cooking oil, wheat-flour and poultry-feed; the Ghana Cement Factory; the Pioneer Food Company, which processes and cans tuna; Lever Brothers (soap and detergent manufacture); the Ghana Textile Manufacturing Company (clothing); Tema Lube Oil, specialized in the processing of motor lubricants and

*An important fishing
and commercial port,
Tema is also one
of Ghana's largest
industrial complexes.*

some industrial lubricants and the manufacture of their containers; Valco Aluminium, a foundry which supplies the sheet-aluminium and roofing materials manufacturer Aluworks Ltd., and the Ghana Pioneer Aluminium Company, which manufactures cooking utensils exported to neighbouring countries such as the Ivory Coast.

Takoradi is the centre of a number of wood-related industries, such as the Takoradi Veneer and Lumber Company, active in lumbering and an exporter of wood products throughout the world, including over a dozen African countries.

The largest Kumasi-based companies include a glue manufacturer and the Tomos bicycle and motorbike plant as well as woodprocessing plants.

A project to manufacture beer from local sorghum, based on research conducted in Germany, is being sponsored by the Accra Brewery Company, Ghana's largest beer producer and the second-largest of sub-Saharan Africa, with an annual output of 10 million cases.

The Industrial Adjustment Programme

Created by the Ministry of Industry, Science and Technology in collaboration with the World Bank, the Industrial Adjustment Programme is intended to maximize the efficient utilization of Ghana's natural resources and raw materials, increase industrial output and facilitate the phasing-out (or streamlining) of the country's unprofitable or badly-managed industries. The programme comprises a number of incentives for the development of private companies, whether producing for domestic consumption or exportation. To facilitate exportation, administrative procedures are being simplified, with manufacturers encouraged to transform their basic products into high added-value goods (such as cooking utensils out of sheet-aluminium, or furniture and wood panelling out of rough-cut logs).

Smaller companies, which are particularly vulnerable to international competition and the obsolescence of their manufacturing processes, are targeted for special support. It is foreseen that small to medium-sized companies will play an increasingly important role in the development of Ghana's domestic economy. Moreover, they represent a potential technological spearhead, respond to the basic needs of the population and are relatively easy to create. To facilitate their development, the government has reduced corporate taxes from 45 to 35 percent. Reforms of the banking system have increased the availability of loans to small businesses, while international investment guidelines have been revised to attract foreign capital. The creation of a free market economy also constitutes an additional threat to Ghana's smaller industries, which up to the present have profited from the government's protectionist trade policies and the high import duties levied against foreign-made goods. Rather than modifying the objective of a free market environment, the government is aiding small businesses to become more competitive and cost-effective.

In terms of employment, the small business sector represents a full 80 percent of the industrial workforce. Given the importance of its contribution to the national economy, the sector will also be the object of a special assistance programme developed jointly by the Ministry of Industry, the National Board for Small-Scale Industries and the World Bank.

It is anticipated that loans and long term financing for small and medium scale enterprises will be provided. The First Finance Company, scheduled to be launched in late 1991, will offer assistance to potentially viable companies and industrial projects.

Lastly, to facilitate their development, small businesses will be exempted from the previously obligatory 25 percent initial deposit on loan-capital: henceforth, the total worth of the company will serve as collateral.

Public works projects

Among the many difficulties that confronted Ghana in the late 1970s was the deterioration of the road system. At present, only an estimated 42 percent of the nation's roads are considered as being in satisfactory condition. The Urban Two Project, created to improve and extend Ghana's urban and regional highway network, will have constructed or renovated a total 260 kilometres of roads in 1991, while other long-range projects for the improvement of Ghana's road infrastructure are in the planning stages. The choice of Ghana as the venue for the 1991 Conference of Non-Aligned Nations has also resulted in the renovation of the runways and passenger facilities of Accra International Airport.

Water distribution remains a serious problem in Ghana, both for domestic use and for purposes of irrigation. At present, small-scale irrigation projects are favoured over those requiring heavy investment.

The financing of feasibility studies for small-scale irrigation projects is being provided by the World Bank and the Canadian International Development Agency (CIDA). One such project concerns the irrigation of the northeastern and northwestern territories; another foresees using lake water from the Kpong Dam on the Lower Volta to irrigate Ghana's northern plains.

Rural water distribution

The distribution of drinking water to rural populations remains a critical problem for the government. For villages with less than 500 inhabitants (representing approximately 20 percent of Ghana's rural communities), the most economical solution is the sinking of fresh-water wells. Four thousand wells of this type will be created by various international organizations over the next five years. Since manually-operated pumps are considered to be the best solution for villages of more than 2,000 inhabitants, it is projected to install some 6,000 new pumps by 1995, in addition to the 8,000 currently in service.

The problem also touches the provincial capitals, larger cities and even Accra's suburbs which often either lack a fully-developed distribution infrastructure or require the replacement of their existing systems.

In 1987, a conference on the problem of Ghanaian urban and rural water distribution was held in Accra. A number of practical and financial approaches were discussed, and feasibility studies organized. Another meeting on the same theme was held in February 1991, with the objective of providing at least 60 percent of the Ghanaian population with fresh water and water-fed sanitary facilities. Communities of less than 5,000 inhabitants were targeted in priority.

To qualify for the programme, they will also be expected to participate in the financing and maintenance of the local infrastructures.

At the same time, low-cost sanitary facilities are to be manufactured by private-sector companies, following a nationwide publicity campaign prior to the launch of the programme in 1992.

National mobilization

It is clear that in the public works sector, as in all others, the government is encouraging the population to address itself to the questions pertaining to its overall well-being as well as to take the initiative of finding adapted solutions. This policy also implies the active support of the government, since projects such as the above require the mobilization of large-scale national and international financial resources, even if the successful implementation of such programmes depends on the participation of all those directly concerned.

For Accra alone, the African Development Bank and the Ghana Water Sewerage Corporation foresee spending 36 million dollars over the next three years for the improvement of the capital's water distribution network, including the construction of underground reservoirs, the laying of an extensive water conduit system and the creation of pumping stations and water towers.

town by town
site by site

accra

■ Although the traditional African mask is rarely worn by most Ghanaians, it nevertheless symbolizes the multiplicity of visages possessed by every human being regardless of his or her origins or nationality. In many respects, a mask would be the ideal emblem for Accra, a secret and even "forbidden" city for visitors who limit themselves to its more superficial aspects.

It is indeed difficult for the casual visitor to realize that beneath its half-traditional, half-modern appearance, Accra contains a practically endless number of different worlds, each one dissolving into or interpenetrating the others like a series of superimposed colour slides. It is only when these images are examined slowly that their meaning — and often their charm — appears: Accra the village, or Accra the skyscraper metroplex; the Accra of banks and finance or Accra of the gods; the Accra of traditional music or the Accra of night clubs; the Accra of fisherfolk and street vendors or the Accra of white-collar workers; Accra basking in its fabled past or Accra of the future...

No city in the world lends itself less to organized tours, complete with loudspeakers and visitors dutifully following a guide...

Accra is a city that is perceived, intuited, imagined, and that surrenders itself — unexpectedly in quick instants, in pauses, in an exchange of smiles and above all, to those possessing a knowledge of its rich history and a love for its inhabitants.

Long ago and far away...

Many hundreds of years ago — no one knows for sure how many — the Kpesi people dwelt on a wild coast battered by violent waves. The Kpesi no longer exist except in the memory and traditional stories of the Ga, who conquered from them the present-day territory on which Accra is built.

The Ga were originally from Nigeria. In the early sixteenth century, small groups of Ga migrated to the southern plains. The migration may well have been peaceful, and the disappearance of the Kpesi can probably be explained more plausibly by intermarriage than extermination.

Although skilled warriors when it was necessary, the Ga were primarily attracted by the region's flat, readily-cultivatable soil. With the arrival of the Europeans, the Ga quickly readapted and turned out to be sharp traders and shrewd bargainers.

They didn't take long to realize that it was infinitely profitable to supply the newcomers with the goods and articles that they had come such a long way to find... especially when the merchandise included slaves.

The many tribal wars which were triggered by the gradual migrations of other ethnic groups from the north and northeast generated large numbers of prisoners, who sadly enough, became a basic staple of the slave trade. The Ga progressively became the middlemen between the inhabitants of the territory's inland villages and the European slavers with whom, in addition to human chattel, they traded gold, palm oil and kola nuts, often against firearms and a variety of implements.

The emergence of a city

To engage in trade, it helps to have a fixed location where trade can be conducted. The Ga thus established themselves west of Korle Lagoon, in a village destined to become the oldest quarter of the present-day capital. The settlement was little more than a fishing village, for it was not possible to live by gold or guns alone. It was thus that the fish caught by the Ga were also sold to the foreigners.

For the Europeans, matters were more complicated. Mere fishing villages were not the sort of accommodations that would do at all. The situation called for strongholds and fortresses for protection from other European rivals, attracted to the region by its commerce in gold and human beings like sharks scenting blood.

At various times, it seemed as if the Gold Coast was literally up for grabs. The Portuguese, despite their efficient habit of beheading anyone who got in their way, progressively lost their monopoly over the region and by the middle of the seventeenth century, a number of other nations were energetically attemping to fill the vacuum.

In and around the site of present-day Accra, the Ga had ceded land to three of these rival nations; to the Dutch in 1650, who constructed Fort Crevecœur, eventually renamed Fort Ussher, east of the present port; to the Swedes in 1657, who erected Christiansborg Castle, located much further east and destined for a dignified career as the headquarters of the British governor and later as the

Overleaf:
Stretching inland from
the seacoast, Greater Accra
is expanding at
an accelerated pace...

presidential palace of the independent state of Ghana; and, in 1673, to the British, who built James Fort. Many years after its construction, James Fort was transformed into a lighthouse whose beams can still be seen over the horizon of the port; as for Ussher Fort, it has since become a prison, while Christiansborg Castle still serves as the government headquarters.

Tactically speaking, it may appear surprising that the Ga so readily accommodated and even aided the Europeans to acquire the strategic positions which made them the effective masters of the region. It must be remembered that at the time, the Ga were at war with their redoutable Akwamu neighbours, whose frequent raids were rendering the Ga's existence increasingly difficult. Not surprisingly, they often sought temporary refuge behind the thick, protective walls of the Europeans' coastal strongholds, whose cannons, marvellously enough, could be turned from their usual positions facing the sea, inland toward the Akwamu enclaves....

Thus, practically within the walls of the three fortresses, there sprung up villages which have continued to exist up to the present day, even if many of their physical aspects have since changed. Osu sprawls at the feet of Christiansborg, and the forts of Ussher and James have engendered Ussher Town and James Town, surrounding the port on the north and west as far as Korle Lagoon, adjacent to the site of the original Ga settlement.

The village of Labadi

Approximately three kilometres from Christiansborg Castle, the village of Labadi is also inhabited by Ga descendants. The village was once almost totally agricultural, since at the time of Christiansborg's occupation by the Europeans, it was necessary to feed both the local population as well as the inhabitants of the fortress. But since those times, Labadi's protective mud walls and verdant fields have disappeared, and the village has been absorbed into greater Accra.

As the Ga were busily gaining an ever-firmer foothold in the region thanks to their activity as middlemen to the Europeans, the ownership of the forts began to change hands.

Four years after its construction, Christiansborg fell to the Danes; it became a Portuguese possession in 1679 only to become a Danish property in 1682. When the dangerous Akwamu gained control of it in 1693, the reaction of the Ga can easily be imagined. In any case, they must have been relieved when the castle was recaptured by the Danes a few months later. Christiansborg became British property in 1850, as did Fort Crevecœur — renamed Ussher Fort — in 1868.

As long as discord had prevailed among the European nations occupying the territory of the Gold Coast, the Ga had been left to quietly pursue their various occupations as middlemen between the Westerners and the indigenous populations of the region. Interestingly enough, and over the long term, these activities produced a new breed of trader — independent, unconcerned with abiding by the authority of the traditional chieftains, and like the Europeans who served as so perfect a role model, basically interested in turning the highest possible profit in the shortest possible time, on a minimum investment.

When the British ruled the Gold Coast, most of their citizens lived on land rented from the local inhabitants in and around present-day Accra (and in Cape Coast, the original headquarters of British administration). When the troubled period of European infighting for dominance of the territory had definitively ended, the former harmony reigning between the resident Westerners and the local population gradually gave way to racial tension, often based on the radically differing lifestyles of the two communities. Efforts on behalf of the local chieftains to compel their subjects to observe minimum health precautions met with little success, and the situation degenerated into a series of heated disputes between the two camps. In 1874, three years after the British had casually annexed the Gold Coast and transformed it into a full-fledged colony, the new governor transferred his administrative centre from Cape Coast to Accra, ostensibly to impose a semblance of order upon the Crown's new subjects.

The emergence of European quarters

In 1862, an earthquake destroyed much of Christiansborg Castle and James Fort. At the same time, the majority of the stone houses inhabited by the Europeans in James Town were reduced to rubble. In consequence, it be-

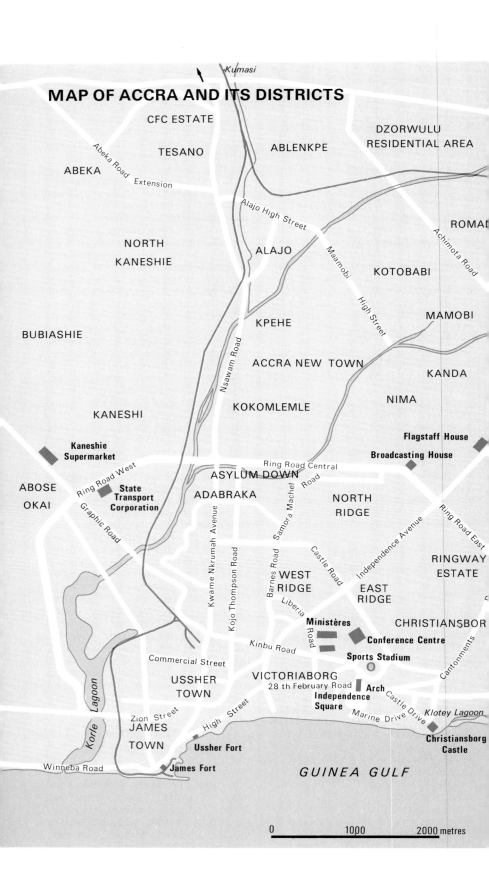

MAP OF ACCRA AND ITS DISTRICTS

Kumasi

CFC ESTATE

TESANO

ABEKA

Abeka Road Extension

DZORWULU RESIDENTIAL AREA

ABLENKPE

ROMAI

Achimota Road

Alajo High Street

NORTH KANESHIE

ALAJO

Maamobi

KOTOBABI

High Street

MAMOBI

BUBIASHIE

KPEHE

Nsawam Road

ACCRA NEW TOWN

KANDA

KANESHI

KOKOMLEMLE

NIMA

Kaneshie Supermarket

Flagstaff House

Broadcasting House

Ring Road Central

ASYLUM DOWN

Ring Road West

ABOSE OKAI

State Transport Corporation

Graphic Road

ADABRAKA

Samora Machel Road

NORTH RIDGE

Independence Avenue

Ring Road East

RINGWAY ESTATE

Kwame Nkrumah Avenue

Kojo Thompson Road

Barnes Road

WEST RIDGE

Castle Road

EAST RIDGE

Liberia Road

Ministères

Conference Centre

CHRISTIANSBOR

Cantonments

Korle Lagoon

Kinbu Road

Sports Stadium

Commercial Street

USSHER TOWN

VICTORIABORG

28th February Road

Arch

Castle Drive

Klotey Lagoon

Independence Square

Zion Street

High Street

JAMES TOWN

Marine Drive

Christiansborg Castle

Ussher Fort

Winneba Road

James Fort

GUINEA GULF

0   1000   2000 metres

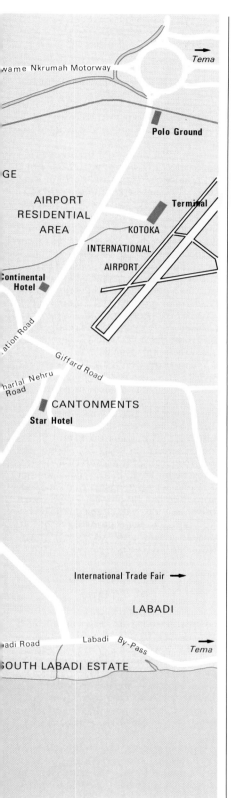

came necessary to draft a reconstruction and town planning scheme, however rudimentary.

Accra's transformation into a colonial capital had resulted in the erection of administrative buildings in the new quarter of Victoriaborg, on the east edge of Ussher Town. This was followed by the construction of bungalows for the Europeans, which resulted in a situation of *de facto* geographical segregation between the native and foreign communities. The separation became even more pronounced when the colonists, doubtlessly weary of their enforced celibacy, began sending for their wives and families. Victoriaborg gradually began expanding inland, where the micro-climate was considered more healthy than the frequently hot and humid coastal regions.

Between 1885 and 1900, a spacious new quarter emerged, filled with gracious residences on pile foundations surrounded by cool gardens. The quarter's development accelerated after 1892, when the acquisition of land by Europeans was officially authorized by law.

A mixed city council

At the same time, the municipal organization of the city was taking form. After the failure of the initial system of assigning the native chieftains with the delicate responsibility of collecting taxes destined for the upkeep of Accra from their subjects, the British created a mixed city council composed of chieftains, the newly-emerging local bourgeoisie and citizens of the Crown. Even then, few tangible results were achieved prior to 1898, at which time the council was comprised of ten members of the three above-mentioned communities.

At the turn of the century, Accra's city limits included Ussher Town, James Town, the European quarter of Victoriaborg and the coastal strip to Christiansborg Castle, which following its restoration, became the governor's residence in 1903.

The Ashanti wars, climaxed by the British conquest of the central region, had by then come to a definitive end. The northern territories had also been annexed by the Crown by means of treaties and pacts with the local chieftains, often negotiated under conditions involving varying degrees of coercion.

The creation of communication links with the interior of the country therefore became imperative. By 1895, a paved road had been laid northwest from Ussher Town in the direction of Nsawam. This primitive thoroughfare was to become the present-day Kwame Nkrumah Avenue (formerly Liberty Avenue), and resulted in the emergence of a series of new quarters and the development of the businesses and shops which line it today. At present, this original business district has expanded to include modern office buildings and the headquarters of most of the airline companies serving Ghana. The Adabraka residential quarter also began to emerge, bordered on the north by Ring Road, currently one of Accra's principal thoroughfares.

Northeast of the city, the construction of the road to Aburi resulted in the creation of West Ridge, East Ridge, Ringway Estate and the immense Cantonments district, lined with embassies and the gracious private residences found on the other side of Captain Thomas Sankara Circle on Ring Road, to the east of Liberation Road.

Much later on, beyond the Cantonments district, Kotoka International Airport was constructed, along with a new residential quarter just opposite.

Any discussion touching on the development of the city should include a mention of the role played by the construction of the country's rail system. This began in 1909, with the laying of lines to Nsawam, Tafo and Kumasi.

A modern city

A modern city had been born, complete with telegraph and postal facilities and a municipal government that was finally fulfilling its function, particularly following a plague epidemic in 1907 which had made the population acutely aware of the necessity of observing appropriate rules of urban hygiene.

From 1919 to 1927, Governor Guggisberg sharply accelerated Accra's construction and urban infrastructure programme. Among other projects, the governor was responsible for the construction of the bridge over Korle Lagoon and Korlebu Hospital, as well as for the creation of the celebrated Achimota secondary school on the northern edge of greater Accra. Under his administration, the northern quarters of Tudu and Adabraka attained their definitive form, as also did those of Korle Gonno and Mamprobi on the west coast, and the European residential districts extending eastward up to and beyond Christiansborg. Another serious earthquack rocked Accra in 1939, necessitating the reconstruction of the eastern districts of Christiansborg and the southern zone of Labadi, which merged shortly thereafter into Accra proper. In the wake of the disaster, the districts of Korle Gonno, Lartebiorkoshie, Abose Okai and Kaneshie were transformed by the addition of modern rental and private housing units.

From 1954 on, Accra began growing increasingly toward the northeast, along Independence Avenue and north of Ring Road. The new communities included Kokomlemle, Accra New Town, Nima and Kanda. Along the coast from Christiansborg, Osu expanded to form a single unbroken stretch of quarters extending to Labadi. Finally, the founding of the University of Ghana in Legon, east of Achimota, resulted in the emergence of a new residential district framed by splendid gardens and a golf course.

Once the history book of Accra's past is closed, visitors should be ready to see for themselves how Accra really looks today. (See map, page 82). Where is the best place to start from? Perhaps from the very beginning: Christiansborg, which by virtue of its age, geographical location and political importance, is the logical starting-off point. When possible, a visit to Accra should ideally be undertaken on a Saturday morning in August, when the *Homowo* festival has given a particularly festive air to all of the city's popular quarters. It is perhaps at this moment, more than any other, that Accra transforms itself into a thousand colourful living images projected against an ever-changing half-African, half-European backdrop.

The fishermen of Accra

Christiansborg is best appreciated from the sea-front to the east, along the beachfront which is traversed by Marine Drive. As the administrative centre of the government, the district is closed to the casual sightseer, but it is from here that the visitor will discover that Accra, a city constructed on a port, has nevertheless deliberately chosen to turn its back to the sea.

From Christiansborg to the jetty that terminates its modest port, the shoreline has remained largely the same since the era when it served as the home to the Ga fishermen and traders. With the exception of the formely palatial Riviera Hotel whose terraces still dominate the beach, not a single modern building mars this perfectly preserved image of the city's past.

The sandy beach, nestling in the hollow of the bay, gives way to a sheer cliff which can be accessed at low tide by using the surrounding rocks as stepping-stones. From time to time the way is blocked, and visitors must then take to the narrow cliff-side paths that lead to the habitations above, where fisherwives smoke the daily catch brought in from the sea by their husbands.

The life here is extremely hard, and given the extreme poverty of the community, it is recommended that visitors make a special effort to respect the dignity of its inhabitants; those tempted by picture-taking should be aware that the price of a single roll of film often exceeds the daily income of the person whose photo you are taking. Cameras are also off-limits in the proximity of Ussher Fort, a short distance away at the intersection of High Street, and situated at the top of a steep stairway leading to the beach. (A word to the wise: for the visitor sitting upon its steps, even so much as writing a postcard may be the occasion for an informal interrogation by over-zealous guards desirous of assuring that the message is of a personal nature and not information susceptible of compromising the security of the state!) The fort itself — formerly Crevecœur Fort — an ancient bone of contention long fought over by the Dutch and the English — is a bit disappointing as are the narrow streets of James Town, overlooking the port.

James Town

An enclave almost entirely inhabited by fisher-folk, perhaps the most surprising aspect of James Town is its unpresupposing, village-like aspect. In general, maritime capitals usually have industrial installations corresponding to their importance.

Once again, Accra astonishes by its indifference to the sea: its port is wholly devoted to artisanal fishing, as the modest surrounding quarters — occupying the place of honour usually given to commerce and international hotels — amply testify. The population of James Town, being very poor, is rather inhospitable.

The atmosphere is totally different — and all the more so during *Homowo* — in neighbouring Ussher Town. As the fever of the celebration mounts with the thundering drums, enthusiastic crowds encircle groups of kaolin-painted traditional dancers.

Everyone here seems to know everyone else: joking and bantering, the onlookers alternate between following the intricate steps of the dancers and the antics of the local youngsters. There's no reason for timidity here, and visitors should not hesitate asking for explanations as to the meaning of the celebrations taking place before them, explanations which will be offered with the greatest kindness on the part of the local population.

Outside the circle of the festivities, the crackle of fireworks and the excited cries of children announces the stirring arrival of the city's chieftains, mounted upon canopy-shaded thrones borne upon the shoulders of their retainers. As firearms of all calibres and ages are emptied in a joyous salute, the odour of gunpowder mingles with that of the free-flowing local schnaps. The resulting scene is a rare vision of a timeless, immemorial Africa, unchanged by modern life and contemporary influences.

Accra's garment district

To visit the shops of Accra's traditional tailors, there's no need to chose a festival day, since here, the party goes on all the time, albeit in a somewhat more subdued manner. The easiest itinerary from James Town is to follow High Street to Lutterroot Street and thence to Lutteroot Circle, which leads to Asafoate Nettey Road on the southern edge of Ussher Town.

Each side of the street is lined with shops selling rolls of locally-made fabrics, caftans, *kente* and a variety of men's and women's clothing of more or less traditional, or at any rate local, inspiration.

"Gyamfi Garments" and "Festus" offer a wide selection at reasonable prices. The incredible Zongo Lane, a few short blocks from the main post office, is a narrow street whose fascinating shops sell everything from rare car parts to designer clothing. Visitors are advised to take their time, for the treasures here range from the odd headlight to extremely pretty, varied and inexpensive items of men's and women's wear. A man's caftan can be picked up (after fierce bargaining) for around 14,000 cedis, with traditional women's dresses starting at 4,000.

Once visitors have exhausted the manifold joys of Zongo Lane, they can continue to Opera Square, bordered by Pagan Road and the GNTC department store. From here, it's just a stone's throw to the main post office square and its clock tower. The square is lined with banks, while tree-shaded Holy Trinity Cathedral can be seen on the opposite side of High Street.

Since Saturday is the day reserved for both traditional funerals and Christian burial services, visitors may sometimes witness a colourful combination of each, with women clad in similar, specially-made mourning robes in traditional fabrics and patterns.

From high finance to fine art

Ghana's financial and legal centre is located on High Street, where the visitor will find, among other financial institutions, the offices of Barclays Bank, Standard Chartered Bank, the Bank of Ghana and Ghana Commercial Bank. Further down the street are the smaller but imposing buildings of Ghana's Parliament and Supreme Court.

The visitor may be struck by the contrast between these symbols of power and wealth and the poverty of the capital's fishing villages only a few blocks distant. In effect, Accra is a city of such contrasts, from the humble souvenir and antique shops of upper High and 28th-February Streets to the brick and concrete buildings facing seawards opposite with, in a vacant lot, a scattered group of horses which graze on weeds in the shade of acacia trees. It's impossible to imagine who they belong to, or even why they are there. Are they the property of the nearby street vendors, or do they belong to the two friends engaged in an animated conversation on the nearby corner? For all one knows, it is possible that they are there simply to accentuate the paradoxical sense of contrast between immemorial Africa and contemporary Accra.

After drinking a refreshing glass of coconut milk served by one of the nearby vendors, the visitor continuing along 28th-February Street will soon arrive at the Ghana Arts Centre.

On Saturday afternoons, the Centre attracts a high-spirited, youthful audience drawn by a varied programme of theatre, traditional dance, rock competitions and rap concerts. Artists such as Koo Nimo and his troupe of musicians are also highly appreciated by both young and old. With a repertory of topical ballads dealing with life, death, marriage, the problems of the family and the joys of nature, Koo Nimo maintains the tradition of educating his audience even as he entertains them. In Ghana, the lessons of the elders are still heeded, and with all the respect merited by their age and experience.

The Arts Centre also offers still other attractions: an annex contains examples of the works of contemporary Ghanaian painters, including several who by the quality of their art appear destined for an international career. Just behind the gallery, another room is given over to the exhibition of hand-crafted gold and silver jewelery, another Ghanaian tradition which is being perpetuated. On the other hand, the sculptured wood statues and the bronze ritual figurines cast by the "lost wax" process, formerly characterized by high levels of creativity and workmanship, are somewhat disappointing. The examples on view are basically copies of older, traditional models. The more innovative, contemporary designs lack the verve and originality often seen in modern Ghanaian painting. Among the more interesting pieces, visitors will nevertheless remark the statue of a woman cast in concrete, created by the artist Alex Sefa, as well as a series of carved wooden statuettes representing contemporary personages. Under a canopy behind the auditorium, potters fire their works in a large kiln, and somewhat further on, the way opens onto a long open-aired passage lined with shops offering an assortment of bric-a-brac, antiquities, fairly well-executed reproductions and in particular, copies of the Ashanti sacred stools. By taking one's time, it is usually possible to discover one or two objects worth acquiring, even if most are available elsewhere in the country.

A timeless world

The tree-shaded avenue leading from the Arts Centre is lined with benches upon which numerous Accrans can be seen napping at all hours of the day, while the more courageous among them have managed to find a somewhat precarious resting-place upon the low branches of the surrounding trees. Here

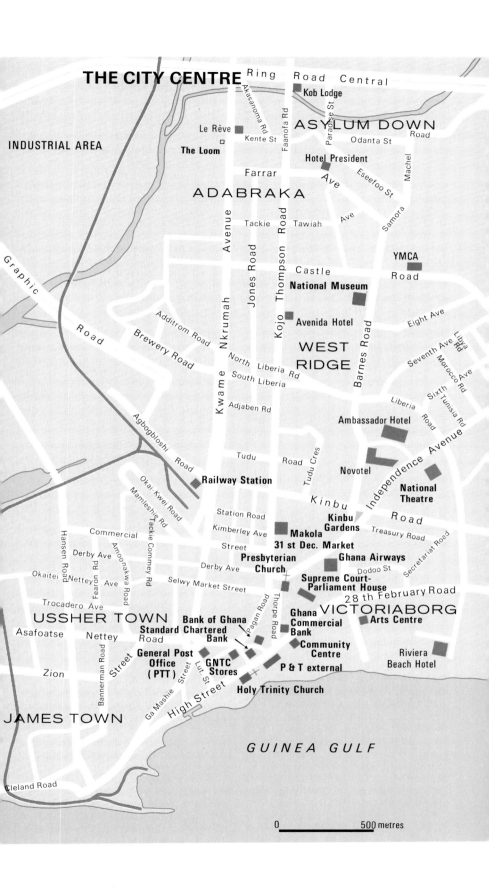

THE CITY CENTRE

Ring Road Central

Kob Lodge

ASYLUM DOWN

Road

Le Rêve

Kente St

Odanta St

The Loom

Hotel President

Faanofa Rd

Paradise St

Eseefoo St

Machel

Farrar Ave

Samora

ADABRAKA

Tawiah

Tackie

Ave

INDUSTRIAL AREA

Avenue

Jones Road

Kojo Thompson Road

Castle

YMCA

Road

National Museum

Nkrumah

Eight Ave

Additrom Road

Avenida Hotel

Brewery Road

Seventh Ave

Libya Rd

WEST RIDGE

Morocco Rd

Graphic

Kwame

Barnes Road

Sixth

Ave

North Liberia Rd

South Liberia

Tunisia Rd

Road

Adjaben Rd

Liberia

Road

Ambassador Hotel

Agbogbloshi Road

Tudu Road

Novotel

Independence Avenue

Railway Station

Tudu Cres

National Theatre

Okai Kwei Road

Kinbu Road

Station Road

Kinbu Gardens

Treasury Road

Mamleshie Rd

Kimberley Ave

Makola

Tackie Commey Rd

Street

31 st Dec. Market

Ghana Airways

Commercial

Presbyterian Church

Dodoo St

Secretariat Road

Hansen Road

Derby Ave

Derby Ave

Supreme Court-Parliament House

Fearon Rd

Nettey

Ave

Selwy Market Street

28th February Road

Okaitei

Amoonakwa Road

Trocadero Ave

VICTORIABORG

USSHER TOWN

Bank of Ghana

Ghana Commercial Bank

Arts Centre

Asafoatse

Nettey Road

Standard Chartered Bank

Pagan Road

Thorpe Road

Community Centre

Riviera Beach Hotel

Bannerman Road

Street

General Post Office (PTT)

GNTC Stores

P & T external

Zion

Ga Mashie Street

Lut. St

Holy Trinity Church

JAMES TOWN

High Street

GUINEA GULF

Cleland Road

0 _____ 500 metres

and there, small groups of men talk together in the slanting rays of the afternoon sunlight, while an adolescent tells a story to a group of children near a man sitting on the grass reading the day's news in the afternoon paper. Regarding such scenes, the visitor may be struck by the impression of having penetrated a timeless, peaceful and dreamlike world, the images of which are unwinding in slow-motion in the heat and torpor of the Ghanaian afternoon.

This impression is accentuated each time the visitor returns to the shaded avenue, for no matter the time of day or the day of week, both the groups and isolated individuals appear unchanged from the preceding visit, manifesting the same attitudes and postures, and apparently eternally engaged in the same activities.

Visitors following the avenue will arrive at an intersection; to the right, a wide unpaved road leads to the Riviera Hotel, while on the left, Liberia Road takes the visitor past the National Theatre, the Ambassador Hotel, and after intersecting Barnes Road, terminates at Kwame Nkrumah Avenue, one of Accra's busiest thoroughfares. From here, 28th - February Road leads to Independence Square and the possibility of another promenade through the city.

Shadow and light

Like an immense open-air stadium without walls, Independence Square is ringed by seating accommodations for 30,000 spectators. Other than on the occasion of a parade or a *Durbar*, the square is practically empty. The nearby Arch commemorates March 6, 1957, the day that Ghana achieved independence. On the other side of Arch Circle stands Accra's sports stadium, where on Saturday or Sunday afternoons, cars, buses, trucks, motorcycles and bicycles discharge hundreds of fans eager to clamour their joy during matches or special celebrations. The same passion for sports animates all of Africa's populations, but here in Accra, it should be remembered that Abedi Pele, one of European soccer's current greats, was born in Ghana. Even if visitors do not share this enthusiasm, they will doubtlessly be impressed by the sheer volume of spectators' cheers, audible throughout, and often well beyond the quarter.

After circling the stadium by Stadium Road, the visitor will arrive in front of the parking lot of the new Conference Centre, constructed in 1991 on the former site of the Accra race track, of which nothing exists but its walls, decorated with painted images of jockeys. The sun floods this treeless street, and visitors desirous of finding a bit of shade should proceed left down Castle Road past the cemetery and the State House gardens. The noise and white heat surrounding the stadium gradually give way to the cool silence of the East Ridge residential district, intersected by shady avenues, some of which are unpaved. East Ridge is lined by ancient colonial-style homes whose vast gardens provide a striking contrast to the neighbourhood that the visitor has just left, filled with imposing buildings but void of vegetation. Here, as in many other of Accra's residential quarters stretching along the southern edge of Ring Road, there are many fine examples of lovely homes, often elevated upon pile foundations. These charming, single-storey residences ringed by verandas were generally constructed prior to the Second World War, and are remarkable by their low-keyed architectural coherence. Thanks to the abundance of shady gardens, the district contributes to making much of Accra a city of open spaces and fresh air.

With the roar of the stadium crowds now definitively behind, the peaceful silence is broken only by the reassuring sound of a ball hitting a tennis racket on the courts hidden behind the luxurious greenery. As the visitor proceeds in the direction of Castle Road, the calm of neighbourhood gradually gives way to the faint music of a carousel in the children's park located between Independence Avenue and Gamal Abdul Nasser Avenue. On Saturday afternoons, the park is filled with joyous youngsters of all ages, accompanied by their families.

Toward the city-centre

A little further on, the Anglican Church stands in solemn dignity on the corner of Egypt Road. On the occasion of a marriage, the area in front of the church is filled by a milling crowd of guests, with the women often dressed in diaphanous European-styled chiffon gowns in all the colours of a pastel rainbow. Just down the street lies Liberia Avenue, lined on its left by a row of ministry buildings dating from the colonial period, constructed by the British to house their administrative offices. The National Theatre stands almost immediately to the right on Liberia Road, followed by the Independence Avenue intersection. It would be reasonable to imagine that as one of Accra's oldest thoroughfares, both sides of the avenue would long have been filled with buildings of all types from one end to the other. This is hardly the case, since from Captain Sankara Circle on Ring Road, and especially from the intersection of African Liberation Square and Castle Road, the avenue is dotted by vacant lots and small gardens planted with corn or banana trees. Against this somewhat stark urban landscape, buildings such as the Bank of Ghana headquarters, the currently-renovated Ambassador Hotel or the Novotel (separated from the latter establishment by a large "no man's land" filled with construction equipment), produce an even more impressive effect.

In terms of contrasts, the recently constructed Accra Novotel which has rapidly become a popular meeting-place for members of the city's business community, is second to none. Particularly when viewed from the bus terminal, as a veritable human tide flows around the observer positioned at the intersection of Independence Avenue and Barnes and Kinbu Roads.

Makola market

Visitors continuing down Independence Avenue to the southwest will soon arrive at what remains of Makola Market, formely one of Accra's largest.

Even if the name of the three interconnected markets that formerly stretched toward Kwame Nkrumah Avenue remains unchanged, their location is no longer the same. But even after being transferred to a new site, the market's atmosphere, odours, sounds and the labyrinth of its narrow stall-lined streets is exactly as before. It is always just as easy (and pleasurable) to lose one's way amongst its milling crowds and to have the impression — which is no longer true — that its surface area is gigantic.

One of the greatest differences can be seen in the section housing the garment and cloth merchants, in which an unusual sense of order reigns. The visitor will also have the surprise of hearing the sound of laughter and joyous singing coming from one of the first day-care centres created by the "December 31 Women's Movement", headed by Nana Konadu Agyman-Rawlings, the wife of the country's Head of State within the market itself. The market entrance located at the intersection of Kojo Thompson and Pagan Roads leads to Asafoatse Nettey Road, lined with the shops of cloth merchants.

Kwame Nkrumah Avenue

One of Accra's liveliest business streets, the avenue runs from the former site of the Makola Market past an open square just after Lutteroot Circle on the right, almost facing the SCOA and UTC department stores.

The avenue is lined with shops covered by a pedestrian gallery opposite a series of ultra-modern buildings such as Liberty House.

On the left, when walking north, the railroad terminal and clock tower seem particularly modest after the sight of these buildings. Approximately at the same level as the railroad terminal, the avenue is divided by a wide median strip obliging motorists to make a long detour to reach the other side. At this point, it is better to simply park one's car, as is always the case for short trips in this traffic-filled city. Although the effects of the country's former economic crisis had for years significantly reduced the number of vehicles seen in the capital, today's bumper-to-bumper gridlock is the tangible proof that the crisis is definitively over.

A little further up the left side of the avenue, Cocoa House is the headquarters for a number of airline companies and various agencies. Next comes Kingsway Stores, doubtlessly Accra's most elegant department store, whose rear entrance leads to the brand new Ghana Stock Exchange, located next to a parking lot.

On the other side of Nkrumah Avenue, Republic House contains the headquarters of the Ghana Export Promotion Council, increasingly frequented by foreign businessmen.

From here to Kwame Nkrumah Circle, the avenue progressively loses its business-like and lively atmosphere, and increasingly starts to resemble the other shady residential thoroughfares lined with modest one-storey homes. Leaving the avenue at the intersection of South Liberia Road and turning onto Barnes Road, the visitor will pass the Ministry of Information and arrive at the National Museum. The museum is a must for any visitor planning a voyage through Ghana's interior.

The National Museum

The exhibits housed under the two-tiered rotunda of the museum comprise much more than Ghanaian culture alone, and include a collection of art objects from the majority of the neighbouring West African countries as well as an archaeological department located in a hall on the first floor.

One of the museum's ground-floor wings is devoted to temporary exhibitions which can range from contemporary dyed fabrics to traditional and even sacred artifacts such as the celebrated Ashanti ancestor stools.

Other interesting exhibits in the ground-floor rooms include richly decorated Ashanti gold-weighing scales adorned with finely-rendered symbolic images illustrative of traditional proverbs. Other aspects of Ashanti culture are widely represented in the form of numerous and beautiful ceramic-ware and pottery, as well as the magnificently-sculptured bronze recipients known as *kuduo* and other ritual objects.

The walls of these exhibition halls are lined with examples of traditional Ghanaian garments known as *kente*, each of whose symbolic woven designs has its own special meaning, and certain of which are reserved for chiefs or dignitaries. The somewhat more subdued *adinkra*, hand-printed with symbolic motifs, are displayed on vertical supports on which appear explanations of their symbolism and manufacturing techniques.

After leaving the museum, it is possible to follow Barnes Road north to central Ring Road which constitutes a dividing line between lower and upper Accra, whose terrain is much more hilly. From Ring Road to the north, the broad avenues leading to Kaneschie, Achimota and Kotoka offer lovely views of the surrounding hills and provide an impression of space lacking in the heavily constructed city-centre.

Visits to attractions such as the Kaneshie Market (a superb view of which is offered from the Winneba highway overpass), arts and crafts manufacturers such as the Akuaba wooden toy company near Achimota or the Pan-African Writers' Association at Pawa House in Roman Ridge, reinforce this impression of open horizons and wide spaces that characterize the quarters located north of Ring Road.

Visitors having had the chance of viewing the collections of contemporary clothing created by Ghana's fashion designers regularly presented at the Novotel, the American Club or even at the University of Legon will assuredly want to pay a visit to their shops and studios.

This is often easier said than done, for finding an out-of-the-way shop like "Ginatu Exclusive", even when one knows that it is situated in North Kaneshie on Mukose Road, can be an exploit. Although no one can tell you precisely how to get there, it's worth the effort involved, and the visitor will be rewarded by an excellent selection of traditional Ghanaian handicrafted cloth, designer batiks with matching handbags and charming home-made dolls.

Accra high fashion

On the other hand, both "Sleek Fashions", theoretically located in Nyaniba Estate and "St Osei" in Labone, are absolutely impossible to find. Ricci Osei, the talented designer of the latter label has closed his first shop, but is planning to open a veritable fashion centre staffed by Accra's finest designers. If nothing else, visitors attempting to track down these elusive shops will have the opportunity of departing from the habitual tourist track and seeing some of the capital's less-frequented but equally interesting quarters.

Fortunately for the fashion-hungry, finding one's way to "Ashia Fabrics", located on central Ring Road next to the main offices of KLM airlines and facing the Nima Police Station is absolute child's play (if nothing else, one can always ask a local policeman for directions!). And if the shop is not exactly what can be termed "high fashion", it nevertheless offers lovely fabrics and panels reproducing traditional Ashanti decorative motifs. "Chez Julie", however, is a fashion boutique worthy of the name. "Chez Julie" is located in the business district of Cantonments Road, southwest of Danqah Circle and Ring Road. The shop offers tailor-made dresses, ready for delivery, if necessary, within 48 hours, as well as long or short caftans and designer jewellery.

Cantonments Road attracts a wide variety of shoppers for other reasons than pure fashion. The Kwatson supermarket at the upper end of the thoroughfare

*One of the first African states
to have achieved independence,
Ghana commemorated the event
with this monumental arch located
in the centre of Accra.*

toward Ring Road is frequented by many of the city's families and is a mecca for visitors planning a trip to less well-supplied regions of the country or projecting a stay in provincial rest houses where it is necessary to bring one's own provisions. The road is also lined with many other types of shops, as well as a number of Accra's best restaurants.

Greater Accra

The most practical way of visiting the outlying areas of Accra is by car, given the distances separating the suburbs from the centre-city.

The ideal itinerary begins to the west, at the Korle Gonno Lagoon. After traversing the adjacent residential district, follow Ring Road to Kwame Nkrumah Circle. From here, the road dips, rising again to continue up the hillside along Nsawam Road which leads straight to Achimota and its surrounding forest. On the other side of a second ring road, Kwame Nkrumah motorway offers rapid expressway access to the Port of Tema located on the eastern end of Accra.

Traffic in Achimota is often heavy, due to the presence of the Kumasi highway. For this reason, it is recommended that motorists keep to the right of Ring Road and detour through the labyrinth of streets traversing the popular quarter of Nima, from where they can rejoin Achimota Road to Roman Ridge, which offers a particularly sweeping view of the city. From here, it is possible to continue in the direction of the Airport and its adjoining residential area. The road leads directly to Legon and Aburi, via the Tetteh Quarshie Circle, to the west of which the distant line of the Akwapim Hills are visible.

Visit to the University

The University of Ghana should be visited not only for its botanical gardens which recent budget restrictions have unfortunately affected, but also for the long palm-shaded avenues lined with gardens and patios, whose curved-roofed

A DAY FOR FUNERALS

In Ghana, the day set aside for burial is quite distinct from the one reserved for the actual funeral services, which in some cases can even be celebrated several years afterwards. Mondays and Thursdays were formerly earmarked for funerals, but for the sake of greater convenience, Saturday has since been adopted, for no one works in Ghana over the weekends. Early in the morning the friends and relatives of the deceased begin assembling at an appointed meeting-place (which is often a village or neighbourhood square), where they are provided with seats and glasses of palm wine or beer or gin. The celebration itself does not get underway before the members of the deceased's family have wended their way through the neighbourhood or village streets in a ceremonial march of public mourning. In some cases, the march is repeated several times before the group definitively arrives at the place where the other guests have been assembling. At this point, things begin looking like a real celebration, complete with music supplied by one or more bands and dancing that can go on until nightfall. Local custom requires that all participants leave a contribution to cover some of the expenses involved. These contributions continue arriving over the following days. It usually takes a week or so to tally up the entire cost of the ceremony, and if expenses exceed donations, the immediate family assumes a major portion of the outstanding costs with the remainder being shared by other members of the clan.

buildings look more like oriental pagodas than examples of local architecture. The university library and bookshop are also well worth the visit, particularly since the latter is the only bookshop worthy of the name in all of Accra. When possible, it is also interesting to meet the students and teachers belonging to the Institute of African Studies. Golfers will certainly want to take advantage of the visit to sample the excellent fairways and greens of the course located adjacent to the student dormitories, in the direction of Achimota.

Leaving Legon by way of Tetteh Quarshie Circle, Liberation and Giffard Road, the motorist will rapidly arrive at the first Cantonments Circular Road and the Du Bois Memorial. W.E.B. Du Bois, a native-born American from Massachusetts whose ancestors came from Africa, was the director of the *African Encyclopedia* founded by President Nkrumah. Following his death in 1963, Du Bois's residence became a memorial and the final resting place of his ashes and those of his wife. Visitors to his former residence can view his library and personal manuscripts, as well as attend seminars on Pan-Africanism.

Labadi and Cocobeach

The International Trade Fair grounds and buildings have long existed just east of the village of Labadi, well outside of the immediate area of the capital. This area, served by the lovely coastal road that begins at South Labadi Estate (the last community within Accra's city limits) and traverses Labadi proper in the direction of Tema, is likely to become increasingly urbanized in the near future.

Rather symbolically a group of chalets near the new labadi Beach Hotel were started in the 1970's and never completed. Then followed the construction of the new four-star Labadi Beach Hotel, which offers 100 rooms and four luxurious suites, as well as a swimming pool, health club and business support services. Along with Trade Fair facilities, the hotel complex undoubtedly represents the beginning of a new urban centre which, as it develops, can be expected to attract increasing numbers of tourists and business travellers. The area is also adjacent to the seaside resort of Cocobeach near the village of Teshie, well-frequented by weekend visitors from Accra and Tema.

The existing complex, consisting of a small nine-bungalow hotel plus a squash court and small swimming pool, is far from what can be termed as a full-blown tourist resort. Nevertheless, its convenient location close to the capital and the improved access which will result from the development of nearby Labadi is certain to attract increasing numbers of visitors. At present, it is already delightful to have lunch under the thatched-straw roof of the beachfront restaurant caressed by a cool sea breeze, while twice weekly in the evenings and every Sunday afternoon, the popular Marriot orchestra attracts a youthful audience to the adjacent dance floor.

The simple but clean hotel bungalows feature showers and locally-inspired furnishings. Just after the village of Teshie, motorists on the road to Accra will notice a wooden signboard in the village of Nungua designating a modest structure known as ''Paa Villiers Six Feet Enterprise.'' By all means, stop in for a visit. Paa Villiers is doubtlessly the world's happiest coffin-maker. Instead of the usual boring and uninspired rectangular boxes stuffed with insipid artifical white satin lining, this veritable artist creates ultra-personalized ''last demeures'' that reflect the profession or special interests of the deceased. Thus, a given coffin may take the shape of a pirogue, a fish, a lion, a chicken, an automobile or even a house. On occasion, the incredible Villiers has even been known to turn out a church - shaped coffin or another in the form of a gigantic coconut! No request is too bizarre for this genial artisan of the unthinkable, whose invariable response is ''No problem!'' It's a pity that at least some of his creations have as yet not found a home in a museum of African folk art, rather than six feet underground...

Kokrobite Beach

In the opposite direction to the west of Accra, another village draws crowds of weekend visitors attracted by traditional African dances and music, sculpture and even New Age techniques designed to heighten the participant's spiritual consciousness. All of this is offered as part of the programme of seminars and events held at Kokrobite Beach, a highlight of which are the courses in percussion instruments given by Mostapha Tetty Addy, the director of the Academy of African Music and Arts. Participants in one of the three-week long cycles which are offered five times a year can chose at will from any of the daily courses and subjects taught during four days of the week.

During the weekend, and particularly Sunday afternoons, spectacles of traditional African dance are presented on the circular dance-floor located between the bar and the restaurant. The dance company that can currently be seen poolside at the Accra Novotel was selected from among the troupes that appear here.

The infinitely charming setting at Kokrobite Beach includes the terrace on which are found the dance-floor, bar and restaurant offering a magnificent view of the jagged, red-hued rocks that dominate the beach. In principle, the sea is safe for swimmers, but the sight of the waves unfurling into the crashing surf can often be unnerving. Nevertheless, merely witnessing this grandiose spectacle is worth the trip out from Accra.

The bar offers cool drinks made from fruits grown on the property (pineapples, papayas, etc.), pressed in juicers running on electricity generated by solar energy. The restaurant serves excellent traditional dishes cooked over wood fires in local clay pottery. The thirty rooms of the hotel are simply furnished, with separate bathrooms. A covered gallery leads from the rooms to a lovely garden surrounded by a conference room capable of accommodating 200 visitors. A series of rustic beach houses on the second beach to the left of the first offer shady retreats from the sun. All of these pleasures are offered for extremely reasonable prices; it can only be hoped that the adjoining shop will soon offer books on Ghanaian culture for visitors arriving between sessions.

For those unable to spend a night or more at Kokrobite Beach, even a day or a Sunday afternoon will offer a pleasantly relaxing experience for visitors in Accra for business or professional reasons. Kokrobite Beach is accessed by the Winneba Road which passes under the Kaneshie Market overpass and continues straight on for thirty kilometres to the Weija Dam and the roadsign indicating the Aama Beach Bar.

Accra
by night

Although Accra offers cinemas, bars, night-clubs and casinos, in the opinion of the Ghanaians themselves, the capital's nightlife is fairly dull during the week and only becomes interesting Friday through Sunday evenings. Further

As car traffic increases, Accra is constantly upgrading its urban road and expressway system.

aburi

more, the best times are not necessarily had at the most reputed spots.

In the popular quarters and near the movie houses featuring Chinese karate and combat films, the night-time atmosphere is rich and colourful. Emotions make the audiences of these films hungry, and when the cinemas let out crowds stream through the streets lined with open-air food stalls where women prepare delicious plates of *kenkey* (smoked fish), *kelewele* (thin, spicy slices of fried plantain bananas) and *tsofi* (fried and spiced turkey wings), served with local beer or Malta, a new and popular malt-based soft drink.

Chants and drums

In Nima, the traditional refuge of newly-arrived Ghanaians from the provinces, groups of nostalgic former villagers improvise an evening of regional dances. These impromptu events regularly change location, which must be continually discovered and rediscovered by those seeking them out.

Sometimes on a dark street visitors will unexpectedly happen upon a cluster of lights and humanity engaged in singing chants accompanied by a drum. These events are often religious gatherings, and the songs being sung are hymns. If the spirit moves them, visitors are welcome to join in; those doing so will be greeted by the friendly smiles of the participants. Spectacles such as these are never lacking, on the condition of avoiding the centre city. In short, when going out for the evening in Accra, do so without preconceived ideas and let chance decide your itinerary.

(*See practical information p. 164*)

■ Who but the British would ever have thought of re-creating a bit of England smack in the middle of sub-Saharan Africa! This is exactly the impression given by a promenade through Aburi Botanical Garden, with its carefully-groomed sweeping lawns, typically English flower-beds and thousands of stately shade-trees. A favorite Sunday afternoon destination for Accra residents, the garden is a mere stone's throw from the capital.

Located approximately thirty kilometres from the suburbs of Accra in the foothills of the Akwapim range, and accessed by a winding road whose every turn reveals a new and glorious panorama of green landscapes dappled by sunlight and the immense shadows of fleecy clouds, both the Botanical Garden and the surrounding regions are blessed with a particularly mild, healthy climate.

Landscapes recalling those of Scotland and Ireland combined with crisp, pure air make Aburi the perfect antidote to the heat and humidity of Accra and its outlying coastal plains.

It was near Kitase that Kwame Nkrumah, Ghana's former president, constructed an official country residence which motorists will pass on the road leading up to the garden entrance. The last stop before arriving, Kitase is a typical African village, complete with roadside stands selling fried manioc, stalkfulls of fresh bananas and juicy, fragrant pineapples.

Upon entering the Botanical Garden, visitors pass the gatekeeper's post, followed by a palm-lined road which leads to paradise. So complete is the illusion of England, that one half-expects to come upon an old lord of the Empire taking his tea on one of the shaded lawns, surrounded by cricket-playing grandchildren and pale young beauties in crinoline dresses.

Aburi Botanical Garden was in fact created by the British in the 1890s. Perfectly maintained over the following years, its young saplings and rare flora, imported from all of the far-flung outposts of the Empire, have since grown into the stately trees and flower-bordered lawns that will contribute to the enchantment of present-day visitors. The garden officials have thoughtfully provided each tree with a small plaque giving both its common and scientific names. This impromptu botanical lesson will be particularly appreciated by those visitors unaware that the impressive *Ceiba Pentandra* near the garden restaurant or the delicious fruit-bearing *Zizyphus* are none other than the common breadfruit and jujube trees....

ada

In many respects, the garden resembles a Noah's Ark of tropical plant-life, with specimens coming from as far afield as Malaya, Mexico, Guatemala, India, China and of course, Africa.

The garden's original purpose was threefold: to serve as the grounds for a school of agriculture, the testing-ground for the systematic transplantation of non-native plant species and to provide plants for agricultural, pharmaceutical and industrial applications as well as for decorative use. The building currently serving as the garden restaurant was originally built as a sanatorium, which is indicative of Aburi's cool, healthful climate.

Lovers' Walk

Visitors of more romantic learnings, for whom neither the garden's history nor its immense Latin nomenclature of botanical species constitute the slightest attraction, will certainly feel their spirits take wing as they simply stroll down its tree-lined paths, and particularly upon entering the shady bowers of "Lovers' Walk." Romantic or not, who could resist being transported by this multiplicity of shapes, odours and colours? And how could anyone fail to be impressed by the solitary splendour of the ancient giant of a tree that reigns upon the summit of the hilltop, last survivor of the primeval forest that once blanketed the entire region?

Aburi's coolness and shade attract heat-weary Accrans during the dry season, but the rainy months also have their own special charm, blending colours and contours that drift apart at the whim of a passing breeze. At these moments the atmosphere takes on an unreal, bewitching quality, as the mist lifts to reveal a backdrop of hills and valleys which were invisible until that very moment. In the wink of an eye, the mist closes in again like a solid wall, or rent by the wind, glides silently through the trees of the distant forests like white silken scarves dappled by unexpected sunbeams emerging from the tormented sky.

Visitors with two days at their disposal can easily combine the trip to Aburi with a visit to the Shai Hills Game Reserve (see description below).

(*See practical information p. 164*)

■ Alexandre Dumas, author of *The Three Musketeers*, would probably have had difficulty imagining the destiny of his grandson of the same name. In effect, Dumas the third, having installed himself in Ada, which was then and still is a small fishing village on the Volta Delta, became one of the richest merchants of the region. His bales of French-manufactured cotton prints were transported upriver by boat, and were enormously successful throughout the entire country. Toward the end of the 19th century, Dumas married an African girl from Ada, had several children, and apparently lived happily ever after. His descendants still live in the area and bear the illustrious name of their ancestor.

Another of Ada's 19th-century luminaries was Geraldo da Lima, a former slave who upon his Brazilian master's death, not only appropriated his fortune, but his wife and name as well. Not satisfied with this, the industrious da Lima assembled a pirate army, declared war on the hapless chieftain of Ada, the residents of Kpong and Accra, and finally on the British themselves! The literary and film rights to da Lima's life have thus far remained in the public domain, pending the filing of a copyright by his descendants....

Any description of the famous or near-famous of Ada would not be complete without the mention of another individual who made the village the front-page news of its time. For it was indeed in Ada that Sir Henry Stanley paused following his celebrated discovery of Dr. Livingstone, accompanied by the legendary Captain Glover, the first navigator to cross the bar of the Volta Delta with an ocean-going vessel and to sail up-river, where he discovered a land then virtually unknown to Europeans.

Today, Ada is still a somewhat sleepy village whose population consider themselves either inhabitants of *Big Ada* , situated toward the interior, or *Ada Foah*, located on the Gulf of Guinea.

The village has seemingly forgotten the heroic period of yore, when it constituted the commercial hub of the entire region. Indeed, a rapid glance at a map of West Africa reveals that Ada occupies an extremely strategic position, at once on the shores of the Gulf of Guinea and the Volta River estuary, and at the intersection of the road network serving both the Atlantic coast and the interior of the Continent.

Unfortunately, since the construction of the ports of Takoradi and Tema, the laying of the great northern highways and the creation of Lake Volta, whose southern tip extends far north of Ada, the village has lost all of its former prestige and strategic importance.

Tourism may bring new life to Ada, since the area is becoming popular with the Ghanaians themselves.

Ada's beaches are particularly safe for swimmers, while other recreational possibilities include boat excursions and fine fishing.

Visitors desiring to spend a day or two in Ada can find basic but quite acceptable accommodations at either the Ada Hotel or the charmingly-named "No Problems" Guest House.

Ada is the point of transition between the scattered vegetable farms of the Accra plain, and the Volta Delta region which extends in a rough triangle toward the Akwapim Hills and Togo. *Songow Lagoon*, to the west of Ada and barely visible from the main road, constitutes a preliminary glimpse of the coastal landscapes that characterize the regions east of the Volta.

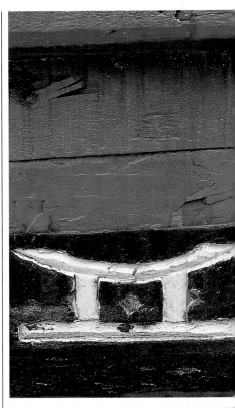

Motorists driving in from Accra may desire to make a short detour east of Tema to visit the extremely modest Prampram Fort, less for the charms of its modernized architecture than for its terrace situated just above a small fishing port. On Tuesdays, traditionally the Ghanaian fisherman's day of rest, the multicoloured beached pirogues amidst the deep blue fishing net spread out on the sand to dry offer a charming subject for photographers.

At the same time, visitors will appreciate the invigorating sea air, and in July and August, attend the *Homowo* festival which is preceded by the official opening of the fishing season on the third Tuesday prior to the opening of the festival itself.

On this doubly-important Tuesday, no one even thinks of putting out to sea, and the village resounds with singing accompanied by ritual gongs. The entire fishing fleet takes to the sea the following morning, in quest of a particular species of fish, the females of which are sacrificed to the divinities of Prampram, Lalue and Dugble.

After crossing the Volta at Ada, motorists can continue east to Keta (see description below), located between the sea and a lagoon. The road from Keta continues to the border town of Aflao and thence to Lome, the capital city of Togo, with its hotels, restaurants, nightclubs, beaches and markets.

(*See practical information p. 165*)

The artistic talent of Ghanaian
fishermen is often expressed by decorating
their canoes with striking motifs
and symbolic designs such as
the stylized royal stool (upper left).

akosombo   amedzofe

■ If placed back-to-back, the succession of projects, orders and counter-orders that preceded the construction of the Akosombo Dam would probably stretch the entire length of the Volta River itself. The story has been documented in James Moxon's *Volta, Man's Greatest Lake*, but it was in 1915 that the English geologist A.E. Kitson saw the potential for hydroelectric power offered by the Volta between Ajena and Kpong. Unfortunately, Europe was then at war, and the necessary resources required for carrying out the project were engaged for the purposes of mass destruction rather than construction.

The idea was revived, modified and shelved in the following decades. All this would probably have gone on forever had it not been for the determination of Kwame Nkrumah, who was convinced that construction of the dam was essential for the modernization and future progress of Ghana.

With Akosombo chosen as the site, both dam and power plant were inaugurated in January 1966, while the associated foundry was constructed in the new town of Tema, on the east coast.

As it backed up behind the immense concrete walls of the dam, the waters of the Volta eventually formed a lake 400 kilometres long from its northern to southern tips, and deep enough to accommodate boats carrying freight, passengers and vehicles on its entire length.

Travellers with or without cars will be fascinated by the lake voyage. The three-day excursion includes stopovers at Kpandu, Keta-Krachi (Volta Region), Yeji (Brong-Ahafo Region) and Buipe, the port of the northern capital of Tamale (Northern Region).

At the outset of the dam construction, a town to accommodate the workers was built at Akosombo. From the great metal bridge that crosses the river over the gorges that continue downstream to Kpong, the road sporadically parallels the course of the Volta River. Beyond Akwamu, it climbs to the top of a hill dominating the workers' quarter of Akosombo, traverses the quarter, and continues past the buildings of the Volta River Authority to the Hotel Volta.

Behind one of the promontories that jut like headlands into the magnificent expanse of the lake lies the port, invisible from town several kilometres distant. Here, travellers will find boats that offer shuttle service northward, with special Sunday excursions including a shipboard lunch and visit to nearby Dodi Island. (*See practical information p. 165*)

■ Perched high upon one of the peaks of the Togo range, Amedzofe is located in an admirable setting a few kilometres from the Togolese border.

From Ho, the capital of the Volta Region, the highway runs via Dzolokpuita and Vane through a landscape covered by incredibly dense vegetation dotted with occasional clearings. In one such clearing, the thick wall of liana and moss-covered trees surrounded by tall tropical grasses gives way to a cemetery lying in the shade of sumptuous, white-flowered trees.

Dzolokpuita marks the beginning of the Avatime district, which forms an enclave within the Ewe territory. Its capital is *Vane*, headquarters of the supreme chief *Adza Tekpo*. Since the rank of this personage is so high, visitors are usually directed to his subordinate, the chieftain of Vane. The latter enjoys recounting the long migration of his ancestors, who arrived from the regions to the west.

After vainly attempting to attain a peaceful coexistence with the inhabitants of Prampram on the east coast, the Avatimes waged war on the autochthonous population of the hills and drove out those who were not ultimately absorbed into their ethnic group. The Avatimes succeeded in carving out a territory encompassing eight towns, including Amedzofe. Having settled in, as it were, they still have no intention of moving away, which is perfectly understandable given the effort they expended in settling here.

Fine excursions

Opportunities for hikes through the region abound, but before setting out, visitors should have a look at the spectacular panorama from the top of the hill overlooking the town. The round, treeless peak in front of the terrace is *Mount Gami*, on which stands a cross erected by German missionaries. On the left, a road stretches toward Kpandu on the shores of Lake Volta, while beyond lies *Fume*, accessible by car or on foot.

Further to the left and in the middle distance, the *Biakpa* range and the towns of *Adomi* and *Anfoega* are visible. The shining line emerging from the background is one of the tributaries of Lake Volta, while spanning the border, the Togo Hills emerge to the right of Mount Gami.

At the top of the hill and behind the rest house, visitors will have a fine view

axim

of the *Kabakaba range, Mount Adaklu* and the *Peki Hills*.

Not all of these peaks are accessible on foot from Amedzofe, but by using a car and some shoe-leather, the average well-intentioned walker can visit many of them without undue strain.

On the other hand, the descent to the waterfall near the village is a real exploit, particularly during the rainy season. It all looks easy enough at the beginning, but this, alas, is merely an illusion. The well-trod path suddenly disappears into tall grasses, while the slope progressively begins to tilt headily downwards and becomes as slippery as ice. At this point, one begins grasping for whatever's nearest, whether a protruding root, low branches or even a handy occasional boulder. With luck, the strategy works, but when it doesn't, the visitor will continue the descent in a somewhat undignified seated position. If you attempt this little jaunt, don't forget to wear sturdy hiking boots and appropriate clothing, as well as leaving your handbag or camera in a safe location. In any event, there is not enough room in the small rockbound area to get a photo of the waterfall in its entirety.

The falls of Wli and Tsatsadu

Amedzofe can also serve as the base for visiting the falls of *Wli* and *Tsatsadu*, further north. Both are accessed by the road to Vane, which runs past Mount Gami on its left.

In general, it is recommended that visitors remain in the immediate vicinity of Amedzofe before returning to Ho, from where the region of Hohoe and its falls can be reached in one day and over good roads.

(*See practical information p. 165*)

■ Located on the western coast, midway between Takoradi and the border of the Ivory Coast, Axim's main attraction is Fort Antonio, constructed by the Portuguese around 1516, and the second oldest fortress after Elmina. Both are among Ghana's original fifty coastal forts, many of which have either disappeared or have been disfigured by the vagaries of time and successive restorations.

Fortunately, this is not the case of Fort Antonio, which has had a typically checkered destiny. Its successive changes in ownership and nationality included the Dutch, who captured it from the Portuguese in 1642 and the British, who were its masters from 1872 until Ghana's independence.

Despite its decaying colonial-era buildings, Axim is a lively town. Visitors will find parking accommodations on the esplanade located on the other side of town, just in front of the fort itself.

From the first courtyard, a vaulted passageway leads to a second, often used by the local fishermen to dry their nets. From there, a stairway leads to the sentry path... and a magnificent view. Even the most jaded traveller will be impressed by the vistas offered by these vantage-points far above the sea.

To the west of Fort Antonio, the lighthouse of wave-lashed *Bobowasi Island* can be seen thrusting proudly skywards from the surrounding reefs.

Were it possible to reach Fort Antonio's upper terraces, the visitor could see the small fishing port to the east, whose presence is nevertheless indicated by the boats entering and setting forth from it. Unfortunately, the upper reaches of the fort are occupied by administrative offices, and are not open to the public. Transformed into a hotel, they would undoubtedly make ideal accommodations for tourists traveling down the coast to Half Assini, on the Ivorian border. In addition, suitably far enough from the boiling surf and reefs of Bobowasi Island, the waters surrounding the fort appear calm and safe enough to provide perfect conditions for ocean-swimmers.

On the other hand, the splendid-looking beaches accessed by the road leading westward from Axim to the mouth of the Ankobra River are totally off-limits to bathers due to the violence of the surf.

Beyond the village of *Awunakrom*, the coconut tree-lined road curves inland, traverses a secondary arm of the Ankobra, and reveals a paradisical site reminiscent of Polynesia. Here, everything justifies the fantasy of thatched

bawku

huts, fish grilling over wood fires and paddling a pirogue up the mysterious Ankobra before disappearing forever into the beckoning, unknown western forests.

If visitors nevertheless manage to resist this temptation, and prior to returning to Axim, they may desire taking a short sidetrip to *Nkroful*, site of the tomb of Ghana's first president, Kwame Nkrumah.

Between Axim and Takoradi the road runs through miles of rubber plantations, coconut, orange and palm groves. And yet, there's nothing monotonous about these landscapes, comprised of rolling hills and gentle stream-lined plains shaded by delicate clusters of bamboo.

Beyond Abura, a signpost on the right of the road indicates the way to *Prince's Town*.

The fortress of Prince's Town was constructed by the Germans in 1683. Originally called Groot Frederickburg, the name of the fort was ultimately changed to Fort Hollandia by the Dutch.

At the time of its construction, the entrance-way was reputed to be the most beautiful on the coast. Today, only a few ruined walls and a sculptured crown mounted into the modern double stairway of the restored building remain to testify of the gateway's former splendour.

The ground floor opens onto a small courtyard to the left, where a low door leads to the vaulted halls formerly used as a prison for slaves.

Despite their sinister history, visitors will admire the delicate architecture of the vaults, whose arches spring from an enormous central pillar. Such subleties were doubtlessly lost upon the unfortunate occupants.

Although the restored fort is not open to the public, visitors have the consolation of being able to walk around it on the broad sentry path which still boasts its impressive array of cannons. The fort itself stands upon a sloping promontory which terminates in a mass of great boulders forming an effective barrier from hostile approaches by sea. West of the fort and nestled in a deep bay lies the village, surrounded by coconut trees as far as the eye can see.

Unlike Axim and its nearby fort, the fortress of Prince's Town is far from the clamour and bustle of the local population. Its total isolation combined with the restless ocean and numerous coconut trees standing sentinal around its walls all contribute to an impression of austerity that penetrates the site.

(*See practical information p. 165*)

■ Just when you think that you've exhausted all desire to visit still another African market, you may happen upon Bawku on a Monday, the town's principal market-day, and your love affair will begin anew.

For travellers arriving from the south, the atmosphere of this small town on the northeastern edge of Ghana seems absolutely new and unique.

Located between Burkina-Faso and Togo, Bawku was for centuries the stopping-off point for caravans arriving from afar, and even today remains a veritable melting-pot of numerous West African ethnic groups.

At the market itself, their faces framed by extraordinary jewellery, Fulani and Peuhl women sell curds. Their men, heads protected from the burning skies of the Sahel by wide, leatherbound conical straw hats, either look on amiably or go about other business. The remarkably tall stature of the inhabitants recalls that of the nomadic peoples to the north.

Enormous baskets overflow with every variety of millet, as well as rice, beans and lentils. Karite — in the form of fruit, nuts, almonds, flour and shea butter — is present everywhere. Tiny wild mangoes, round as apples, are sold as the flavouring to sauces. Delicacies such as oranges, bananas and kola nuts add their color and perfume to the ivories, reds, yellows and dark browns of the cereals.

Perhaps the most delightful symphony of colour emerges from the stalls selling fabrics, and particularly the multi-hued pagnes and grege cottons, destined to be sewn into flowing caftans and shirts.

At this point, the visitor will notice that here, clothing manufacture is no longer the exclusive province of men. Gathered beneath a convenient shady tree, small groups of women laugh and gossip as they work fabrics into garments upon pedal-driven sewing machines, while within their shops, the village tailors ply their trade in solitary dignity.

Bawku can be reached by road from either *Bolgatanga* on the west or *Nakpanduri* to the south. It's more interesting to make the trip from north to south, for as motorists traverse the plain, they have the pleasure of seeing a series of rocky ridges that progressively loom up from the west, ultimately filling the horizon with their rocky crests. In any case, photographers will find the winding road that twists up the mountain to Nakpanduri offers many opportunities for picture-taking.

(*See practical information p. 165*)

The cannons of Fort Axim,
still aiming seaward,
recall the centuries of bitter
European rivalry for
the mastery of the Gold Coast.

bolgatanga

■ The small regional museum created in 1991 constitutes the main attraction of this provincial capital located in northeastern Ghana, at the confines of Burkina-Faso and Togo. With a focus on ethnology rather than history, the museum represents an interesting complement to Accra's National Museum. Displays include the tools, ritual objects, arms and insignia of the peoples of the northeast as well as those of other regions. The fairly limited number and extremely high quality of the objects on display represents a welcome change from similar museums whose halls are often overcharged with articles of mediocre provenance.

Bolgatanga's little museum

Among the gems of Bolgatanga's little museum are the carved darkwood stool representing a reposing man; an extremely beautiful sculptured bronze Akan *kuduo* , or ritual vase, used in ancestor worship; the carved reclining chair decorated with human and animal motifs, and the elegant statuette of a seated woman in a style reminiscent of Modigliani's. Most of the exhibitions are arranged thematically, and include music, animal hunts, jewellery, weaponry and the traditional attributes of power of the kings and chieftains. Not to be missed is the superb multi-bladed ceremonial sword and the astonishing Ashanti combat tunic, covered in leather charms for the protection of its wearer.

Located in the Frafra country of Ghana's Upper East Region, Bolgatanga only began to prosper towards the end of the 1930s. With its modest population of 12,000 inhabitants, the city appears to be somewhat more of a backwater than other regional capitals. Except for the old city centre with its market and single business street, the rest of the town, which occupies a fairly wide area, fails to convey either a precise sense of purpose or activity. A number of construction projects are nevertheless either in the planning stages or actually underway, and it can be expected that the development of entire new districts will gradually fill up the empty lots that currently dot the city.

Recently completed buildings already give an idea of Bolgatanga's future aspect. In particular, the impressive Catering Rest House with its 24 well-appointed rooms, bar and restaurant, represents — among the numerous other new, small, basic and inexpensive visitor accommodations — one of the city's best hotels.

Bolgatanga also boasts the charmingly-named "Comme ci-comme ça" Restaurant, featuring an elegantly decorated, air-conditioned dining room and a reputation for fine food that extends throughout the entire region.

Bolgatanga's sports facilities include tennis courts and an all-purpose stadium. Car-weary visitors can even rent a bicycle at the stand opposite the marketplace and peddle off on a leisurely tour of the accommodatingly level city and outlying areas.

But before setting off, have a look around the business district. In the marketplace, artisans work leather goods while tailors offer striped shirts made of locally-woven cotton. The shirts are for men, but women visitors seem delighted with them, as by the men's straw hats, the handsome stone bracelets and leather goods sold by the handicraft shops lining the city's main street.

By taking the Tamale road to the first police checkpoint and then turning left, visitors can bicycle to the village of *Tongo*, the site of a nationally celebrated phenomenon.

The oracle of Tongo

Throughout the entire year, Tongo draws pilgrims from every corner of Ghana, and particular members of the Ashanti ethnic group. All come for the experience of the oracle-spirit, whose predictions, issued from a mountain cave overlooking the village, are reputed to be infallible.

During the period of the Ashanti migrations toward the north, their warriors transported a protective fetish in the form of a black, long, flat rock. Upon approaching the present-day site of the oracle, they were attacked by a fierce swarm of bees. In consequence, the Ashanti attributed a greater power to the local divinity than to that possessed by their fetish. Abandoning the latter — which is still preserved as a relic by a local family — they transferred their faith to the spirit inhabiting the cave.

Consulting the oracle involves compliance with a ritual decreed by the juju priest, or medicine man, who lives on the lower reaches of the mountainside. Depending on the importance of the consultation, offerings of poultry, rice or money are made. Pilgrims ask the ora-

bosumtwi (lake)

cle for advice and predictions, and frequently request cures as well. Whole fortunes are offered by childless women, while seriously ill patients are borne on litters to the foot of the mountain, from where they continue on foot, supported by friends and relatives.

After the priest has determined the appropriate offering, the pilgrims set off up the mountain. The voyage to the cave is punctuated by numerous ritual halts along the slopes leading to the three plateaus that occupy the centre of the horseshoe-shaped mountain range. When the group finally arrives at the entrance to the cave, additional offerings may be necessary before obtaining a response.

The Talensi villages

Aside from the evident fascination of witnessing such rituals, the excursion into these mountains is certainly worth the half-day's time necessary for a visit. A fairly stiff climb brings visitors into range of the Talensi villages, whose 12,000 inhabitants are scattered over the three plateaus.

According to Talensi legend, their ancestors sprang forth from the earth itself. Ethnologists have concluded that the Talensi are an authentically autochthonous people, most likely driven from the plain they originally occupied by invading Namows, a Mamprusi subgroup. The change of environment can be considered salutory in terms of scenery. The *Tongozugu*, their present habitat, dominates the entire plain, while from the last plateau overhung on the south by sheer rock walls — the view extends into Burkina-Faso.

(*See practical information p. 165*)

■ Visitors motoring from Kumasi to the Obuasi gold mines in the Ashanti country may wish to make a rapid detour to Lake Bosumtwi. Strangely enough, this majestic lake situated south of Kumasi is practically unmarked on most road maps. Accessed by a complicated series of mountain roads, it suddenly appears, as round as a monocle, circled by the surrounding hills. Stranger still is the fishermen's custom of lying prone or sitting astride on tree trunks and paddling with hands or feet over its surface...

The beauty of the lake, when first perceived from the rest house constructed on the summit of one of the surrounding hills, is absolutely breathtaking. According to the scientists who have studied similar lakes in Cameroon, its almost perfectly round form is due to an extinct volcanic crater that has progressively filled with water.

The underwater villages

During the rainy season, water pours steadily into this natural funnel. Lacking a runoff, the waters gradually rise year after year, with the result that in recent years, at least several entire villages have been swallowed up and since disappeared under the lake. Composed of hairpin turns and sheer drops, a rough track winds down to the shores of the lake and one of the last remaining villages. In time, this village is also destined to vanish beneath the waters, and in anticipation of the fatal moment, some of its inhabitants have already moved to a new, government-constructed settlement located on one of the neighbouring hillsides.

The novel use of tree-trunks rather than traditional pirogues by the local fishermen is explained by an ancient legend which states that the lake bottom is inhabited by a divinity named Twi, who long ago took human form in order to engender the ancestors of the present-day inhabitants. In exchange for this favour and his ongoing protection, Twi imposed two particularly severe taboos. The first forbade the use of anything resembling a traditional pirogue on the waters of the lake; the second prohibited fishing with the accessories usually employed for this activity. The problem of remaining in Twi's good graces while fishing the waters of the lake was resolved in a particularly ingenious manner by the population. The use of tree trunks (without paddles, for extra

*The former capital of
the Gold Coast under
the Bristish, Cape Coast, now
a provincial town,
still reminds of colonial days.*

busua

measure) circumvented the first taboo, while the second gave rise to a technique of fishing based on the use of special stationary nets, initially transported on rafts made of tree-trunks bound together with the vines of a local plant. As for the tree trunk "pirogues," maintaining the balance of one of these unusual craft is far from easy, especially when lying in a prone position with only one's arms for paddles.

Bekwai, a coffee-growing centre

On the return trip to Kumasi, it is possible to visit *Bekwai* , a coffee-growing centre. This pleasant little town was founded at the turn of the century, and is situated on a hillside offering a beautiful view of the surrounding landscape. Its numerous Ashanti-style dwellings with central colonnaded loggias are curiously similar to the covered ground-floor verandas of the old colonial-era homes built for the former European residents.
(*See practical information p. 165*)

■ This ideally-located seaside paradise is the perfect place to rest and recuperate after a few days of travel through Ghana's interior. Located on the Gulf of Guinea a few miles west of Takoradi, Busua offers weary travellers one of Ghana's finest palm tree-shaded beaches.

Visitors are advised to avoid Busua on weekends, when this charming little resort town is literally invaded by the residents of Sekondi and Takoradi, whereas finding accommodations in the local bungalows and guest houses during the week poses no problem.

Aside from its marvellous beach, Busua is also reputed for the excellence of its shellfish. Almost immediately upon their arrival, visitors will be approached by small children selling lobsters, which they will offer to cook on the spot for you, accompanied by yam chips. Those not succumbing to this temptation will find a well-supplied fish market at nearby *Dixcove*, virtually Busua's twin city.

Rays, sharks and sawfish

The mere sight of the bustling little port of Dixcove is worth the visit in itself. A multitude of sea-going pirogues discharge their cargo of enormous rays, sawfish, thread-fins and the occasional shark. Getting there is half the fun, since a well-frequented path covered in tropical vegetation takes you from the far edge of Busua beach directly to the port itself, and is even faster than driving. Yams, tomatoes, onions, bananas and everything else necessary for preparing a delicious fish dinner can be found at the port's adjoining market.

On the other side of the promontory which borders the beach from Busua, a small sheltered lagoon offers marvellous bathing in its clear waters, while inviting paths lead off into the surrounding tropical forest.

In addition to all of the above, Dixcove holds an even further attraction for the visitor, for if instead of following the Busua-Dixcove path directly to the port, you turn left up the hill and redescend toward the sea, you will have the agreeable surprise of discovering one of the region's finest fortresses dressed upon an esplanade.

Constructed by the British from 1691 to 1697, the fortress — like most others in Ghana — subsequently passed into the hands of many other nations, but fortunately under peaceful, non-destructive circumstances.

cape coast (oguaa)

Occupying a remarkably strategic position on the hill overlooking the sea, the fortress is flanked by a cove on the left, and to its right, by the bay and rocky bar that shelter Dixcove port.

The rocky promontory between Busua and Dixcove is softened by groves of different varieties of trees, while a handsome stone stairway, punctuated with five landings, leads up from the village to the esplanade and main entrance of the fortress.

A four-star fortress

The atmosphere is that of an improbable, fairy-tale African castle, since the fortress is inhabited by a large Ghanaian family and, from time to time, by foreign visitors.

As you pass from courtyard to courtyard, it is not unusual to come upon such familiarly-domestic scenes as an entire group of women hanging out the laundry or preparing a meal, entirely oblivious to the presence of total strangers bristling with sophisticated photographic equipment. The interior of the fortress contains a number of cells which were formerly used for imprisoning slaves, and which — entirely remodeled, of course — now serve as hotel rooms. On the exterior, the guard's walkway offers superb views of the Atlantic ocean, and in the evening, the unforgettable spectacle of magnificent tropical sunsets.
(*See practical information p. 166*)

■ Even when forewarned, visitors are always agreeably surprised by the nostalgic charm of Cape Coast. Like every ancient city marked by history, the past seems more present than the present itself. Everything here is evocative of Cape Coast's checkered history: old creole-style houses, a totally unexpected Italian palace, and the equally startling statue of a doughty Queen Victoria in the middle of one of the town squares. In addition, there are no less than two fortresses, complete with their rusty cannons still aimed menacingly seawards, as if in expectation of the arrival of some improbable enemy armada.

An entire history book would not be enough to contain the story of Cape Coast's fascinating and varied past. Despite the very British ring to its name, this charming little town on Ghana's west coast was in fact originally christened Cabo Corso (probably signifying "Corsaire's Cape") by the Portuguese. The name later became Cap Corso under the French, and was ultimately transformed into Cape Coast by the British. It was here, during the period of the opening of the celebrated African trade route to India in the fifteenth century, that the Portuguese first established themselves on the Gold Coast and instituted commercial relations with the Fanti population, whose name for Cape Coast was *Oguaa* .

This multiplicity of names for a single site is symbolic of Cape Coast's destiny during the centuries that it was fought over — as were most of the other strategic points on the coast — by successive waves of European adventurers and traders. For the purposes of security, the British erected a stronghold in 1662, although in the opinion of certain historians, the fortress had actually been built by the Dutch and captured by the Swedes before falling into their hands. But whatever the exact sequence, it is a fact that the British held it for three centuries, and that Cape Coast was also the first capital of the former British Gold Coast, well before Accra.

Not that the British occupation was without incident. Stories concerning the conflicts between the governors of Cape Coast and the Fanti population are innumerable, with the advantage often temporarily gained by the latter.

To improve the defensive capacities of their precious stronghold, and possibly to eliminate a potential rival, the British purchased a neighboring Danish fort, considered dangerously close to their own. Situated at Amandul, little remains of it today, whereas *Fort Victoria*, constructed for the protection of the initial fortress on a hill to the west of Cape Coast overlooking both the present-day college and the more distant city of Elmina, may still be seen. Its totally gutted hulk, looming impressively from the hilltop, is in total ruin, and according to local rumours, spirits have taken possession of its crumbling walls. Although this is difficult to assert, it is certain that the ancient fort has become the home to the lizard-infested weeds growing in profusion before its entrance.

Fort Williams, the contemporary of Fort Victoria, is a narrow, rounded structure situated on a nearby hilltop that dominates the sea. The position made it the ideal site for a lighthouse; in 1838, one was built, and still serves today.

Formidable fortifications

If Cape Coast's star attraction is certainly its fortress (Ghana's largest, and even more spectacular than that of Elmina), motorists arriving on the Accra-Sekondi highway are nevertheless advised not to make a bee-line for it upon arrival in the city. Instead, after parking your vehicle and relaxing over a cool drink at the Savoy Hotel, walk down to the sea, turn right on the beach, and follow the shoreline up to the port. From here, if you zig-zag your way around the beached fishing boats and succeed in avoiding getting drenched by the incoming breakers, you will arrive at a large rocky promontory jutting out into the sea like a great jetty. And all at once, fending the boiling surf below, the silhouette of the immense and impressive fortress looms into view high over its esplanade.

Much here has remained unchanged since the days when the ancestors of Cape Coast's high-spirited and voluble inhabitants, taking their lives and destinies into their own hands, massed before the gates of the fortress in futile efforts to overthrow its masters. Visitors making the effort to retrace the route of their discontent will be rewarded by an added dimension of meaning upon their visit of the fortress, the tour of which is conducted by a capable and well-informed guide.

The guided tour of the fortress includes a visit to the airless and lightless vaulted cellars into which as many as 1,000 slaves were packed during the one to two-month waiting period prior to their shipment abroad. An underground passage leads from the cellars to the beach, where formerly, slave ships put in

A nostalgic reminder of
Cape Coast's colonial past,
this ancient palace formerly occupied
by Europeans now serves as a primary
and secondary school for local youngsters.

for the loading of their human cargo.

In the main courtyard, visitors will notice three tombs. One contains the remains of a slave who succeeded in obtaining a higher education overseas and returned to Ghana with numerous academic honours. The two others are the final resting-place of Governor MacLean and his wife, Laetitia Elizabeth Landon, the celebrated English poetess.

The museum and library

The public is not admitted to the buildings that surround the second courtyard behind the governor's residence, since they currently serve as a prison. The left wing off the entrance houses the West African Historical Museum, whose permanent collection includes numerous engravings representing Ghana's coastal forts down through the centuries. Another exhibition retraces the history of the slave trade, and displays the everyday objects and furniture formerly belonging to the European traders established on the coast. Other items of interest include swords, firearms, chests and cabinets, and a number of objects made by Ghanaians during the same period, such as chieftains' stools, Fanti funeral drums and clay pipes.

Some of the display cases contain a collection of pottery and iron utensils dating from the seventeenth century. At that epoch, the Fanti of Oguaa were under the influence of their parent city, *Efutu* located several kilometres to the north of the present-day Cape Coast. In 1973, a number of precious golden ornaments were unearthed during an archaeological dig at this site, which is still believed to contain as yet undiscovered treasures.

The souvenir of Queen Victoria

A small square facing the sea to the west of the fortress contains a bust of Queen Victoria. One side of the square is occupied by a handsome building dating from the colonial era, whose entrance is guarded by two carved stone deer. A large stone staircase leads to an impos-

THE CENTRE REGION DEVELOPMENT PROJECT

Ghana's Central Region, which extends along the coast west of Accra, is currently the object of an ambitious project destined to totally transform its socio-economic structure. With the financial support of the PNUD, studies have been undertaken to determine the vast potential for the development of the region, and in particular, the area between Cape Coast and Elmina, which is considered as ideal for the creation of one or more resort complexes. By the beauty of its landscapes, the safety of its sheltered beaches and the presence of three ancient fortresses (one in Cape Coast and two others in Elmina) classified by UNESCO as international historic patrimony, the area offers everything capable of pleasing even the most exigent of visitors. The adjacent tropical forest and wildlife reserves of Kakum and Assin-Attandanso are exceptionally rich in animal species, seventeen of which enjoy totally-protected status.
The multiple objectives of the project include the renovation of the three fortresses by specialized architectural teams, the transformation of the forest and wildlife reserves into national parks, and the creation of a coastal resort complex at Brenu Akyin, 10 kilometres from Elmina. Although strongly tourist-oriented, the project also emphasizes the protection of the environment and its abundant wildlife. To this end, and as a related economic activity, the project calls for the creation of a seed-culture facility whose output will serve for the reforestation

elmina

ing crenelated door. Further in town, the Italian Renaissance-style palace and its park, occupied by an Anglican school, are also worth the visit.

Wildlife parks

Several animal reserves are being developed in the Cape Coast area, and in particular, the Kakum River National Park, to the west of the city and the Assin-Attandanso Wildlife Reserve. Another project foresees the creation of a forest and animal reserve some 30 kilometres from Cape Coast, open to visitors but primarily destined for scientific research and the protection of certain species menaced by extinction. Other wildlife inhabiting these reserves will include elephants, forest buffaloes, crocodiles, civets, the rare Bongo antelope, and more than 80 species of birds.
(*See practical information p. 166*)

■ For visitors arriving from Accra on the coast highway, the sight of the Fortress of Elmina on its wave-beaten promontory can be a moving experience. The first impression of the spectrally-white edifice, when glimpsed through the surrounding curtain of palm trees and surf-misted sunlight, is that it is a mirage. But as the visitor approaches, the outlines of the fortress — Castelo Saõ Jorge da Mina for the Portuguese and the Chateau de la Myne for the French — emerge, revealing the details of its perfectly preserved fifteenth-century architecture. Many of the old parchment maps of the first navigators to Ghana contain representations of its banner-crowned towers, along with the legendary King of Mali and his golden crown and the mythical lion of Sierra Leone.

Transformed into a museum, Elmina Fortress is one of the best-preserved of all of the coastal fortifications constructed by the Europeans from the fifteenth to the nineteenth century. Out of approximately 60 of these, only 20 or so still exist, with some in a state of near-ruin.

Elmina, however, remains the irreplacable souvenir of the first Por-

and embellishment of the greater Cape Coast region.
The local economy is being studied in an effort to create
structures permitting the creation of parallel activities
complementing the traditional occupations of the inhabitants. The
importance of avoiding an over-dependence on tourism has
become a central priority for the region, even if the renovation
and development of existing hotels and visitor accommodations in
Cape Coast and Elmina is being encouraged.
As a counter-balance to a mono-economy based on tourism, the
region's enterprises, when judged sound, will be eligible for
government aid. Existing fisheries, plantations and small
industries will thus receive adapted financial support permitting
their ongoing development, with future plans calling for the
creation of a small factory manufacturing handbags, belts and
footwear out of snake and crocodile hide, associated with a
breeding station for the supply of the skins and a marketing
structure to facilitate the merchandising of the articles produced.
Other plans call for the construction of a distillery for the
extraction of citronella essence in Breman-Asikuma. The essence
produced will then be marketed as a perfuming agent to the
several detergent and cosmetic firms already established there.
Other provisions of the project include the creation of training
centres in which women or unskilled younger workers will be
taught specialized techniques of fabric dying, the manufacture of
construction materials and building construction. At present, six
teams of young workers have already been constituted, one of
which is currently building a research centre at the entrance to the
Kakum Nature Reserve. The teams are being encouraged to form
trade cooperatives.

*Fishing, commerce
and commerce have
transformed Elmina into
a prosperous and charming
seaside village.*

tuguese navigators, and the living embodiment of the period of trade and commercial exchange between Europe and Africa in the centuries that followed.

At the request of king Dom Joao Il of Portugal, the construction of an initial stronghold was commenced at Elmina in 1482, some twelve years after the first contact of the Portuguese navigators with the Fanti of the Ghanaian coast and eighteen years before Vasco de Gama opened the celebrated sea route to India via the Cape of Horn in southern Africa. A few years earlier, Christopher Columbus had sailed to the New World, an event which was to have enormous repercussions for Africa in general, and Elmina in particular. The colonalization of the Caribbean, followed by North America, resulted in the massive deportation of African slaves. As will be seen throughout this guide, the fortresses of the Ghanaian coast not only served as warehouses for stocking the riches of West Africa prior to their transport to Europe, but also as prisons and holding pens for the human cargoes awaiting shipment to the plantations of the New World.

For the Portuguese, Elmina was initially little more than a landing-point for their caravels, offering the possibility of taking on fresh rations and drinking water. It soon became apparent, however, that the region contained immense natural riches — in particular gold (Elmina literally signifies "the mine") — as well as enormous herds of elephants whose ivory tusks represented another source of considerable wealth. It was thus that the first fort — initially of modest size and less for defensive purposes than commercial — was constructed at Elmina. The choice of Elmina was particularly strategic, since the site offered the natural protection of a small rocky promontory situated on a river estuary where ships could safely anchor. In addition, the fresh sea winds and temperate climate of the coast were infinitely more agreeable than the heat and humidity of the inland regions, infested with disease-bearing mosquitoes.

The initial fort, christened Saõ Jorge, was occupied by the Portuguese until the third decade of the seventeenth century. After period engravings, the fort bore a strong resemblance to a medieval castle, complete with round, crenelated towers capped by a conical roof and heavy, defensive ramparts pierced by gun emplacements. It was considerably enlarged by the Dutch, who took it in 1637, thus marking the definitive end of Portuguese mastery of the Ghanaian coast. Elmina subsequently became the African headquarters of the celebrated Dutch admiral De Ruyter during the Anglo-Dutch territorial war of 1666. The defensive capacity of the fort was accordingly strengthened by the construction of new walls and the installation of additional and more powerful cannons. During the same period, the nearby smaller fort of Saint Jago, renamed Coenraadsburg by the Dutch, was also renovated. A further transformation of the main fort occurred in the late seventeenth century, at which time it began to take on the size and aspect of a veritable fortress. The final metamorphosis was achieved by the Dutch in the early nineteenth century, when following further renovation, the fortress took on its present-day aspect. But the winds of change had already shifted....

With the abolition of slavery, a considerable source of wealth forever disappeared. As the cost of the upkeep and maintenance of the fortress of Elmina became increasingly prohibitive, the Dutch ceded it to the British in 1872, at the same time that they definitively retired from the Gold Coast.

For motorists arriving on the coastal highway from Accra or Cape Coast, the fortress of Elmina is accessed from the west, defended along its full length by two parallel moats separated by a sentrywalk. The original drawbridge over the first moat has been replaced by a stationary overpass, while the second is spanned by a small stone bridge. This unique double-defense system was constructed in the nineteenth century by the Dutch.

A vaulted passageway on the other side of the stone bridge leads to the enormous central courtyard. It is obvious that the imposing building on the visitor's left formerly served as the governor's apartments. Two broad stone staircases lead up to a terrace, above which two more flights rise to a loggia protected by a wrought-iron railling. The formal parquet floors and the dimensions of the enormous rooms suggest that they were used for official purposes, while a gallery traversing the second courtyard connects them to the chapel.

To the west, a colonnaded balcony overlooks the double moats, and offers the perfect vantage-point for regarding the neighbouring river, lagoon and salt marshes, as well as the surrounding wooded hills. The visitor will find it easy to imagine the romantic vision of a lovely woman, doubtlessly the wife or, since she's really a beauty, the mistress of the governor, watching the full moon rise over the seacoast on a warm summer's evening. Unfortunately for the romantically-minded, during the colonial period, few women even set foot on the balcony, since neither the Portuguese nor the Dutch ever thought of bringing their wives (or mistresses) to what was then considered as a dangerous and uncivilized territory. In reality, the balcony was more likely used by the governor for the more prosaic purpose of verifying that his sentinels were still awake and guarding the approaches to the fortress, rather than for admiring full moons over the Gold Coast.

As for the other buildings in the main courtyard, the edifice opposite the main stairway formerly served as a chapel for the Portuguese until the Dutch transformed it into a warehouse. Just behind it lies the famous Bastion de France, but to this day, its purpose or function remains unknown.

A ship on the roof

But the fortress is not Elmina's sole attraction. It is recommended that visitors desirous of discovering some of the town's further charms take the time to talk with the local inhabitants, who are generally delighted by the interest shown in their surroundings.

After a leisurely stroll through Elmina, the visitor may also want to hike up the hill for a look at *Fort San Iago*, located just opposite the fortress on the other side of the narrow river that runs between the lagoons and salt marshes and between the port and the ocean.

In 1638, the Dutch transformed what was originally a hillside chapel constructed by the Portuguese into a small fort equipped with four batteries of cannon and a watchtower. For present-day visitors, the creation of Coenraadsburg was a capital idea, since it now serves as a rest house for tourists, while the emplacement itself offers an even better view of Elmina and the surrounding region than that of the fortress, which it overlooks.

And by looking attentively from the watchtower, visitors will be able to make out what will appear to be the outlines of a ship perched upon the roof of the house northwest of the fortress; as will later be seen, this illusion is in reality a *posuban* .

After redescending from their vantage-point in the tower, visitors may desire to question the caretaker as to the signifi-

cation of a ship apparently anchored on the rooftops of Elmina. The caretaker, a charming individual totally devoted to assuring the comfort and peace of mind of the rest house guests, will be pleased to explain all this and more, and thus informed, the visitors will doubtlessly find themselves on their way through the narrow streets of the town for a closer look at the house whose roof is adorned with an entire ship complete with statues of a phantom crew of European sailors. As if this were not already enough, the ground floor of the curious house is surrounded by a loggia containing still other life-sized statues, but in this case, representing traditional Fanti warriors standing guard over the entrance.

In the same street, two other buildings of similar construction are crowned by statues of Biblical personages, mythical animals, African chiefs in full regalia, and such sundry other items as a helicopter, a cannon and a clock-face that appears to have been transported directly from an English country church!

Visitors questioning their sanity will be relieved to learn that these surreal apparitions are actually altars to the divinities of the Asafo, a warrior tribe that formerly inhabited the region, after being driven from their homeland in the Akan territory by the English. After migrating to the coast, and eventually intermarrying with the indigenous Fanti population, the Asafo constructed their strange altars, under which they prayed for protection and victory before going into battle.

The fact that the inhabitants of Elmira were amongst the first to make contact with the Europeans and their missionaries explains the origin of most of the heteroclite array of objects and personages found upon the roofs (the helicopter, however, still remains somewhat of a mystery). Nevertheless, all the knowledge of a specialist is needed to decipher their ultimate symbolism and meaning, especially since the population's grasp of their significance is gradually fading.

As extraordinary as the posuban are, there is still another highly-interesting spectacle which may be witnessed for an hour or so every morning : the return of the pirogues after the night spent fishing the waters off the coast.

This can be best viewed from the jetty that borders the narrow channel leading to the port. One by one, the boats enter the channel and make their way to the port, each flying a bright-hued flag attached to the prow. The dominant colour of the flag is repeated in the hats of the crew members and the helmsman, while the hats themselves vary from one boat to another, and include an incredible array of miners' helmets, snap-brims, dark-knit bosuns' hats, sailors' caps and practically every type of headgear ever conceived by man. Visitors will not soon forget the vision of an immense helmsman standing imperturbably in the stern of his pirogue, crowned by a bell-shaped striped cloth cap and draped in a brilliantly-coloured traditional garment ressembling a Roman toga. As the boats silently make their way to the port, the impassive crews are the object of the admirative gaze of the local spectators gathered on the jetty, and it soon becomes clear that what is being witnessed here is in reality a ritualized competition based on the size of the catch, the excellence of the splendid decorations painted on the flanks of the vessels and of course, the *chic* of the crew members' outfits.

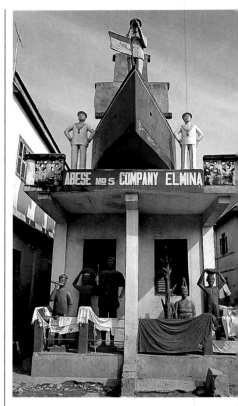

The ultimate challenge consists in crossing the bar that separates the channel from the high seas, a daily exploit that tests the skill of even the most experienced crew. By small groups, the boats await the wave that will carry them safely over the bar and into the calm waters of the channel, each helmsman aware that the slightest miscalculation will send his craft hurtling into its neighbour, resulting in the capsizing of either or both vessels.

To best get the feeling of this charming little town and its myriad attractions, visitors should try to obtain a room at the above-mentioned San Iago Fort which has been converted into a pleasant rest house. Since at the writing of this guide, San Iago does not offer meals, its guests are obliged to either eat in the local restaurants or to buy provisions at the market. In either case, your contact with Elmina's inhabitants will be rewarding, and give the opportunity to enter more completely into their colourful daily life.

For visitors desirous of more than basic comforts, the solution is to check into one of the new resort hotels that dot the region between Elmina and Cape Coast. The objective of the Centre Region Integrated Development Programme (CERIDEP), launched by the regional administration of Central Ghana in collaboration with the Ghana Tourist Board is to transform this portion of the coast, and in particular, Brenu-Akyinm Beach near Elmina, into a "Ghanaian Riviera" offering world-class tourist facilities.
(*See practical information p. 166*)

*Formerly serving as traditional shrines,
the "posubans" reveal a wide variety of artistic and cultural
influences: here Adam and Eve are surrounded
by traditional Ghanaian chieftains, as a cortege
of steamships and airplanes pass overhead.*

gambaga (escarpment)

■ Running for 65 kilometres across northeastern Ghana's grain-belt, the Gambaga Escarpment is an admirable geological formation offering superb views of the neighbouring savannas and the Volta River. The entire cliff-like escarpment owes its name to the little village of Gambaga, accessed by the Bolgatanga-Tamale road via Walewale. With its population reduced to just a few thousand inhabitants, Gambaga has lost much of its ancient splendour, and today's visitor will have difficulty in imagining that this sleepy village was once a proud regional capital and centre of the Mamprusi nation.

After supplanting the autochthonous tribes of the region, the Mamprusi, who were originally from Chad, were in turn decimated by internal dissention and dynastic wars.

The Mamprusi fatherland

One of the largest remaining groups, headed by chief Tohogu, initially settled in *Mamprugu*, from whence their name Mamprusi, and afterwards migrated to Gambaga. The village was henceforth considered as their spiritual fatherland, as well as that of the Dagombas, a different tribe many of whose members are the Mamprusi's blood relatives.

The Mamprusi chieftain, or *Nayiri*, is traditionally the sovereign leader and supreme chief. Prior to the construction of the main road from Belgatanga to Bawku, Gambaga was a regional centre of trade, and the site of passage for the Mossi tribes from nearby Burkina-Faso. The city was also the seat of the colonial government of the northern district until 1907; its decline occured after the transfer of the administration to Tamale and the construction of a new network of regional roads.

Gambaga is nevertheless experiencing renewed popularity as a tourist destination, thanks to the sheer loveliness of the region.

The town of *Nakpanduri*, situated further to the east near the Togolese border and equally situated upon the high Gambaga Plateau, is also attracting increasing numbers of visitors seeking wide, open spaces and breathtaking vistas visible from the terrace of the rest house, which admirably dominates the vast plain to the north.

At night, when the contours of the surrounding countryside become less distinct, the far-off lights on the low plains punctuate the darkness like those of ships, and the illusion of being on the edge of a great sea is total.

The pottery houses

For the visitor arriving in mid-afternoon, the enchantment is complete ; the terrace lies in an expanse dotted by great, easily-climbable boulders, while the rocky ledges surrounding the rest house and dominating the plain offer an inviting vantage-point for travellers weary of regarding the scenery through the windows of their car.

The region also features the unique traditional dwellings of the Mamprusi, constructed of earth and hand-modeled like beautiful pottery. The surrounding countryside is also lovely, and visitors will be tempted by the pathways that lead off between the tall, golden fields of millet. On a fine, late afternoon when the soft rays of the setting sun play over the landscape, one can only be impressed by the serenity of the inhabitants and elegant harmony of their hand-crafted dwellings. And as the night falls over the spotlessly clean inner courtyards of the *kraals*, women can be seen preparing the evening meal, the occasional lights of other distant villages and cooking-fires twinkle in the mysterious expanse of the invisible plain far below.

(*See practical information p. 166*)

ho

■ The capital city of the southeastern Volta Region, Ho is the perfect base for side-trips through the rolling green hills that stretch from Ghana to Togo. The large and prosperous agricultural centre of a region producing cocoa, tobacco and teak, Ho was originally an enclave of villages inhabited by the Ewe, drawn to the location by its strategic position on the caravan route from the north, at the junction between the coastal plains and the wooded mountain highlands. The site was chosen by the Germans, the first local colonizers, as the seat of their administration. Ho was also the centre for a number of Protestant missions ; the arrival of the British, following World War I, further increased the importance of the city already endowed with a healthful climate and immense agricultural possibilities.

The Kaba Hills, which rise above the city, can be accessed by a road leading to their summit, topped by a modern television relay station. The view extends over the whole city to the distant southern plains, while trails leading over the crests provide an attractive, easy-to-follow itinerary for hikers.

Origin of the "kente"

The traveller arriving from Keta will have already passed through the small locality of *Kpetoe*, to the east. If not, the distance from Ho is short, and well worth the trip. Lovers of kente will discover numerous weavers specialized in the creation of the traditional garment. According to the inhabitants of Kpetoe, the kente originated with the Ewe rather than the Akans, and the local population takes particular pride in having won the national kente competition during the visit of Queen Elizabeth II. Furthermore, the Ewe even claim that their ancestors invented the very name, derived from *ke*, meaning open, and *te*, signifying closed, the combination of which symbolizes the back-and-forth movement of the loom's shuttle.

A number of excursions can be made from Ho, including *Kpandu* to the northwest, which has developed into a busy port since the creation of Lake Volta. The port, which is charmingly picturesque, boasts an interesting local market complete with fresh fish and an impressive parade of "mammy trucks". The name has never been more richly merited than in Kpandu, since the trucks are filled to the roof with local fisherwives intent on rapidly selling their catch in all the major cities of the country, including the capital.

In the morning and evening, large ferry-boats operate between the villages on the east shore of the lake, and adventurous travellers can take advantage of the service to spend the night in one of the villages before returning the next day. There is also a boat that makes a weekly round-trip voyage between Kpandu and Buipe, located on the extreme north of the lake, and Akosombo on the southern end. In the port of Kpandu, it is also possible to make your own arrangements with a local fisherman for a motorboat visit to the various islands dotting the lake, and if you so desire, to fish for the tiny tilapias — delicious when fried, or the big mud fish, excellent when sliced and grilled over a wood fire.

Tsatsadu Falls

Tsatsadu Falls are located between Kpandu and *Hohoe*, the second-largest town of the Northern Region. Motorists are advised to avoid taking the usual road between the two towns, since the best itinerary is the small track to *Dzogbedze* and *Kpame*, and thence right to Hohoe. Once arrived at *Abehenease*, it is recommended that you ask a local youngster to serve as a guide. In the dry season, it's possible to drive nearly to the end of the road that leads up to the hill overlooking the falls. But even during the rainy season, when the state of the road necessitates leaving your car outside of the village, it's little more than a fifteen-minute hike to the falls.

The path that leads from the hills down to the base of the falls may look discouragingly steep, but is in fact easily descended due to the strategically-placed rocks which serve as a natural staircase. Rather than falling in a sheer wall from the top of the cliff, the waterfall forms a series of cascades, splashing from one ledge to the next before flowing into a rocky basin which in turn gives onto a narrow gorge and the valley beyond. Although the effect is less spectacular than the free-falling cascades, the site itself — a perfect composition of green plants and mossy rocks — gains in sheer beauty and enchantment whatever else it may lack in terms of impressive power.

The track east from Abehenease leads to Hohoe, which vies with Ho as an agricultural centre, and particularly for cocoa and rice.

keta

When in Hohoe, visitors should not miss the breathtaking trip to *Agumatsa Falls*, an hour's walk from *Wli*, and accessible by a path that skirts the Togolese border via Afagame.

A perfumed forest

The falls and the surrounding forest form a small national park, best visited in the company of a guide to avoid getting lost in the maze of paths that lead through the incredibly dense vegetation. The going is easy enough, since the way winds through the bottom of a valley ; on the other hand, the river formed by the falls has to be forded several times. Despite this minor inconvenience, the visitor will find the trip enchanting, particularly since the forest air is permeated by a sweet perfume similar to orange blossoms. Upon reaching the vast clearing with, in the background, the roar of the great mass of water plunging down, the first sight of the falls is all the more thrilling, since up to that moment, the curtain of vegetation has masked the sheer cliff from which it descends. During the day, thousands of sleeping bats can be seen clinging to the rocky protuberances of the cliff wall.

It is not possible to access the hills surrounding the waterfall during the rainy season, but from December to April the excursion enables visitors to discover an extraordinary panorama. The highest crest of the range lies farther south, at *Kpoeta* near the Togolese border, while getting there requires all the traction of a four-wheel drive vehicle, followed by a ten-kilometre march.

(*See practical information p. 166*)

■ Located on the east coast of Ghana upon a sandy spit constantly eroded by the ocean, Keta is a splendid site that will enchant anyone attracted by the sea and water sports. This small Ewe village occupies an extraordinary position between the Gulf of Guinea and the Keta Lagoon. The contrast between the often raging sea and the calm waters of the lagoon is astonishing. The lagoon itself is frequented by local fishermen who use a number of interesting techniques, ranging from classic nets to enclosures made of branches, including an ingenious system of small earthern dikes which trap the fish in the narrow channels of the lagoon.

The peaceful beauty of the landscape nevertheless hides a particularly poignant drama, for Keta is menaced by the inexorable progression of the sea. Its several thousand inhabitants are trying their best to survive here, but it is not certain for how much longer this will be possible. Of the port constructed during the last century by the Germans for the exportation of palm oil, rubber and slaves, nothing remains today.

After the arrival of the British, Keta nevertheless remained the region's main port before being swallowed up by the sea. Today the town, which still boasts an important commercial, administrative, medical and educational infrastructure, is slowly going the way of the port. Its buildings, constructed on a sandbank offering little resistance to the unending violence of the incoming tides, are progressively collapsing row upon row like houses of cards. The local residents claim that within their memory, ebb tides have already destroyed fifteen kilometres of formerly-inhabitable land, while several dikes have crumbled and vanished. One of the last of the remaining dikes is beginning to crack, while it is sad to note that on the other side of the road that runs alongside of it, regularly submerged during storms, many half-finished buildings have been abandoned even before completion.

The plight of this town is also common to a number of other Ghanaian villages located upon the Gulf of Guinea, with the problem extending to Togo and Benin. Within the context of the "Sea Defense Project", international agencies have sent specialists to diagnose the situation, and certain defensive measures are currently being implemented throughout the region.

Given the situation, the atmosphere of the town is somewhat strange, in which the laughter of children mingles with the continual misgivings concerning the fu-

As everywhere else in sub-Saharan Africa,
women play a vital part on every level of Ghanaian society
and are a key factor in the development of the economy.
But whatever their activity, they never lose
their legendary sense of humour and innate dignity.

ture expressed by the adults, and all of this over the ceaseless background music of the roaring breakers. The sight is particulary impressive when the highway passes over the narrow tongue of land that remains the sole obstacle preventing the ocean from breaking through to the lagoon that spreads broadly out behind Keta.

It's easy to see that once the sea becomes rough, there is little to prevent the waves from sweeping over the road to the neighbouring waters of the lagoon, and even where the adjoining strip of land is broad enough to accommodate farmhouses and fields, their occupants are frequently required to flee by boat when the area is submerged during storms.

For motorists arriving from Accra, Keta is accessed by the Tema highway via Dawheny, Sege and Kasseh Ada. From the latter town, one continues to Sogakofe, traverses the Volta, and a smaller road on the right leads to the coast.

« Fufu »,
a national dish

At *Sogakofe*, visitors appreciative of Ghanaian cuisine should stop near the bar on the left of the highway, just beyond the bridge. Around great open-air cauldrons in the courtyard, women will be seen serving up highly-spiced meat or fish dishes onto broad leaves that are used as plates. Near the bubbling pots of stew, other women are occupied in pounding plantain bananas into the paste serving as the basic ingredient of a popular national dish known as *fufu*.

For visitors desirous of sampling other regional specialities, the nearby market offers skewers of fresh shellfish from the Volta River.

The shellfish, which resemble small oysters, are found on rocks submerged in the deepest waters of the river. After being brought to the surface by local divers, the shellfish are buried in well-marked plots along the bank of the Volta until they attain maximum size. The Volta also holds many other treasures for those fond of fresh and salt water fish, including Nile perch, barracuda and tilapias, which are grilled like sardines and sold in the marketplace.

Beyond Sogakofe, the main coastal road runs past a pretty lagoon ringed by onion fields. To fish in the lagoon, locals use a system of water enclosures made of tree branches to trap their catch. When the door of the enclosure is lowered into the water, all that remains is to lift the fish onto the bank of the lagoon.

After Dabala, the road swings right to Anyanui, located on the banks of the Volta, and then continues to Anloga and Cape Saint Paul, the site of Ghana's oldest functioning lighthouse.

The extraordinarily lively Ewe villages that line the coastal road are full of the brilliant colours of an abundance of garden - grown fruit and vegetables.

Although livestock breeding does not constitute one of the region's local industries, the road is nevertheless cluttered with more sheep, goats and chickens than most motorists see in a lifetime of driving.

After Anloga and Cape Saint Paul, a road leads over a sandy spit to Keta. On the trip back, visitors have the opportunity of stopping off at *Blekusu*. This tiny palm-shaded village surrounded by fields is particularly charming, and fortunately, less threatened than Keta by an eventual disappearance under the ocean. Due to their somewhat more protected shorelines and more stable soil, this is also the case of the villages extending beyond Blekusu to the Togolese border.

At *Denu*, the Tuesday market offers a sampling of products and produce from the entire region. From here, the highway runs northeast to the formerly small border town of Aflao.

A real city
in the making

Long a sleepy border village between Ghana and Togo, Aflao is fast developing into a real city offering excellent accommodations to travellers arriving from both countries.

Its strategic location on the Pan-African coastal highway which links Ghana to the Ivory Coast, Togo, Benin and Nigeria make it a natural intersection for visitors to West Africa, while tourists will appreciate the beauty of the splendid coast.

(*See practical information p. 166*)

kibi   kintampo

■ If increasing numbers of visitors are coming to Kibi, a peaceful village located on the banks of the Birim River in the Eastern Region of Ghana, the main attraction is less the town itself than its surrounding wooded hills, a veritable paradise for nature-lovers.

Some ten kilometres north of Kibi, just before a signpost indicating Sagyamase, a dirt road leads off to the left into the forest, and progressively rises to a 750-metre peak.

Although the road is negotiable, the best way to appreciate the *Atewa Atiwirebu* forest that spreads over the hills for 259 square kilometres is to leave your car near the summit of the crest and continue on foot to the top.

From here, the magic of the forest is total, and as the visitor walks in the dim tropical half-light filtering down through the trees, he may have the luck of catching sight of the celebrated *papillio antimachus*, Africa's largest butterfly. The forest is also the habitat of numerous other species of butterflies, giant ferns (over 150 different varieties, including tree ferns), innumerable rare plants, and 300 species of trees. The forest also contains a mysterious waterfall which can be heard, but which up to the present, no one has ever succeeded in locating.

Visitors to the forest should also be prepared to encounter at least one representative of the forty varieties of serpents that inhabit the undergrowth, even it some of the resident insect population can often be even more intimidating. The forest is the home to one of the world's most diversified range of ant species, as well as monsters such as the frighteningly enormous winged beetles known as Goliaths or the more innocent-looking twig-like phasmidae. If after all of this, visitors understandingly prefer to cast their gaze heavenwards, they will be rewarded by the more reassuring sight of innumerable species of monkeys and tropical birds in the trees above.

Visitors having a particular interest in botany or zoology may desire contacting one of the specialists in either of these two disciplines at Legon University, located in the suburbs of Accra, or at the Tafo Cocoa Research Centre northwest of Koforidua. Kibi is also the home of the supreme chief of the Akim, a small ethnic subgroup of the immense Akan population of Ghana. A visit to the chief's headquarters offers a unique opportunity to observe the extent to which secular traditions coexist with the modern world.

(*See practical information p. 166*)

■ Of extreme archaeological interest in Ghana, Kintampo is a small town located on the Kumasi-Tamale highway. Kintampo is also the name given to an ancient civilization whose vestiges were first discovered a few decades ago in the grottoes of the neighbouring Boyase Hills. Dating from approximately 1500 B.C., the ruins of the habitations that were unearthed are contemporary with those discovered at Begho, near Hani, somewhat to the west of Kintampo itself.

In the vestiges of the clay and wood dwellings, archaeologists have uncovered polished stone axe-heads and receptacles containing traces of palm oil, fruit and peas. The discovery of the bones of domestic animals indicates that the former population were adept at livestock raising.

Kintampo pottery is hand-decorated by wooden combs drawn across the unfired clay, a technique still current in other African countries. These finds indicate more than one thousand years before the present era, an authentic civilization had developed around Kintampo, even though the region was later marked by the influence of northern traders, followed by that of the Akans.

Iron implements, which first appeared in the region of *New Buipe*, on the Black Volta north of Kintampo, approximately 1,300 years ago, undoubtedly existed here at the same time, or possibly even earlier. This hypothesis is founded on the idea that the heavily-wooded nature of the immediate environment would have logically elicited an adapted technological response.

Fuller Falls

The hills surrounding Kintampo run from north to south and form a transitional zone between the northern landscapes and the adjacent forested regions that extend into the mountains. Located on the northern extremity of the range, Kintampo offers numerous opportunities for walking tours of the surrounding countryside. Of particular interest is *Fuller Falls*, located a few kilometres northwest, whose waters mysteriously disappear underground before unexpectedly re-emerging far from the original site.

Visitors travelling from Kintampo to Techiman are advised to make a side-trip to the villages of *Boabeng* and *Fiema*, despite the frequently poor condition of the road beyond the village of Jema. Af-

koforidua

ter turning left at Manso, follow the road to Tanko, clearly indicated on a signpost, and then turn right. From here, the track rapidly takes you to the house of the custodian of the small Boabeng-Fiema Wildlife Sanctuary, that is home to four different species of monkeys, including 2,000 black and white colobus and 14,000 monas.

With the exception of village festival days, when the monkey population of the adjoining sanctuary prefer the tranquillity of their natural forest habitat, the visitor will have the pleasure of seeing them roaming confidently through the streets and courtyards of both Boabeng and Fiema, much as if they were an extended family of the villagers themselves.

If the monkeys of the sanctuary are accorded such favours, it is because they have always been considered as sacred by the local villagers. The monas and colobus, in particular, are considered by the native priests to be representatives of the god Abujo, who is thought to inhabit the Daworo River which flows through the forest. Killing or merely harming them constitutes a sacrilege, and when a monkey dies, it is given a funeral worthy of a human being. On such occasions, the rites include the sacrifice of a sheep, whose blood is used to colour a funeral shroud in which the body of the monkey is wrapped before burial in an appropiately-sized coffin.

A few years ago, the gilded existence of these furry "children of God" was menaced by hunters who violated the local tradition. The villagers consequently requested that the district council issue a special decree ensuring their legal protection, and the measure was duly adopted.

A number of fruit trees and banana groves are specially reserved for the monkeys, while the villagers'vegetable gardens and crop fields are located far from the feeding grounds of the sacred animals. At least in on this small part of the planet, it can be said that man and beast live in perfect harmony.

One of the most attractive features of the visit consists in the peaceful walk through the enchanted forest lying between the two villages. Amidst the exuberant tropical vegetation, visitors will be particularly charmed by a remarkable tree that puts forth brilliant red blossoms. No one knows whether the soft fragrance which is often noted in the immediate area comes from these flowers or the surrounding vegetation.
(*See practical information p. 167*)

■ The late afternoon sun casts golden rays upon the hillside over which the rooflines of Koforidua emerge, crowned by the silhouette of a white church. This is the ideal time of the day to arrive at this hospitable town, whose population — for the most part composed of members of the New Juaben ethnic group — welcomes visitors with particular enthusiasm and friendliness.

The New Juaben are an Ashanti subgroup whose ancestors migrated to this region, at the junction of the Densu and Pawnpawn Basins, and founded a state in 1876.

Having implanted themselves here, the New Juaben adapted to the new conditions of life skilfully, despite the problems engendered by the arrival of a mysterious plant disease in 1939, which decimated many of the cocoa plantations, the region's economic mainstay.

In addition to possessing an important market for agricultural produce, Koforidua is also a vital administrative centre and the capital of Ghana's Eastern Region.

Traditional funeral ceremonies

Throughout the Akan homeland, Saturday is reserved for funerals, and if you happen to be in Koforidua on that day, you're more than likely to witness the traditional ceremonies that accompany these important events.

The town's largest square is particularly well-suited for accommodating the festivities that follow the funeral services. If the deceased was a member of an important family, a large crowd will be present, with music supplied simultaneously by various groups, including comtemporary bands. Participants of all ages will be seen dancing to the sound of drums and often unusual brass sections, with even the village elders and chiefs joining in. On the occasion of a funeral, social rank, the dignity of age and differences in fortune are temporarily banished.

The delicate golden and green foilage of the stateliest tree on the square provides both shade and the perfect backdrop to the gilded thrones of the local dignitaries. The police are also decked out in their finest apparel, topped by a curious headgear made of golden plates secured by leather chin straps. Aside from adding supplementary local colour to the event, these guardians of the peace are responsible for keeping the par-

kumasi

ticipants' increasing exuberance within reasonable limits.

Welcomed by the smiles of the villagers, visitors will find themselves irresistibly caught up in the general enthusiasm, with explanations of the ritual celebration generously offered by the friendly onlookers.

Boti Falls

From Koforidua, the nearest point of interest lies northeast, in the direction of *Nkurakan* and *Huhunya*. Before reaching the latter village, a clearly marked track leads to Boti Falls, which has the particularity of being framed by a magnificent rainbow after each rainfall.

Everything here, from the soft, tree-shaded site to the small pool formed by the falls before it flows off to join the *Pawnpawn River* make this the ideal spot for a picnic or a siesta. Several felled tree trunks offer natural benches, while the afternoon light filtering down through the cool air is perfect for photos of the falls, the meandering stream and its rich vegetation.
(*See practical information p. 167*)

■ Before the spellbound onlookers, the high priest Okumfo Anokye invokes the heavens and slowly lowers the magnificent golden stool upon the knees of King Osei Tutu. The stool contains the *sunsun* (spirit) of the entire Ashanti nation, and is perhaps their most sacred and jealously-guarded ritual object. As is often the case, the legend which tells of the founding of the most powerful of the West African kingdom is based on tangible reality, since the famous golden stool (*sika gwakofi*, in Akan) actually exists in a well-guarded room of the Ashanti royal palace in Kumasi. And as will be seen below, the golden stool is a tangible incarnation of history itself.

Other than on extremely special occasions it is impossible for visitors to see the golden stool, which is displayed only during the coronation of a new Ashanti king (*Asantehene*), as was the case after the death of Prempeh II in 1970, who was succeeded by Asantehene Otumfo Opoku Ware II, Ghana's former ambassador to Italy.

All of the traditional pomp of the ancient African kingdoms is deployed for these ceremonies, during which the gold-clad Ashanti chiefs of the entire territory pay homage to their new sovereign. The precious thrones of the chiefs are carried in a solemn march, but no object receives more attention than the venerated golden stool. Not even the new king himself is permitted to sit on the sacred stool, which is provided with its own special throne.

To satisfy their curiosity other than on the rare occasion of a coronation, visitors will have to content themselves with the photo of the golden stool exhibited at Accra's National Museum and the Cultural Centre of Kumasi.

One of the more interesting stories surrounding the golden stool concerns Governor Frederick Mitchell Hodgson, sent by Queen Victoria to the Gold Coast with the mission of subjugating the Ashantis. After requesting that the sacred stool be brought before him, Hodgson expressed the ill-inspired wish of sitting upon it before the Asantehene and the members of his entire court. The reaction was immediate, as to a man, the Ashantis took up their arms and attacked the British fort of Kumasi, where Hodgson was forced to flee.

The ensuing battle, which took place in 1900, was long and bloody. Hodgson and his troops had to be rescued by a supplementary detachment of British soldiers from Accra. In a strange twist of fate, Major Baden-Powell, the founder of the Scout movement, took part in the destructive attack which reduced Kumasi and its royal palace to a heap of smouldering cinders.

To celebrate their victory, the British sent what they believed to be the veritable golden stool to the British Museum. Fortunately, the British were unaware that before dying in the flames of their palace, the valiant Ashanti defenders had substituted a copy for the original. And when Asantehene Primpeh I, who had been deported to the Seychelle Islands returned to rule as king over his nation in 1924, the genuine golden stool reappeared from its hiding place as by magic. This time, however, the British wisely refrained from claiming it as a battle trophy, and thus avoided the necessity of waging a new war for its possession.

The present palace — where visitors will be received upon prior request to the private secretary of the Asantehene — is prominently located on a hill overlooking Kumasi. Unfortunately, the entire structure was completely rebuilt after the visit of Major Baden-Powell and his troops, and bears little resemblance to the original.

A period print in Accra's National Museum represents the fort of Kumasi being attacked by Ashanti warriors, who are seen emerging from Manhya Palace and advancing across a deep ravine. The ravine has since been filled in, but the palace esplanade offers an excellent shortcut for visitors on their way to the fort, a trip which otherwise requires a roundabout walk back to Kejetia Circle and another climb up the hill opposite that from which you've just come.

The original palace has been described and illustrated by a number of contemporary witnesses. The walls of the royal chambers, constructed around a series of inner courtyards, were completely covered by carved panels, while the shutters enclosing the Asantehene's bedroom were richly decorated in gold and silver. The old city surrounding the palace included four main avenues lined with private residences whose walls echoed the decorative motifs of the palace itself, while their facades were graced by colonnaded loggias destined for the reception of guests.

Although all of this has since disappeared, the use of loggias is still current throughout the region, even in contemporary homes and buildings.

The fortress of Kumasi fared much better in the battle of 1900, and has remained in perfect condition. The proverbial stone's throw from Manhya Palace by the above-mentioned shortcut, the fort now serves as a military museum containing a fascinating collection of firearms. The museum also offers a well-documented exhibition devoted to the exploits of Ghanaian troops, and particularly their contribution to the Burmese offensive during World War II. But certainly the most interesting exhibit deals with the traditional Ashanti warriors and the ill-fated battle of 1900. In particular, the visitor will be struck by the evocative portraits of the then-reigning Asantehene and his nemesis Governor Hodgson, stiff as a British ramrod among his troops and a number of their women.

The Cultural Centre

Visitors desirous of learning more about the rich heritage of Ashanti traditions will find that the Kumasi Cultural Centre is a veritable treasure-trove of information, and a city within the city itself.

The oldest of the centre's buildings and probably the most impressive is the library which is offering nearly everything that has been written or published concerning the Ashanti civilization.

Further up the hillside pathway, and on the same side as the library, a wide esplanade contains the buildings of the Primpeh II Jubilee Museum. The architecture replicates a traditional chief's residence on a somewhat smaller scale, and consists of four separate buildings that open onto a rectangular inner courtyard. As may be expected, the museum walls are decorated with traditional carved Ashanti symbols, while an *Edwene* tree — representing wisdom — graces the interior of the common courtyard.

The four wings of the museum display a splendid collection of traditional objects, including clothing, jewellery, royal insignia and furniture. One of the star attractions is a bronze *kuduo* and its carved lid, believed to have belonged to the legendary Asantehene Nana Kofi Karikari. The kuduo was taken as a war trophy by the British, who eventually returned it to the present Asantehene who in turn graciously donated it to the museum.

Directly facing the esplanade and museum buildings, a great lawn terminates in a raised platform on one of its extremities. It is here that the present Asantehene sits to receive the homage paid by the regional chiefs and his subjects during *Durbars*, the incomparable festivals which will mark one of the high-points of your journey, if and when you have the good fortune to witness one.

To the right of the central pathway, the museum shop sells local handicrafts and art. While the selection is not what could be termed extraordinary, visitors will find fairly tasteful and inexpensive suitable things for gift-giving or as souvenirs.

Further along and to the left of the pathway, a large outdoor auditorium offers seating for one thousand spectators on the occasion of concerts, dance performances and plays. The auditorium is a perfect symbol of the vitality of Kumasi's cultural life, which is harmoniously integrating both the past and the present, even while helping to shape the future.

The very crest of the hill is devoted to the studios of potters, weavers, ivory and wood sculptors and leather crafters. Of special interest are the weaving rooms, where some ten young people turn out *kente*, each of which surpasses the next by the mastery of colour and design. The visitor will soon realize that the amount of time-consuming and painstaking concentration required to produce just one of these sumptuous garments totally justifies what at first may appear to be their somewhat exorbitant prices.

After leaving the Cultural Centre and turning right, the *Royal Mausoleum* will be seen on the left side of the avenue leading to the Bantama quarter. The current mausoleum bears only a slight resemblance to the original, which formerly contained the remains of eight Ashanti kings bound in gold. With the exception of the golden stool, few relics were as revered in the Ashanti homeland.

Following the avenue in the opposite direction from the mausoleum, the visitor will arrive at Kumasi's central intersection, Kejetia Circle and its fountain. The Kumasi Zoo is located somewhat further down the hill to the left. Unlike the Accra Zoo, the animals residing here principally consist of impressive local or regional specimens such as monkeys, squirrels, antelope, lions, leopards, buffaloes, crocodiles, snakes and birds. The zoo grounds are filled with shade trees constituting a green belt particularly appreciated by residents and visitors, while those in search of a good meal will find that the small but excellent restaurant is also worth a visit.

One of Kumasi's most prominent buildings is a two-steepled Catholic church perched on the summit of a hilltop above the city. While the church is of no special interest in itself, it does offer a convenient landmark for locating the street containing the shops of the local goldsmiths. As befits so noble a calling, these gentlemen are anything but early risers. The shops are rarely open before 10 in the morning, and even then, work has usually not yet gotten underway, for likely as not, the artisans will be busy fortifying themselves for the day ahead over a substantial meal.

At the opposite extreme, the nearby central market will already be going full blast by 8 a.m. For a bird's-eye view of all the activity, head for the top of the hill overlooking the market, one of Africa's largest, and which extends in all directions along the small valley as far as Kejetia Circle.

Before venturing back down (by following the stairway that winds from one landing to the other) to the street where the metal-workers' hammers send up an incredible cacophony, the visitor will have the pleasure of witnessing the impressive sight of a veritable human tide ebbing through the market below. In this ever-changing sea of humanity and vividly-coloured garments, only the countless thousands but even-brighter red ripe tomatoes offer a fixed point of reference.

A symphony of colours and perfumes

Once in the market proper, everything competes for the visitor's attention. The stalls overflow with the green bouquets of broad leaves used as plates, kitchen utensils decorated with gaudy motifs, piles of madly-yellow, red and green pots and bottles, spices of all colours and every conceivable type of fresh produce. Hand-carts rattle past at maximum speed, bearing heaped loads of green and gold bananas or violet-hued pyramids of yams that totter but never fall, artfully dodged by passersby intent on completing their purchases. Incredibly enough, the carts often make better time than the picturesque freight train which wends its way through this utterly discordant symphony of noises, odours, colours, people and merchandise.

It's possible to lose one's way here for hours on end, just for the pleasure of walking between the stalls filled with enticing spices, exotic herbs, unknown liquids and even — as if from another planet — gigantic snails sold either alive or roasted. If the visitor's appetite remains intact after confronting one of these beauties, the market also offers a

The streets of the hillside city of Kumasi, Ghana's second-largest and the capital of the Ashanti homelands, bustle with life far into the evening.

near-infinite number of occasions for sampling the local cuisine. Everywhere, food-stalls propose tempting dishes capable of satisfying every possible taste, all the way from the hardworking stevedores to the majestically-ambling housewives who pause in the middle of an intersection to gossip, heedless of the bottleneck they're causing.

It's no wonder that amidst all this sound and subdued fury, temporarily-dazed visitors welcome the occasion to pause and accept the chair offered by a merchant lacking the change due on a purchase. While the shopkeeper dashes off to locate someone to change your banknote, the neighboring merchants and their friends will gather around the "broni", as they call Westerners, and bombard you with an endless stream of good-natured questions concerning your nationality, origins, profession, family, and above all, your impression of Kumasi !

The once-in-a-lifetime atmosphere of this extraordinary market is one of the principal attractions of the city, and even the Westerners who live here permanently never get tired of discovering it further.

After having wandered through its maze of noise and colour, visitors may find that they have somehow found their way to the fountain of Kejetia Circle. And here, another fantastic experience awaits, for directly opposite the stands and stalls that ring the circle, lies the launching pad for the "tro-tros" and "mammy trucks", otherwise known as the Kumasi bus terminal. Although by this time, visitors should be habituated to the presence of these surrealistic vehicles, every new confrontation can be the occasion for a further dose of pleasurable culture-shock. From Ghana's most modern highways to its smallest villages, the ubiquitous vessels provide both transportation and endless cause for wonder and hilarity. But here, as in Accra, it's their juxtaposition that makes for even greater pleasure. Individually, covered in mottoes and cryptic messages, they comprise a veritable mobile compendium of Ghanaian folk wisdom. Grouped together in the bus terminal and read consecutively, they begin to compose the pages of an epic novel whose style, alternating between realism, resignation and a healthy dose of ironic sarcasm, perfectly mirrors the popular spirit, capable of metamorphosing the starkest reality by dint of pragmatism and imagination.

In addition to the open-air agora of popular wisdom represented by the bus terminal, Kumasi also boasts an excellent technical and scientific university located on the outskirts of the city.

As its name indicates, the University of Science and Technology offers specialized courses in all aspects of both disciplines, while training the future executives who will eventually serve in the country's manufacturing and industrial companies.

The lovely grounds of the university rival those of the Aburi Botanical Gardens to the north of Accra, while the campus is also equipped with fine athletic fields and tennis courts in addition to a riding club and a swimming pool open to non-students. Other sports facilities in Kumasi include the officers' mess, which offers squash, ping-pong, billiards and badminton, and a golf course belonging to the Ghana Social Club, one of the city's principal athletic organizations.

The Owabi Wildlife Sanctuary

Formerly, Kumasi's only source of drinking water was the Owabi River, located to the west of the city. When the river was dammed to create a reservoir, the resulting watershed extended deep into the city's nearby forests. The reservoir and forest have since become the natural habitat for many species of the region's wildlife, as well as for a number of migratory birds. To protect this abundant animal population, Ghana's Game and Wildlife Department created the *Owabi Wildlife Sanctuary*. Located on the Akropong road, some 16 kilometres west of Kumasi, the sanctuary is closed to car traffic but accessed by footpaths, and may be visited in the company of a guide.

Even with the obligatory guide, the sanctuary's antelope are difficult to find and even more difficult to observe, due to their extreme shyness. At present, one of the basic pleasures of the sanctuary consists in the opportunity of visiting a fine, well-preserved forest that gives an idea of how the region used to look before intensive logging began.

Certain craftsmen in the Kumasi suburbs and particularly in *Asawaki*, on the Accra highway, make kente that are somewhat simpler than those produced at the Cultural Centre. In consequence, the prices are also much lower. The only drawback is that the kente must be ordered in advance, which is to say about three weeks ahead of time.

At *Ahwiaa*, visitors can observe traditional stool carvers working along the

larabanga

roadside, under straw overhangs. The completed stools, which are generally top-quality articles, can be purchased a short distance away in several different shops. Once again, the problem remains as to how to fit one into your suitcase.

A little farther down the road, the village of *Ntonso* is specialized in the manufacture of *adrinka*, another traditional Ghanaian garment, of which numerous models can be seen drying in the sun on either side of the road. The adrinka can be purchased at one of the village shops, where they are displayed with lovely and considerably more expensive kente as well as other types of simpler but attractive handwoven cloth.

Banfabiri Falls is located in the small *Boumfoum Reserve* and accessed via a good road leading through Ejisu and Kumawu.

Another and often preferred itinerary to Banfabiri Falls is via *Bonwire*, the capital of kente production, reached via the Mampong road, followed by a right turn onto Asonommaso road. Since weaving is the principal activity of Bonwire, visitors will have the opportunity of seeing the production of every conceivable type of design.

The town itself, located in pleasantly rolling countryside, is an interesting stopover. Almost all of its buildings are constructed in traditional Ashanti style, with enclosed inner courts and loggias on the main facades. The taller buildings often boast beautiful double stairways leading to their loggias.

The Boumfoum Reserve

After having divested themselves of several pounds of Ghanaian cedis in exchange for the royally sumptuous kente of Bonwire, visitors can continue their exploration of the region by taking the road to Boumfoum, just before Juaben.

Although the tarred road continues to the entrance to the Boumfoum Reserve and practically to Banfabiri Falls, cars must be left at the reserve entrance, after which visitors proceed on foot. Since the park is a recent creation it's still too early to know whether guest accommodation will eventually be available here, as is the case for Mole National Park, where visitors can rise at dawn to observe the wildlife. But the proximity of Kumasi, with its numerous hotels, readily compensates for the reserve's current lack of accommodation.

(See practical information p. 167)

■ The ancient mosques of Larabanga and its surrounding region constitute an admirable discovery for visitors travelling through northern Ghana. Painted in strikingly contrasting tones of black and white, their upper reaches bristling with wooden stakes serving as perches for birds and flanked by soaring, missile-like minarets, the mosques resemble abstract sculptures or the inspired creations of the Catalan architect Antonio Gaudi. The small volumes of these veritable jewel-boxes echo the larger mosques found at Djenne and Mopti in Mali, and the Sultan's palace of Agadez in Niger. Often constructed under shade-trees, Larabanga's mosques are cool sanctuaries particularly conducive to meditation and prayer.

The surrounding village habitations are of equal interest, owing to the unique hand-printed decorative motifs, pressed into the still-humid earthern walls.

On the outskirts of the village, visitors can see the locally-celebrated "magic rock," which occasioned endless problems for the engineers constructing the road through Larabanga. The rock, which constituted a sizeable obstacle, was transported to a new site, only to magically reappear on its original emplacement the following night. After repeated attempts to find a new home for the strong-willed rock, the engineers surrendered to the occult powers that seemed to be animating it, and modified the new road so as to bypass the site. Since then, the rock is leading the peaceful existence proper to such objects.

After an excursion to Mole National Park, visitors can continue their discovery of several of the other mosques located in the northern region, notably at Sammabo Ga, between Swala and Wa, and to the west of Larabanga. The smallish mosque of Sammabo Ga features a splendid enclosure made of intertwined tree branches that have been stripped of their leaves, and whose tormented natural forms have been left intact. The twisted enclosure, topped by the jagged outline of the branch-ends, provides a savage but harmonious counterpoint to picket-like decorations gracing the upper reaches of the mosque. The striking silhouette of the entire ensemble is enough to stop most visitors to this Dagarti enclave in their tracks.

The habitations of Sammabo Ga are also unique. Rectangular in design and constructed with a flat roof serving as a terrace, the houses are often accompanied by a huge cone-shaped silo covered on three sides by a canopy supported by a framework of tree branches protected by a thick layer of hard-packed soil. Under the canopy hang large hollow gourds which serve as nests for the local pigeons.

On the outskirts of Sawla at the intersection of the northern highway and the road leading to Mole National Park, visitors will be struck by the presence of an astonishing tree. Its immense truck and cascade of aerial roots are half-hidden by dense foilage in the midst of which appear windows giving onto the sky above.

Visitors must refrain from giving in to thes temptation of exploring it until having obtained the authorization from the local inhabitants, since the tree is believed to be the home of a spirit. Curiously enough, this robust vestige of animism exists in a region dotted with mosques, and long islamized by Mande traders.

After Sawla, the most interesting examples of local earthern architecture are found at *Wa* and two other nearby villages, the first of which is also a Wala enclave.

Visitors will notice that the village located on the left of the road is characterized by habitations whose overall volumes are much larger than the *kraals* (traditional family compounds constructed out of hard-packed earth and clay bricks) previously seen in the northern region. In general, the latter serve as the home to a single family, and are often separated from one another by a field of millet and the traditional laced-branch corral serving to enclose the domestic animals at nightfall. While the distance between these habitations is often too great to give the impression of a village, here each family is separated from its neighbours by narrow walkways with a central channel for draining off rainwater. The inner courtyards, although neatly swept, are not quite as spotless as the *kraals* whose courtyards have been treated with a special coating to harden the soil. The entryway to some of the habitations features a decorative cone-shaped object resembling the motifs seen on the local mosques. Many of the external earthern walls are also carved with series of spiral, straight or broken lines, while the rough clay brickwork is occasionally left in a natural, unfinished state. Contrary to the kraals which are totally closed to the exterior, the habitations in this village are pierced by small square windows flanked by shutters, giving onto the street.
(*See practical information p. 167*)

*Resembling abstract sculpture
and bristling with decorative
wooden stakes, the earthern-walled
mosques of Northern Ghana are
marvels of indigenous architecture.*

mole national park

■ Located in the heart of the Northern Region, Mole National Park has offered visitors the unique experience of its "foot (trekking) safaris" since the early 1980s. Thus, instead of being confined to a four-wheel drive vehicle (from which it is often prohibited to descend) as frequently occurs in other African wildlife reserves, visitors are encouraged to set off on foot along the numerous paths that traverse the park. The result is a first-hand, direct contact with nature, during which visitors will gradually learn the ancestral art of tracking and approaching animals as silently as an Apache. The time that one spends here is accompanied by the progressive realization that even if one manages to master the instinctive fear of wild animals, it is apparent that on the other hand, the latter have not gotten over *their* instinctive fear of man. And rightly so, if the sad experience of their wholesale slaughter during the great African hunting safaris of recent history is any lesson.

Possibly for this reason, visitors are rarely able to approach them at really close range, since the slightest movement or odour signifying a human presence will usually send them running as if their lives depended on it, which of course, was formerly the case. Nevertheless, to minimize any potential risk, every trekking safari is accompanied by an armed guide perfectly familiar with the park and the habits of its animal population.

The reserve, which is administered by Ghana's Department of Game and Wildlife, covers some 2,330 square kilometres, a portion of which are traversed by the Mole River. Current wildlife includes numerous varieties of antelope (Defassa or Buffon bucks, guibas, reeboks, bubales, etc.), warthogs, monkeys (cercopithecus, baboons, red patas, blue and black colobus), elephants (fairly difficult to approach), a multitude of African buffalo, the occasional lion, and scads of leopards, hippos and hyenas. Over 300 bird species live permanently in the park, while 150 additional migratory species regularly touch down, along with the intermittent visits of eagles and bee-eaters.

Visitors desiring to observe these animals generally hike to either of the two principal watering-places, or are driven in the park Land Rover to Camp Lovi, 30 kilometres distant, to spend the night. Both trekkers and camp guests must bring their own food and camping equipment, since the park's unique stone shelter is totally unfurnished.

If the Land Rover is unavailable, other than during the rainy season there is generally no problem in attaining either Camp Lovi or Konkori (situated at the base of a cliff in the northeastern section of the park) in an ordinary vehicle.

The vestiges of ancient villages

The cliff overlooking Camp Konkori dominates a great, rolling and wooded plain dotted with clearings and rocky outcroppings. Even during the rainy season, the thin topsoil generally prevents the grass and vegetation from growing high enough to conceal the wildlife. The landscape is lovely in all seasons, with red-coloured succulents and scattered clumps of brilliant yellow wildflowers contrasting with the green sea of the tropical grasses.

Along the track leading to Konkori, visitors will occasionally notice the presence of a maze-like network of cavities and underground passageways, frequently used as a natural refuge by some of the park's wildlife.

Prior to the tribal wars which swept through the region in the 1870s, the area contained a number of villages, the vestiges of which are still visible in the form of the above-mentioned declivities.

To the south of the park in the vicinity of Larabanga, a safari-hotel has recently been constructed. The hotel complex contains accommodations for 35 guests in private bungalows, a restaurant and a currently unfilled swimming pool. Lights go off at 10 p.m., possibly to ensure guests get plenty of sleep before rising at the crack of dawn, the most favourable moment for observing the local wildlife.

Although Mole National Park is open throughout the entire year, the rainy season frequently transforms the paths into muddy swamps, while high grasses can complicate the viewing of the reserve's wildlife. For these reasons, the best period for visiting the park is from December to May.

Don't forget to bring along appropriate gear and clothing if you are planning a trekking safari. Clothing should be either neutral or jungle-camouflaged to provide low-visibility to the skittish animals. Sturdy boots, a hat and sunglasses are also essential, as is a water canteen and a pair of binoculars. Photographers should equip themselves with a telephoto lens, while campers should not forget the indispensable butane lamp or battery-powered flashlight.
(*See practical information p. 167*)

mpraeso

■ In terms of tourism, the destiny of the *Kwahu Plateau* on the southern shores of Lake Volta is becoming increasingly clear, since the heavily-travelled Koforidua-Kumasi highway runs nearly parallel and provides rapid access to all of the region's marvellous sites, including Mpraeso.

In many senses, more than the town itself, the scenery offered by the route from *Nkawkaw* to the top of its neighboring escarpment is the area's real attraction.

This impressively high cliff, formed by rocky outcroppings, changes its aspect with every step the visitor takes. Its grandiose scale becomes somewhat more reassuring once you reach the top, but the visitor is once again dazzled by the view of the valley offered at its abrupt edge. After parking their car at the base of the television relay station which is visible from southern Mpraeso, visitors may desire to follow the path leading off through the underbrush which terminates at the very rim of the plateau.

The plateau itself is anything but flat. From Mpraeso, a road winds off through the valley and its gently sloping hillsides dotted with the palatial villas of *Obo,* the favourite summer residence of affluent Kwahus who flock there for its fresh air, stunning scenery and pervasive calm.

Motorists traversing this region are often overcome by the quite understandable urge to leave their cars and set off on foot across this truly sumptuous landscape. Unfortunately, the trails are not clearly marked, and hikers must either take the time to localize them or be guided by a local resident.

Either before or after Mpraeso, depending on whether you arrive from Koforidua or Kumasi, the main highway traverses *Bunso*, whose rest-house may be reserved from Koforidua.

Sparkling liquid stalactites

From Bunso, a sidetrip to Begozo Falls is imperative. This small village situated southeast of Mpraeso upon the Kwahu Plateau is accessed by the road from Osiem. From here, the tarred road cuts across the plain to Bosuso and then rises as it traverses a densely-forested region. At Begoro, the road attains the summit of the plateau, and from here, visitors should engage a local guide for the walk to the falls, located two kilometres from the village.

It's only a ten-minute walk through a grove of seedling oil palms and blue and yellow blossom-filled yam fields, followed by a descent on the left through tall tropical undergrowth and a forest extending to the face of a rocky bluff. The bluff overlooks the path and forms a natural amphitheatre for the falls, whose diaphanous curtain of water descends in sparkling liquid stalactites to the pool at its base. From a height of 125 metres, the myriad silver filaments plunge down along the irregular, moss-covered sides of the falls. The effect is most spectacular when viewed through the rays of the late afternoon sun.

A rare species of fern

The site is also the habitat of an extremely rare species of fern whose scientific name is *Oleandra Ejurana*, the unique pteridophyte common to Ghana.

Visitors emerging from the sun-dappled and verdant hollow will revel in the walk back up to the lighter atmosphere of the plateau. The calm and peace is total, while the fronds of a lone papaya tree whisper gently in the breeze. Behind the surrounding fields, which accentuate the impression of openess and space, the distant forest beckons under the last rays of the setting sun. Of such visions are dreams made...
(*See practical information p. 167*)

navrongo

obuasi

■ In this northern region of Ghana (Upper Region), where both Islam and animism are strongly implanted, the sight of a cathedral, and, in the middle of the bush, a replica of the Grotto of Lourdes may be enough to prompt visitors unprepared for this encounter to pose certain questions concerning their susceptibility to mirages and hallucinations. In fact, these admirable works are the result of the long presence of the celebrated "White Monks," whom the French Cardinal Charles de Lavigerie sent on missions of evangelisation throughout all of Africa beginning in the late 1860s. In Navrongo, the Canadian priest, Father Oscar Morin — sent by the Vicar of Ouagadougou in Burkina-Faso — founded a mission in 1906 before initiating the construction of the Cathedral of Our Lady of the Seven Sorrows in 1919.

The cathedral's humble tin-covered beamed ceiling is possibly its least impressive feature, but visitors will be captivated by the compelling beauty of the nave, whose pillars and earthern walls are covered with naive frescoes. The white, brown and black-hued paintings were executed by the women of the village, who deliberately chose natural colourschemes created out of a mixture of local soil and karite oil (serving both as the medium and a varnish). The images represent saints, religious symbols and geometrical designs, while a frieze that runs completely around the interior depicts troops of animals and everyday moments of village life. A particularly striking series of scenes painted under the entryway represent the Nativity, Saint George and the dragon, the Virgin Mary, Adam and Eve banished from Paradise and in a somewhat more familiar mode, a local mother with her child on her back, hard at work pounding millet into flour in a mortar.

Behind the altar rises a great, stark wooden cross framed by two vertical strips composed of brown, ochre and pink triangles.

During the Sunday services, the singing of the local choir is accompanied by the beat of the drums which can be seen standing along the pillars.

From Navrongo, visitors can continue northward to Burkina-Faso via Paga, a small border village celebrated for its sacred crocodiles (see description of Paga). To the east of Navrongo, the region is dotted by lovely fields of millet, punctuated by *kraals* (traditional earthern dwellings) entirely hand-decorated in painted geometrical or animal motifs. (*See practical information p. 168*)

■ Before arriving at Obuasi, the gold-mining centre of the Ashanti homeland, some visitors may imagine that they're going to discover a dusty frontier city straight out of the legendary American West, complete with gunslingers, local saloons and hard-bitten prospectors ready to lose a nugget or two over a glass of whiskey and a bad hand of cards. This romantic vision is rapidly dissipated by the sight of the sobre, peaceful and well-organized city, situated in a valley surrounded by wooded hillsides. A number of Obuasi's inhabitants have never even seen a nugget, since the ore is industrially extracted from the millions of tons of dirt, rock and sand that are brought up like coal from mine galleries some 1,500 metres below the ground. In this respect, the visitor contemplating Obuasi's gold mines from one of the surrounding hillsides will be struck by their similarity to the coal mines of Birmingham in England.

Once brought up from the underground galleries, the raw ore is transported across the city on an overhead conveyor-belt, where it arrives at the immense processing plant of the Ashanti Goldfield Corporation. From here, it undergoes a complex series of transformations which include washing and crushing before becoming the dark, concentrated paste which will be baked in high-temperature ovens. But even at this point, the faintest glimmer of gold has yet to be seen, for the ore is still as black as pitch. The next step of the refining process takes place in an inner sanctum containing furnaces and crucibles, and whose thick, double-locked iron doors are guarded by heavily-armed security personnel. Visitors will finally have the impression that something vitally important is going on in the withering heat that can already be felt beyond the entrance to the room, and this time, they are right.

The golden bowls

Brought up to white heat in the ovens, the liquified ore is poured into small, bucket-sized crucibles. A worker covered from head to toe in heat-resistant clothing then turns the crucible over, releasing a heavy, glue-like substance looking like nothing so much as black molasses. After its solidification, the crust is broken, revealing a bowl-shaped lingot of approximately nine kilos of pure gold. The lingots are then hosed down to room temperature and rapidly transported to

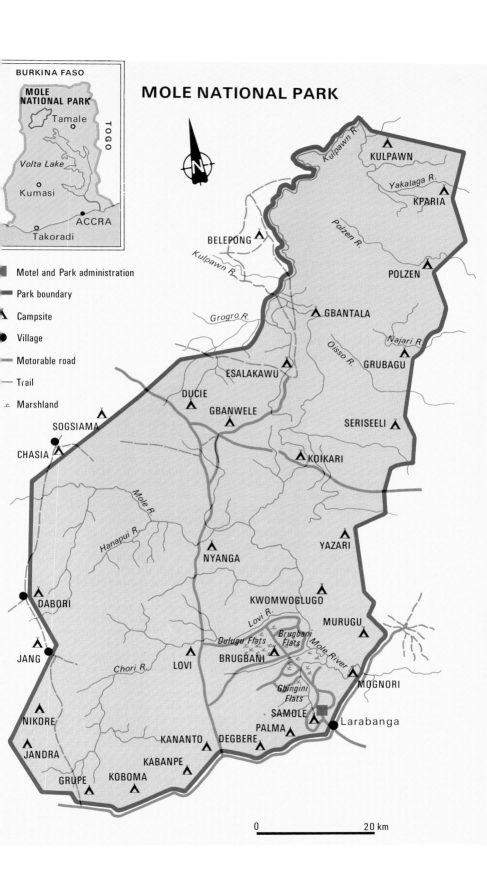

MOLE NATIONAL PARK

BURKINA FASO

MOLE NATIONAL PARK

TOGO

Tamale

Volta Lake

Kumasi

ACCRA

Takoradi

Kulpawn R.

KULPAWN

Yakalaga R.

KPARIA

Polzen R.

BELEPONG

POLZEN

Kulpawn R.

Grogro R.

GBANTALA

Najari R.

Oisso R.

GRUBAGU

ESALAKAWU

DUCIE

GBANWELE

SERISEELI

SOGSIAMA

KOIKARI

CHASIA

Mole R.

Hanapui R.

YAZARI

NYANGA

KWOMWOGLUGO

DABORI

MURUGU

Lovi R.

JANG

Dulugu Flats

Brugbani Flats

Mole River

Chori R.

LOVI

BRUGBANI

MOGNORI

Gbingini Flats

NIKORE

SAMOLE

Larabanga

PALMA

JANDRA

KANANTO

DEGBERE

KABANPE

GRUPE

KOBOMA

- Motel and Park administration
- Park boundary
- Campsite
- Village
- Motorable road
- Trail
- Marshland

0   20 km

paga

a safe, prior to shipment to Germany for further processing.

A visit to the processing plant takes up the better part of a morning, but the long wait inevitably yields its expected reward, and from this point on in their lives, visitors can consider themselves as belonging to the select club of those who have actually witnessed, if even for only a few seconds, the creation of a lingot of this fascinating and precious metal.

For obvious reasons of security, visitors desirous of visiting the mines and processing plant must send a written request to this effect to the Ashanti Goldfield Corporation, whose company headquarters are located in the Diamond House building of Accra. Without have received this authorization, visitors will be politely but firmly turned away by the mine's security guards.

From Obuasi to Lake Bosumtwi

Aside from its mining activities, the town of Obuasi contains little of real interest. Most of its 20,000 inhabitants are employed by the AGC, which has constructed amenities ranging from a golf course to company restaurants and hotels for its personnel. The popular quarters of the town are filled with small hotels, bars and dance-halls whose picturesque names recall those painted on the "trotros" and "mammy trucks." The visitor possessing an eye for local colour will also appreciate the signboards adorning many of the small shops, whose artwork is often charmingly naive.

From Obuasi, it is possible to make a rapid sidetrip to Lake Bosumtwi, some 60 kilometres to the northeast. From here, it's just a short hop to Kumasi, the capital of the Ashanti homeland.
(*See practical information p. 168*)

■ This small village situated in the Upper-East Region on the Ghanaian-Burkina-Faso border is best known for its sacred crocodiles. Visitors to the region should make of point of turning off at Navrongo for the sidetrip to the home of these semi-tame monsters.

Although the local tradition is progressively giving way to the imperatives of tourism, the crocodiles were originally the object of a veritable cult among the inhabitants of the region. Nevertheless, a number of Ghanaians continue to make the pilgrimage to the crocodile pond where they sacrifice a chicken or two in exchange for the "blessings" of its toothy denizens. In general, the crocodiles are called upon to aid in the realization of a wish of some sort, be it for rain during a dry spell, an abundant harvest, the fertility of a wife or even passing a university examination.

Practices involving the divine intervention of crocodiles are current elsewhere in Africa, as for example at Sabou, near Ouagadougou in Burkina-Faso or in the Bassar country of northern Togo.

Today, the once-venerated pond and its crocodiles have lost much of their sacred mystique. The phenomenon is directly proportional to the increasing arrival of both tourists and the merely curious, and it may be expected that soon, the site will be attracting whole busloads of visitors participating in organized tours of the region.

Despite all of this, the visit is still well worth the effort, and if nothing else, the sight of a horde of eager crocodiles responding to a call as good-naturedly as the family dog is one which the visitor will not soon forget.

After having climbed out of their pond at the summons of the attendant, the crocodiles lend themselves to the inevitable photo-sessions wherein visitors are "snapped" seated upon a scaly but docile back, or in the attitude of the fearless crocodile tamer, with one cautious foot lightly posed on an outstreched tail. It's all in good fun, and when the local youngters are not splitting their sides in laughter over the antics of both man and beast, they offer an interesting side-show, composed of tail-pullings, sarcasms and various forms of body-to-body contact with their erstwhile playmates. As for the crocodiles, it would appear that they are delighted by all the attention, and in particular, for the endless supply of sacrificial chickens whose purchase by visitors constitutes the relatively modest entry-fee.
(*See practical information p. 168*)

sekondi-takoradi

■ Even though they have become sister-cities, both Sekondi and Takoradi have maintained their individual personalities. Sekondi, the provincial capital of Ghana's Western Region, remains a small town full of old-fashioned charm, while Takoradi has grown into Ghana's principal commercial port with an activity even greater than that of Tema. Collectively, both cities count some 250,000 inhabitants.

As may be expected, Sekondi, which can be accessed by the coastal highway leading from Accra, offers a much slower pace of life than its sister-city Takoradi.

This is most apparent in what is called the European quarter, dominated by Fort Orange (constructed by the Dutch in the seventeenth century) and sloping down in the direction of Sekondi's fishing and military ports. The quarter's colonial-style, somewhat decrepit private residences offer a nostalgic vision of a more gentle but distant past, while several spots afford fine views of the irregular shoreline of Sekondi Bay, the activity of the fishing port and the neighbouring beaches. The harbour of the adjacent naval base generally has several military ships of light tonnage riding at anchor, while the nearby shipyard constructs fishing boats.

Despite its air of having seen better days, Sekondi is anything but a ghost town. Capital of the Western Region and an administrative centre of the government, the town is also the seat of the Western Regional House, an administrative body comprised of both the regional chieftains and the supreme chief. The head offices of the Ghanaian Railroad are also located here, and it was thanks to the construction of the rail line connecting Tarkwa, Obuasi and Kumasi with the coast in 1900 that Sekondi enjoyed a long period of prosperity and development even more pronounced than that of Takoradi.

The Railroad Workers Union, whose headquarters are also in Sekondi, remains one of the most powerful labour organizations in the country.

The emergence of Takoradi

Up to and just after the turn of the present century, all of Ghana's exported goods transited through the port of Sekondi. This commercial activity attracted a fairly large population of Westerners and the subsequent construction of the above-mentioned European quarter in Sekondi, while the local workers' residential area extended inland and to the west, toward Takoradi.

The destiny of the latter city definitively changed in 1920, when Takoradi, then a small fishing village, was chosen as the site of a new and modern port, which has since grown into Ghana's largest and most active. As workers streamed in from all over the country, new housing was constructed. While the Europeans, true to form, took possession of the most attractive residential districts adjacent to coast, the African quarter grew inland, perpendicularly to the port. It ultimately became necessary to draft an urbanization plan to ensure the rational development of the mushrooming city. The results of the plan are still visible today: the downtown area of the African quarter is formed by a circular marketplace into which the city's main avenues intersect, while each neighbourhood was provided with additional land to absorb eventual growth. The plan also called for the creation of separate industrial zones, which today house sawmills, plywood factories, paper mills, metalworks, a cigarette and tobacco company and a cocoa-processing complex.

A panorama of the port

Although more business travellers than tourists are lured to Takoradi by this array of industries, visitors may well enjoy viewing the activity of the port, part of which is specialized in the preparation and loading of the huge logs trucked in from inland localities such as *Samreboi*, Ghana's "timber city" with a wild-west flavor.

But despite its heavy accent on industry, Takoradi has an exceptionally open, countrified feeling about it, probably as a result of its rolling terrain and the dense tropical vegetation that invades any available square centimetre of unbuilt land.

The coastline is somewhat less attractive here than at Sekondi; however, the coastal highway running between the two cities affords beautiful views of the surrounding landscapes, as does the road running north of *Ensie Lagoon*. The latter route extends along the Adiembra district, the Sekondi hospital and an industrial zone before intersecting at a traffic circle and John Sarbah Road, which like Liberation Street and all the adjacent avenues, leads to the central market.

Takoradi's touristic infrastructures are concentrated in the former European

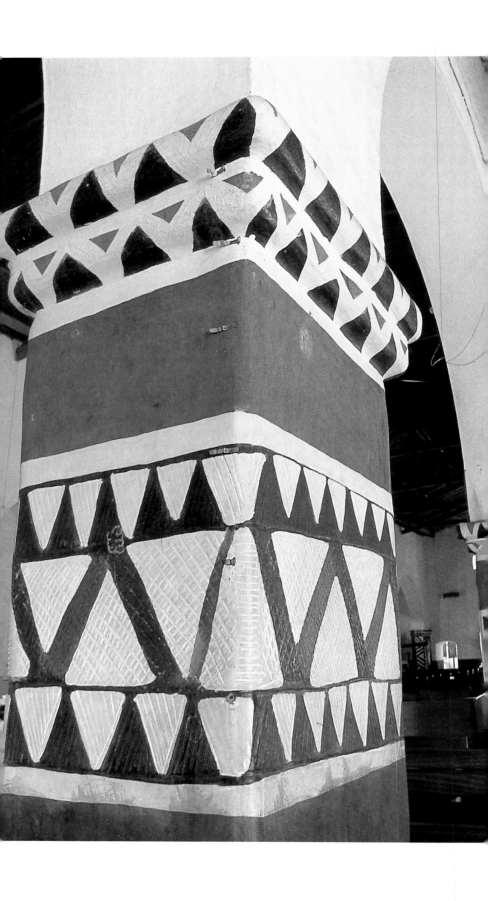

*In Northern Ghana, the women of the village
of Navrongo use a mixture of soil-based
pigments and karite oil to decorate the walls
and pillars of the church with
vividly-coloured frescoes and bas-reliefs.*

quarter on the seafront. The tall Atlantic Hotel building, complete with night club, restaurant and shops, is fronted by a large terrace and bar overlooking the beach. A short distance away is the smaller but cosier single-storey Midwood Hotel.

Somewhat further inland but particularly well-located on a hilltop overlooking the port, the Harbour View Restaurant offers a superb view of the entire coastline. Its bar and terrace are the informal meeting-place of Takoradi's business and intellectual community, while the nightime vistas of the glittering lights of the seaside and port are unforgettable.

For visitors appreciative of such creature comforts, Takoradi can serve as the ideal base for excursions into the surrounding region, including Samreboi and many of the coastal fortresses, of which all, from Axim to Elmina, can be round-tripped in a single day.

The closest of all is Shama, located just a few kilometres east of Sekondi.

The unfortunate destiny of Doctor Amu

Fort San Sebastian was constructed by the Portuguese some four centuries ago on an unprotected sandy promontory so flat that the fortress appears particularly enormous. From the ramparts above the main gateway, a great conical stairway with time-worn, rounded steps leads down to a small square planted with handsome cactaceae… and the grave of Doctor Amu, one of the first native Africans to have received a European education in the eighteenth century. Upon returning to his homeland, Doctor Amu found he had become a misfit; rejected by both his countrymen and the European community, the doctor led a hermit-like existence within the walls of the fortress until death finally released him from his solitude.

The fortress, one of Portugal's largest, subsequently passed into the hands of the Dutch and then into those of the British, and continued to be exchanged or fought over between them from time to time. History is mute over whether Dr. Amu ever shared the fortress with the Europeans or whether it remained uninhabited after definitively becoming a British possession in 1872. It can only be hoped that the unhappy doctor found peace and contentment here, which is not unlikely given the intimate living quarters contained within the walls of the fortress.

The proportions of the inner courtyard are particularly attractive, as is the gallery that runs along the upper storey, at a right angle to the entranceway. To the left, the entry way gives onto a sentry path which widens into a terrace, and to the right, a handsome double-flight stone staircase. Its simple dark-blue wooden framework contrasts elegantly with the surrounding white walls, producing an effect similar to the patio of a private residence rather than that of a great courtyard in a fortress.

The second sentry path offers a fine view which is invisible from the first path, semi-enclosed by walls pierced by narrow gun slits.

Komenda Fort

On the western shore, the small covered market, main street and village houses bring everyday life right up to the foot of the castle. To the east, the scenery takes on the grandiose proportions of the mouth of the river Pra. The river, which has remained discretely invisible up to now, flows into a lagoon from which it is separated by a narrow sand spit before veering abruptly off to the right where it flows onto the bar. The contrast between the violence of the surf and the calm waters of the river along with the beauty of the surrounding rolling, wooded countryside, plunge the onlooker into a state of fascinated contemplation.

Once the enchantment dissipates — or even to prolong it — visitors may desire to arrange a boat trip up the Pra with a local fisherman, or to visit Komenda Fort further east. Unfortunately, the only vestiges that remain of the latter are its foundations, a portion of which have been incorporated into modern habitations, with other sections used as shelters by the local fishermen, who have pierced doorways and windows into its enormous walls.

(*See practical information p. 168*)

shai hills game reserve

sunyani

■ Created in 1974, the Shai Hills Game Reserve is a small wildlife sanctuary occupying 5,180 hectares north of Tema in the Greater Accra Region.

To get there from Accra, take the Tema expressway straight to the end, followed by the highway to Ho. On the right, just beyond the Shai Training Centre, the main entrance of the reserve leads to the building where visitors' passes are issued and the mandatory guides assigned.

Guides are not only obligatory, but also indispensable. As in Ghana's other wildlife parks and reserves, visits on foot are both recommended and encouraged. But only a trained guide, perfectly familiar with the habits of the animal population and the nature of the territory can ensure that visitors will profit from their excusion to the maximum.

During the rainy season, even experienced guides can hesitate over which path to take amid the tall tropical grasses of the reserve. As visitors will soon discover, these grasses are anything but gentle to the touch, and after a single thorny encounter, one is only too happy to let an experienced companion reconnoitre the area in search of wildlife or simply the right direction to the next stopping-off place.

The guides also know how to find the elusive vestiges of a series of villages inhabited from the thirteenth to the nineteenth centuries by huntsmen and their families. Occasional fragments of ruined walls indicate the former presence of dwellings, while elsewhere, innumerable pottery shards or intact earthenware receptacles offer mute testimony of the lives that were led here.

In more remote historical periods, the Shai dwelt in the caverns of the surrounding hills. Ulteriorly, these same caves were used as temporary refuges and strategic strongholds during the episodic wars between the Shai and the Ga.

As wildlife rarified during the early years of the twentieth century, the Shai huntsmen progressively abandoned the hillsides for the surrounding villages which their descendants inhabit today.

At present, the reserve's animal population includes monkeys (baboons and cercopithecus), water bucks, royal antelope, cephalophes, oribus and wildcats, while the lovely surrounding hills offer the possibility of hiking, camping and excursions on horseback.
(*See practical information p. 168*).

■ Approximately three hundred years ago, Ghana's dense western forest was the home to an abundance of wildlife. The site of the town of Sunyani (population 60,000), which is the present-day capital of the Brong-Ahafo Region, was formerly the site of a hunters' camp and an ivory depot. The name is thought to derive from the Akan expression *ason ndwae*, signifying the place where elephants are stripped of their hides and tusks.

Kola nuts, one of the region's leading products, eventually attracted traders from the north. As commercial activity increased, a permanent zone of habitation developed.

In 1909, the region's colonial administration transferred its headquarters from Odumase to Sunyani, whose central location was particularly convenient for the reorganization of its various departments. The topography of the site, a broad, basin-shaped plain surrounded by forests, was considered especially attractive by the Europeans.

Sunyani came into its own following the introduction of cocoa culture, and particularly after an epidemic decimated the near-totality of the eastern plantations. Cocoa was then progressively introduced into the Ashanti territory and the Brong-Ahafo Region, currently among Ghana's leading areas of production.

The timber empire

In *Bekyem*, located between Sunyani and Kumasi, the Cocoa Production Division's experimental farm occupies one hundred hectares, and it is here that the results of the research conducted by Ghana's Tafo Institute are tested under actual growing conditions. A number of different species are cultivated, from seeds to young plants, as well as full-grown trees.

A visit to the farm can be a fascinating experience. Ordinarily, cocoa trees are planted in a rather haphazard fashion, whereas here, the trees form neat ranks planted an ideal distance from one another. The result is an endless series of inviting, shade-dappled passageways filled with deliciously cool leaf-filtered light.

Sunyani is also the heart of the region's lumber industry. The town and the outlying areas are dotted with sawmills and logging centres, the largest of which is found at *Mim*, accessed via an often rough track that begins south of Berekum.

The headquarters of a chieftainry, *Berekum* boasts a palace anything but traditional, since it was constructed in the 1930s, when the town's total population was only 2,000. Like Sunyani, Berekum benefited from the cocoa boom, and as workers poured in from all parts of the Ashanti homelands, the town nearly outstripped Sunyani, which nevertheless retained its leadership due to its position as an administrative centre and the presence of a training school for forest rangers.

The school, which is growing every year, is devoted to protecting and improving Ghana's timber reserves, and in particular, the development of country's secondary forests. Between Sunyani and Kumasi, the forest is somewhat sparse, but still offers fine stands of rare species which have been placed under the protection of the authorities.

Nearly virgin timberland

The most recently-created forest tracks to the south and southeast provide the unforgettable opportunity of penetrating a nearly-virgin timberland.

In contrast to the immemorial peace of these tracts, the trucks that one encounters toiling up the steep slopes of the Kumasi highway loaded with enormous logs which seem as if they're going to roll off the truckbed at every turn of the road, can be an unnerving experience for the motorist just behind them.

To facilitate the transport of the felled trees, the original road is being widened, with great pieces of land being sliced out ot the ochre and red clay of the surrounding hills to accommodate the new route. The combined sight of the huge earth-moving vehicles and the outsized lumber trucks moving through these amputated spaces — whose colour contrasts emphatically with the soft green hues of the surrounding wooded hills — has something terrifying in its striking symbolism of nature being violated by mankind.

(*See practical information p. 168*)

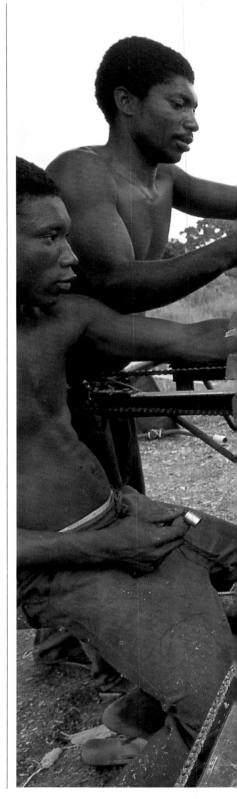

*The economy of Central and
Western Ghana is essentially
based on forestry and
the transformation of wood into
beams, boards and planks.*

tamale

■ The capital of the Northern Region, and surrounded by immense tropical savannas, Tamale (population 170,000) is Ghana's fourth largest city, after Accra, Kumasi, Sekondi-Takoradi and Tema.

Like Kumasi in the centre of the country, Tamale represents the heart of a star formed by roads coming in from the four points of the compass.

A region of rice and cotton

After becoming the administrative headquarters of a province that included the entire northern territory up to the border of Burkina-Faso in 1907, the city developed rapidly. This period was marked by the construction of a road network designed to link Tamale to all the other urban centres in this vast region, and the creation of the city of *Yapei* on the White Volta. Within a few short years, Yapei became Tamale's port on Lake Volta. Yapei's role as port was significantly reduced after the construction of the excellent Tamale-Kintampao-Kumasi highway and the Yapei Bridge which replaced the former river ferry. At present, both oil tankers and passenger boats arriving from Akosombo put in at the new port of Buipe, 60 kilometres to the southwest of Yapei.

Today, Tamale ships its agricultural produce by both road and lake transport. The products include traditional produce such as yams, millet and peanuts (a portion of which are transformed into oil by an on-site processing plant), and non-indigenous items such as rice and cotton, whose cultivation has attained considerable importance in the north.

More than half of the nation's rice crop comes from the two northern provinces. On the outskirts of Tamale, a plant has been constructed to hull the harvested grains, which are transformed into whole or broken rice, with the residual waste products converted into pig feed.

Cotton was introduced into the region only a few years ago, and is already enjoying increasing popularity as a cash crop throughout the country. At present, the annual yield supplies approximately two-thirds of Ghana's needs.

Both rice and cotton are now firmly established in the northern regions. During certain months of the year, the tender green shoots of the rice, the white and pink blossoms of the cotton and the bright red or yellow tractors used on the vast plantations (along with the occasionally-matching headgear of their drivers) produce what can literally be termed "local colour" on an impressive scale.

Since Tamale is located in the region of the great savannas, visitors may imagine an encounter with stark, monotonous lanscapes. On the contrary, nothing is less uniform than the savanna, with its isolated trees spaced as if to emphasize their uniqueness, and no two of their silhouettes alike, or appearing in uncluttered groves through which the rays of the sun filter with greater dramatic effect than in the denser southern forests.

In addition to the slender, soaring teak trees and the upredictable, fantastic forms of the baobabs, the lanscape is marked by irregular rows of karite trees whose modest size and foilage recall orchards of pear trees. There are also acacias, including the fragrant blossoming nims; eucalyptus and anacardia (cashew nut trees), plus countless other species unknown to Westerners, and whose names change from one village to the next in this patchwork region of ethnic groups.

An eighteenth-century tourist resort

Motorists taking the Yeji ferry rather than the highway that leads directly to Tamale can visit *Salaga*, one of the Northern Region's largest cities. Salaga offers a traditional market in which Haoussa Muslims from Niger used to trade cotton garments, leather goods and slaves in exchange for the gold and kola nuts of the south. Although the city was formerly a tributary to the supreme chief of the Gonja of Kpembe, Salaga eventually grew far more important than the latter.

Nevertheless, during the period that the Ashantis — the principal suppliers of kola nuts — were at war with Britain, Salaga nearly vanished from the map as a trade hub, and for many years it was only the presence of the British colonial administration that permitted the city to maintain a certain level of activity.

Today, Salaga remains important as a trade, administrative and regional health centre, but has lost everything related to its past, while even its two mosques (including the so-called "old mosque") are of recent construction. The few examples of traditional habitations constructed in laterite earth and fine gravel offer an interesting effect of rounded relief. The city is also dotted with fine mango groves and scattered coconut palms, all the more surprising in this distinctly northern setting. Another particularity of the city is its population of goats, as agile as cats, and which can be seen prowling about everywhere, as if keeping watch over the countryside when they are not meditating over the fate of their town in the shade of a convenient wall.

Visitors busy exploring the city or just enjoying a tasty fried millet cake may have the luck of seeing a traditional procession of women bearing multicoloured enamelled dishes balanced upon their heads, preceded by a drum player. There are the relatives of a newly-married bride, on their way to celebrate her arrival in her new home with gifts of food the day after the wedding. In this heavily Islamic region, where women no longer enjoy the importance traditionally assigned to them by the Ashantis, the dowry paid by the bridegroom to his parents-in-law is only a quasi-symbolic bag of rice or millet, or at the most, a goat.

After Salaga, the road north to Tamale traverses the Gonja country via the Dagomba homeland, whose capital city is Yendi.

Tamale also has its local palace, known as the *Gulkpe Na*, and located on the square into which intersects the avenue on which the catering rest-house and city library are situated.

Gulkpe Na's Palace

The palace consists of approximately 25 thatch-roofed buildings surrounded by a low wall which prevents views of the interior of the compound.

Near the palace and located in the centre-city, the Tamale Cultural Centre offers a variety of attractions, beginning with the "Sparkles," undoubtedly one of Ghana's best restaurants. In the courtyard of the centre, merchants sell a wide array of handicrafts, ranging from woven baskets to traditionally-worked leather goods (handbags, wallets, sandals, etc.), and carved wooden statues.

The local market is also worth a visit. Located near the palace, visitors will enjoy roaming among its colourful stalls amidst the odor of exotic spices. The catering rest-house, with its 30-odd bungalows, bar and restaurant, serves as Tamale's main hotel as well as the inevitable meeting-place for appointments and get-togethers.

At any given moment, Tamale is also host to a number of visitors from neighboring Burkina-Faso. Relations between the two countries are cordial, and athletes from Ouagadougou and Tamale frequently compete in well-attended matches at the town's sports stadium.

The kraal buildings

Only a few kilometres north or east of Tamale, visitors will discover the first northern-style *kraals* set amidst their surrounding millet fields. These traditional habitations are totally different from those of southern Ghana, and also vary from those in the rest of the country. In the Dagomba territory, all the kraal buildings — both habitations and granaries — are covered with straw roofs in the shape of conical hats. Upon their first visit to a compound, visitors are often impressed by the cleanliness of the courtyard, divided into separate areas containing living quarters, livestock shelters or sanitary facilities. The ground, harder and smoother than cement, is composed of clay blended with cow dung that serves as a bonding agent. After application of this mixture, the surface is pounded down by women or children singing traditional chants and wielding wooden mallets. It is then further smoothed with a layer of liquid mortar.

The rounded openings in the dwellings are often surrounded with multicoloured ceramic mosaics, which on closer inspection, reveal themselves to be the skilfully-salvaged fragments of chinaware. Just in front of the threshold of the houses, a shallow ditch connected with a system of gutters provides a means for the evacuation of rain and waste-water from the habitation area to the surrounding fields.

The women's huts are filled with piles of brightly coloured traditional pottery or modern decorated enamel utensils, while inside the men's quarters, hunting arms are fastened onto the straw roof-tops and various ritual objects are ensconced in niches in the walls.

(*See practical information p. 168*)

*Small-scale agriculture
and large-scale industry
make Tema one of the most important
economic centres of Ghana,
as well as its largest seaport.*

tema

■ Visitors arriving in Tema by the Accra-Tema expressway rather than the more scenic coastal highway, will encounter an endless series of high-tension electric pylons serving as the backdrop to a landscape of construction booms and modern buildings. Ghana's second-largest port after Sekondi-Takoradi, Tema is also a dynamic industrial city which owes much of its past and present growth to the gigantic Akosombo Dam.

Akosombo's associated hydro-electric complex supplies all of Ghana with inexpensive electrical power, and has immeasurably aided the development of light and heavy industry. For practical and logistical reasons, most of this industrial activity has deliberately been concentrated in the greater Tema area, and particularly — given the presence of a deep-water port — in interprises involved in the exportation of raw materials. Ghana's industrial infrastructure is one of the most developed among those of the Third World countries. Tema boasts an enormous foundry which transforms Ghana's bauxite into aluminium as well as a cement plant, an oil refinery, huge agro-food complexes (flour mills, fish processing and animal feed plants) and several chemical, textile and food processing plants. A number of well-known multinational corporations are also present, including Nestle, Air Liquide, Kaiser Aluminium and Unilever.

Tema, Ghana's second-largest port

Tema's port has recently grown into a multi-purpose complex, specialized in the rapid loading or off-loading of large volumes of raw materials such as coal, cement or sugar, and possessing modern equipment (ro-ro and container shipment) for handling of a wide range of other imported or exported goods.

Visitors to the port will be fascinated by the impressive spectacle of the gigantic cranes and travelling gantries plunging into the holds of ships from Germany or Asia and bringing out loads of flour, sugar, livestock or computers. Swinging high over the docks, containers and palettes of merchandise are delicately lowered onto the beds of waiting semi-trailor trucks, which transport them throughout Ghana and to neighbouring countries such as Burkina-Faso, Togo and the Ivory Coast.

The port's large warehousing and refrigerated storage facilities permit the stocking of every type of perishable and non-perishable produce, including meat products from the ranches of northern Ghana and fresh fish from the adjacent fishing port. Tema has no less than two fishing ports located within its immense commercial and industrial port complex. The first is the home of the city's modern fleet of fishing boats, while the second — preferred for obvious reason by tourists — is filled with hundreds of slim, marvellously-decorated traditional pirogues. It's always a pleasure to see these frail craft pass over the bar onto the frequently rough sea in quest of sole, red mullet, tuna or crayfish.

« Bedroom communities »

Given the number of persons working either in the port or employed by the innumerable companies located in Tema's industrial zone, it was necessary to construct what amounted to entirely new cities and residential districts. Starting from this basic concept, and desirous of avoiding over-crowding and the saturation of Tema's municipal infrastructures, Ghanaian authorities designed a series of "bedroom communities" generously scattered throughout the greater Tema area. Today, rather than by slums and shantytowns, the city is dotted by open spaces and crisscrossed by a network of roads leading to several adjacent urban centres. The result is a metroplex resembling — on a smaller scale — Los Angeles or Brasilia. Thus, instead of a unique city centre surrounded by closely-packed residential zones, greater Tema is composed of some ten residential districts, each comprising several neighbourhoods of approximately 5,000 individuals occupying private homes, multi-family dwellings and small apartment buildings.

The green belt

Each district is equipped with shops, schools and markets, and surrounded by parks and fields that provide open space and a real-estate reserve for future construction. The green belt they constitute is one of the dominant characteristics of western Tema, while on the east, they are bordered on their entire length by the industrial zone that extends to the port area.

Although the Accra expressway is the fastest route to Tema, most visitors will prefer the coast road which follows the

tumu

shoreline from Christiansborg Castle. From here, and always parallel to the coast, the road runs past the International Trade Fair buildings and through the lively Osu district, marked by a strikingly colourful signboard indicating the manufacture of royal parasols and the traditional insignia that the district's tribal chiefs and subordinates continue to wear on ceremonial occasions.

Homowo celebrations

Visitors in Tema during July and August can attend the *Homowo* celebrations that take place in Osu, during which the ritual objects displayed on the signboard are carried and worn by tribal dignitaries dressed in predominantly red ceremonial garments, the fetish colour of the Ga ethnic group inhabiting the locality.

From Osu, the coastal road parallels several ponds surrounded by tropical underbrush. At roadside stands, the fish netted by anglers who can be seen working in the distance are sold as soon as they are caught, extra-fresh, by women and children.

The Acapulco Club at *Teshie* is a pleasant stopping-off place, especially for lunch. Its swimming pool and vast terrace overlooking the sea are adjacent to a restaurant featuring highly varied cuisine. Although the weather can be on the cool side during the rainy season, the club and the surrounding area is an ideal spot from November through May. On Friday evenings, a barbecue dinner is prepared on the beach.

(*See practical information p. 169*)

■ A main leg of the northern journey from Wa to Bolgatanga, Tumu is located in the heart of the rolling savanna country. The town is of particular architectural interest, since the form of its traditional *kraals* are rectangular and flat-roofed, rather than the round, straw-roofed compounds typical of Bolgatanga and the Upper East Region.

The habitations and buildings of Tumu's kraals are generally constructed at the four angles of the *bonia*, the name by which the local Kasena ethnic group designate a kraal.

Visitors should make a point of visiting one of these bonia, each of which contains a central area for domestic livestock, surrounded by the habitations grouped in series of three to four units forming "apartments" separated by low walls accessed by stone steps or tree-trunk stairways. The walls serve to protect the impeccably clean, hardpacked earth of the inner courtyards from fouling by the domestic animals, while stairways provide access to the flat rooftops of the dwellings, which are often interconnected. During hot weather, the entire family sleeps on the rooftops, while in the harvest season, grain crops are spread out upon them to dry in the sun.

Among the Kasena, household decoration is entirely the responsibility of the women of the family, who extract a liquid from the long pods of the *dadawa*, a local tree, and apply it directly upon the walls of the habitations, giving them a brown colour and a smooth finish.

The half-sphere that can occasionally be seen protruding from the ground in some of the inner courtyards is the tomb of the eldest female of the family. To construct it, a vertical shaft is dug to a depth of about one metre, whereupon a horizontal gallery is dug out into which the body is placed, lying on its right side. The shaft is then filled with earth and capped with the sphere, which is covered with the same protective coating as the rest of the courtyard floor and positioned exactly over the heart of the deceased.

The *Gbele Game Sanctuary*, located near Tumu, is home to wildlife such as monkeys, African buffalo and antelope. In principle, hunting is allowed, but before doing so, it's best to contact the Tumu District Council for the current regulations. As throughout the entire savanna region, the visitor will remark both the infinite variations of the landscapes and the modifications in the domestic architecture.

(*See practical information p. 169*)

*Market-day in the village of Wa:
in Ghana, as in the rest of Africa,
these colourful and traditional
open-air markets are of
special interest to visitors.*

wa

■ Visitors desirous of meeting one of Ghana's traditional chiefs can request an audience with the *Wa-Na* (sovereign) of Na. A particularly outgoing and hospitable individual, chief Na-Momora Bondiri II receives his guests according to the traditional protocol employed by all of Africa's high-ranking dignitaries. At the entrance to the palace, constructed in the style of an ancient mosque and flanked by soaring towers, the chief's head of protocol will accompany you from the vestibule to an interior courtyard and thence to a small audience chamber where the Wa-Na awaits seated upon a simple folding chair and surrounded by a small group of aged retainers on goatskin rugs at his feet.

For extremely important or official occasions, the Wa-Na sits upon a platform set up in the great court with a leopard skin draped over a large leather ottoman and a second cushion under his feet. On such occasions, the chief wears a sumptuous cape of white silk with a red lining and a gold-brocaded cap.

Out of respect for the Wa-Na's rank, visitors do not address him directly. Several interpretors transmit questions and responses back and forth, during the course of which the chief usually speaks of his past as a member of the British Army of India and his service in the medical corps in Burma during World War II. Although the descendant of a long line of princes, the chief's position is not hereditary, and he was elected by the council of elders following the death of the former Wa-Na in 1978. Contrary to appearances, traditional chiefs have little chance of becoming veritable despots, due to the influence exercised by the ever-present elders. In addition, the creation of modern governmental structures throughout most African countries following their independence has considerably attenuated the power of the traditional monarchs, who no longer have the right to impose taxes or possess a personal army. At present, their functions are limited to judging certain civil and family disputes such as divorces and inheritances, with the exception of criminal cases.

The days when the Walla of the Mamprusi ethnic group waged bloody territorial wars with their neighbours have long since vanished. As the Wa-Na explains to visitors, his ancestors from eastern Ghana who settled here after a dynastic quarrel between two brothers were obliged to battle the Lobi for the right to inhabit the territory comprising the future city of Wa.

wenchi

The Lobi were pushed to the west, while the remaining members of the Dagarti ethnic group submitted to the new arrivals, who founded the city and completed the islamization of the local population. The imprint of Islam is clearly visible not only by the presence of the city's handsome mosques, but also by the fact that the *Damba*, Wa's most important traditional festival, commemorates the birth of the Prophet Mohammed.

At present, some of the exiled Lobi have returned to Wa and intermarried with the Dagarti, while those who have elected to remain in the enclave between the Wala and the Burkina-Faso border are nevertheless under the authority of the Wa-Na.

Like so many other towns, Wa owes its founding to its location along the caravan route leading from northern Sahel to the coast. The locality already boasted a market in the seventeenth century, and the town, which was gradually islamized by the passage of northern traders, became celebrated for its mosques, which were considered to be among the most prominent of all of northern Ghana. Two of these mosques are still standing.

The surrounding region is far less populated than the northeastern portion of the country, despite similar climatic conditions and fertility of the soil. This is partly due to the effects of "Cyclone Samory," a quasi-legendary brigand and slave trader who instituted a reign of terror from the Ivory Coast all the way to Wa in the latter decades of the last century.

Although the region is no longer menaced by Samory, the effects of long-term drought conditions and the presence of the parasitical Guinea worm in the stagnant waters of the local ponds are nevertheless taking their toll on the inhabitants' lives. Fortunately, a large-scale governmental programme is doting the region with new wells, which have contributed to reduce disease and mortality in the Upper West Region over the last few years. Aided by the presence of new sources of water, the region's vegetation is thriving, while visitors will remark the lovely gardens of Wa, certain of which contain numerous varieties of vegetables, including a number of non-indigenous Western species.
(*See practical information p. 169*)

■ The small village of Wenchi, located in the Brong-Ahafo Region, was formerly on the route of the ancient northern trade caravans, which probably accounts for its founding. Today, the village draws visitors interested in its archaeological vestiges. Begho, located near Hani, contains the region's most important archaeological finds of recent date. It is accessible via a track that runs from the left of the road between Sampa and Wenchi.

Kokua, a small village located slightly further to the west and some ten kilometres from Sampa, can be accessed by the same route. The village has been the object of anthropological and ethnological research concerning its interesting population mix and the local manufacture of spindles (tipped with clay balls decorated in white, red and yellow stripes applied with quill-tipped brushes). The entire region is inhabited by families of traditional potters, whose customers flock to Kokua's Thursday market from all over the region to purchase the unique spindles. Although it is possible to procure equally efficient items elsewhere, the overwhelming regional preference for the traditional spindle is a phenomenon which remains to be satisfactorily explained.

Two ancient villages

One clue to this mystery may be the discovery of remarkably similar spindles unearthed by archaeologists at the Begho dig, only a few kilometres from Kokua. The find implies an historical if not traditional continuity between the present-day potters and their Iron-Age predecessors.

The sites of two other ancient villages near Begho have also been excavated, revealing the vestiges of small, rectilinear dwellings. The bones of domestic animals have been unearthed, as well as several clay figurines. Carbon-14 techniques permit their dating at approximately 1500 B.C., making these villages among the oldest sedentary settlements ever discovered in Ghana.

The site has already yielded much new data to archaeologists, and in particular, the reasons for its lengthy human occupation. These include its proximity to the formerly abundant forests between Niger and the Volta River, the presence of plentiful wildlife, fertile soil and the gold deposits and kola trees whose fruits, along with the precious metal, where highly-prized commodities sought by the caravaneers.

yeji

At Begho, archaeologists have attempted to trace the evolution of objects and the soil conditions, while studies are being conducted on the current linguistic structures and the oral traditions of the surrounding villages, revealing a coherent historical continuity from the distant past up to the present.

A concordance has been observed between the regional dialect of Begho, which represents a limit of Islamic influence due to its former role as a stopping-off place for the northern trade caravans, and that currently employed by the inhabitants of Hani. In Begho itself, the population speak Brong, a southern Akan dialect, whereas immediately to the north the predominant dialects are more or less derived from the linguistic family spoken by the Mande traders centuries ago.

The rectangular dwellings of the ancient villages unearthed near Begho were built around inner courtyards, with walls probably made of clay and wood similar to present-day habitations. Archaeologists have also uncovered pottery, copper and iron-ware, beads, chinaware, traces of fabric and fragments of carvings. This evidence points to the existence of a flourishing civilization in and around ancient Begho, many of whose principal characteristics and traditions have been maintained in the present-day villages.
(*See practical information p. 169*)

■ The small village of Yeji, located on the shores of Lake Volta, lost much of its activity following the construction of the main north-south highway from Kumasi to Burkina-Faso. The well-paved road offers rapid access to Tamale without the former necessity of taking the ferry at Yeji. While motorists pressed for time will appreciate this progress, other visitors may wish to follow the old route from Kumasi to Tamale via Yeji, where the faithful Volta ferry, as charmingly erratic and dilapidated as ever, still awaits its passengers and cargo. The hours between each voyage are long, and visitors may find that they'll have to wait until the following morning to embark once the ferry has docked for the evening. But these inconveniences are minor compared to the pleasure of the voyage and the opportunity of exploring the other shore of the lake, whose villages include Salaga, Bimbila and Yendi.

Before the construction of the Akosombo Dam and the creation of Lake Volta, Kete and Krachi were the site of annual pilgrimages in homage to the divinity Dente, who was worshipped in both villages. The villages, which have since vanished beneath the waters of the lake, were located above the rapids of the Volta River. Since the two villages were doomed by the creation of the lake, their inhabitants were transferred to a new town near the village of Kantajuri, which has since merged with the modern city of Kete-Krachi and its lakeside port. Access to the latter is generally via the boat running between Akosombo, Yeji and Buipe.

In both Kete-Krachi and Yeji, visitors can organize fishing expeditions with the local boat owners, who will transport you in their pirogues to the best fishing sites. It is also possible to traverse the lake from Kete-Krachi to the opposite western shores and the 3,120 square kilometres of *Digya National Park*. Although lacking visitor infrastructures other than mandatory guides, the park nevertheless offers a wide variety of savanna wildlife, including herds of antelope, a large monkey and warthog population and a smaller number of lions and elephants.

Visitors traveling from Yeji to Kumasi will traverse the Brong-Ahafo Region (Atebubu), followed by the Ashanti homelands. Prior to arriving at Kumasi, the village of *Kampong*, located in the heart of coffee, cocoa and tobacco plantations, offers lovely vistas from the top of its escarpment.

Still further south, near the road leading to Kumasi, visitors can visit the curi-

*With consummate art, the constructors
of "kraals" in Northern Ghana decorate
the walls of their traditional family
compounds with geometrical motifs and stylized
representations of African wildlife.*

yendi

ous "fetish houses" (temples) scattered in the small villages of the area.

One of these traditional temples is located in the village of *Kenyasi*, which is accessed via the northern road to Abuaso and thence by the track leading left to a series of villages engulfed in vegetation. From here, a track perpendicular to the preceding one leads to Kenyasi, flanked on the left by the village of Abirim, which is also the site of a temple.

A few habitations along the principal street of Kenyasi still display the traces of traditional decorations. Unfortunately, the temple was disaffected following the death of its officiating priest. The building containing the altar has a facade covered with carved decorations, while six panels above the doorway depict, among other symbolic representations, a wheel signifying the sun's rotation. The temple in question formerly offered the sole remaining example of traditional carved panels, but the majority of these have since vanished, prior to the adoption of the measures which now protect such monuments. Some of the village inhabitants still speak with admiration of the marvellous carved decorations representing birds and foilage of an almost Byzantine complexity.

At *Abirim*, the site of the traditional temple is indicated by an official Historical Monuments sign. Visitors can photograph the courtyard and outer walls of the sanctuary, but photos of the interior and altar are prohibited. Two-thirds of the facade of the building housing the altar is covered by wooden shutters extending from either side of the entranceway. The latter are covered with carvings, as is the upper panelling. To the left, behind a black-panelled wooden door, a stairway leads to a low room used by the priest. The wooden stick planted in the ground in front of the door to the room offers the same signification as the candles found in Catholic churches. The room receives air and light from a fine open-work colonnade some 30 centimetres high.

In the environs of these two villages, two other similar temples can be seen at *Saaman* and *Bosore*. The first particularly merits the visitor's attention, since it is almost entirely intact. Its carved motifs are of high artistic interest, and include an unusual representation of a spiral branch on the lower portion of the altar walls. On either side of the outer door, panels represent stylized images of priests, their raised arms curiously brandishing antique muskets.

(*See practical information p. 169*)

■ Located off the main north-south highway and adjacent to the Togolese border, Yendi is the historic capital of the Dagomba homeland. Yendi can be reached via Tamale, the administrative centre of the Northern Region.

As a city, Yendi began its development in the seventeenth century, following the arrival of the Dagomba, who had abandoned their former capital of Diari in the wake of territorial conflicts with their Gonja neighbours. The origins of the Dagomba are probably the same as those of the Mamprusi farther to the north, whose common ancestors arrived from the Lake Chad area around the thirteenth century.

Yendi became a popular stopover for the caravans from Dahomey (the present-day Benin), Togo and Nigeria, bound for Salaga, Kete and Kintampo.

An open-air audience

The growth of Tamale has clearly diminished the regional importance of Yendi. The city nevertheless remains the residence of the supreme chief of the Dagomba. It is possible to arrange an audience with him by submitting a request to his secretary, bearing in mind that protocol prohibits visits before 4 p.m.

Another possibility also exists. On Monday and Friday mornings, an open-air audience is held under a canopy placed outside the chief's residence, in the courtyard enclosed by his wives' apartments. On these occasions, the chief receives the homage of his subordinate chieftains and confers with them on local matters. He also hears the grievances of private individuals, and often settles minor disputes. Visitors attending these sessions will find them an excellent opportunity for gaining an insight into the traditional patterns of life in the region.

Yendi is also of interest insofar as it is located at the intersection of three major itineraries. The first leads north to the Gambaga Escarpment, the second to Togo in the east via the ferry across the Oti and Zabzugu, while the last runs due south to Bimbila and Kpandae, where after being ferried across Lake Volta to Dambai, motorists can continue towards Jasikan, Hohoe, Ho and the coastal region.

(*See practical information p. 169*)

zebilla

■ The entire Northern Region of Ghana (including the Upper West and Upper East Regions) is reputed for the beauty of its earthern-walled habitations, known as *kraals*, a name taken from houses of the same type found in the Republic of South Africa.

Visitors will have the pleasure of discovering numerous kraals decorated with geometric motifs in the vicinity of Wa in the northwest, as well as on the road from Tumu to Bakwu, via Navrongo and Bolgatanga. Although the choice is immense, the best examples are found in the villages of Zebilla and Amkwalaga (between Bolgatanga and Bakwu), which also offer a number of supplementary local attractions.

A good tarred road followed by a fully motorable dirt track run from Bolgatanga to Zebilla, 45 kilometres to the east. Especially during the rainy season, the itinerary reveals a joyous landscape of millet fields and pasturelands dotted by herds of goats and cows. The residence of the local chief, situated just off the road leading from Zebilla, is fairly unimpressive when seen from the exterior. But once inside the compound, visitors will have the pleasure of discovering that the round-shaped habitations of hard-packed red laterite are covered with painted frescoes whose motifs range from triangles to diamonds, and include extremely stylized, striking representations of animals outlined in black ink. Chief Symon Apidogo Akparihilla and his family are particularly hospitable ; the kraal is the home to both the former chief's wives as well as those of the present sovereign and his brothers. Each group occupies a traditional round habitation occasionally featuring an adjacent granary and cooking area enclosed by a wall delimiting an inner courtyard. As the family expands, new living units are added on, each with their own small courtyards. The ultimate impression is not unlike the cross-section of a bee-hive, in which the younger and often polygamous families construct their habitations and walled courtyards on the periphery of the central and semi-collective residential core, occupied by the older members of the family.

In addition to its decorations and the traditional disposition of its habitations, the compound of the chief of Zebilla also offers other interesting features. In reality, the kraal is a self-contained universe providing its occupants with shelter, an area to prepare and take their meals, granaries for stocking crops, and courtyards and enclosures reserved for domestic animals. Other areas within the compound are given over to the manufacture of handicrafted pottery and the preparation of millet beer. The brewing process, generally the responsibility of the women of the families, is particularly interesting. Within one of the courtyards, visitors will discover immense clay jars bubbling over upon the coals of a fire, usually watched over by an elderly woman who, from time to time, stirs the thick red mixture with a long wooden spatula. This is the next-to-final phase in the long brewing process of *kpaya* (millet beer). The entire operation takes a number of days, beginning with raw, harvested millet grains which are spread out upon the floor of the courtyard and finely ground to accelerate their fermentation. After being dried and cleaned of its husks, the millet is poured into great jars of boiling water, where it simmers for two full days and nights. The resulting liquid is filtered to drain off the residue, while its alcohol content is raised by the addition of organic yeast. Millet beer is particularly perishable and must be consumed within 48 hours, after which it becomes bitter and undrinkable. Since Chief Akparihilla's home brewery produces far more kpaya than can be reasonably consumed by his extended family, the remaining jars are sold in all the surrounding regional markets. Prior to transport, the surplus beer is stocked in a small warehouse adjacent to the kraal, which also serves as a bar.

The latter is particularly charming, often full of visitors who have made the trip to Zebilla in bush-taxis. According to the chief, a gourd or two of kpaya is an excellent kidney tonic, while also constituting an infallible means of reducing fevers. Whatever the state of their health, visitors should make a point of dropping into the bar for a taste of this veritable ''home brew'' before leaving the village.

Somewhat further from Zebilla in the direction of Bawku, the village of *Amkwalaga* (along with Tongo to the south of Bolgatanga), is a pole of attraction for pilgrims from the entire region who come to consult the local divinities in the event of droughts or other calamities.

Like the kraals of Zebilla, the family compounds of Amkwalaga are of special artistic interest for their beautifully decorated walls and the perfect organization of their interior areas.

The elegant pattern of the incurved separating walls enclosing the spotless courtyards and rest areas reflect the innate sense of harmony of inhabitants whose instinctive sense of urban planning will enchant visitors.

(*See practical information p. 169*)

practical
information

Accra

LOCATION AND ACCESS : 165 km (paved) from Ho ; 85 km (paved) from Koforidua ; 270 km (paved) from Kumasi ; 640 km (paved) from Tamale ; 810 km (paved) from Bolgatanga ; 400 km (paved) from Sunyani, via Kumasi ; 144 km (paved) from Cape Coast ; 218 km (paved) from Sekondi ; 29 km (freeway) from Tema.

BY AIR : Kotoka International Airport, northeast of the city ; tel : 777.61.71. Flights to Europe, North America and other African capitals by nine airlines. Domestic flights to Kumasi, Tamale and Sunyani by Ghana Airways ; Cocoa House, Kwame Nkrumah Avenue ; tel : 22.19.01.

BY ROAD : (Coach travel) The State Transport Corporation, Ring Road West, P.O. Box 7384, serves all the regional capitals and many of the smaller cities ; coaches from the Omnibus Services Authority and the City Express Services.

BY RAIL : Accra-Kumasi line via Koforidua, New Tafo, Asuboni, Konongo ; Accra-Sekondi via the Huni Valley with spurs to Oda and Kade. Railway station : lower end of Nkwame Nkrumah Avenue, opposite Kinbu Road.

VISITOR INFORMATION : Ministry of Information, tel : 22.80.11 ; Ghana Tourist Board, Ramia House, Kojo Thompson Road, tel : 22.89.33 ; Ministry of Commerce and Tourism, tel : 66.54.21 ; Department of Game and Wildlife, P.O. Box M.239, tel : 63.793 or 66.61.29.

HOTELS : See list of hotels at end of volume and Ghana for Business Travelers.

RESTAURANTS : Ghanaian cuisine : *Afrikiko restaurant*, next to the French Embassy, Liberation Road, tel : 22.99.97. — *Cocobeach restaurant* at Teschie Nungua. — *Edvy restaurant* and *Providence Catering*, off Dankwa Circle. — *Flair*, at Rangoon. — *Country Kitchen*, in the Ringway Estate. — *Home Touch*, on the road to Burma Camp, near the airport.
Chinese cuisine : *Golden Dragon*, Cantonments Road. — *Regal*, Cantonments Road. — *Kung-Fu*, Danquah Circle. — *Mandarin*, Ring Road East. — *Pearl of the East*, off Cantonments Road. — *Shila* (Korean), Ring Road East.
Indian cuisine : *Maharadja*, Cantonments Road.
European cuisine : *Accra Novotel* (French). — *Marie-Lou*, in the hotel of the same name, Cantonments Road. — *Annabelles*. — *Club 400*, Jones Road, off Castle Road in Adabraka. — *Chez Mammie*, lower Cantonments Road. — *The Ritz*, Graphic Road.

ENTERTAINMENT : *Night clubs* : *Appolo Theatre*, Ring Road Central, off Kwame Nkrumah Circle. — *Blow Up*, located in the same area. — *Tip-Toe Gardens*, off New Town Road. — *Le Reve*, Kwame Nkrumah Circle. — *Le Must*, Caprice Building off Dankwa Circle. — *Fine Style*, on Ring Road. — *La Cave du Roi*, Osu.
Cinemas : *Orion*, on Kwame Nkrumah Circle. — *The Globe*, Adjaben Road. — *The Go-Bliss*. — *The Roxy*, near Kingsway Stores on Kwame Nkrumah Avenue. — *Ghana Films and Industry Corporation*, off Captain Sankara Circle. — *Opera*, Pagan Road. — *Rex*, behind Parliament House.
Casinos : Hotels *Continental*, *Golden Tulip* and *Ambassador* ; the two latter establishments scheduled for reopening following renovation in early 1992.
Theatres : *National Theatre*, *Art Centre* : University of Legon.
Main Post Office : Kwame Nkrumah Avenue.

CAR RENTAL : *Vanef-Europcar*, 29 Sobukwe Road (Farrar Avenue, tel : 22.63.65 ; fax : 66.82.65, or at the Novotel). — *Budget Rent-a-Car*, Republic House Annex, Kwame Nkrumah Avenue, tel : 22.68.16 ; fax : 22.45.07. — *Avis*, tel : 22.77.44 ; telex : 2300. — *Conca Car Hiring*, tel : 77.21.78, with offices at the Shangri-La Hotel.

TRAVEL AGENCIES : *Akuaba Tourist & Travel Agency*, Republic House Annex, Kwame Nkrumah Avenue, tel : 22.80.20. — *Pan African Travel & Tours*, Republic House, Kwame Nkrumah Avenue, tel. : 22.68.16 ; telex : 2349. — *Sunseekers Package Cargo Services*, Kotoka Airport. — *Universal Travel & Tourist Services*, Republic House.

MUSEUMS AND CULTURAL INFORMATION : *National Museum*, Barnes Road. Open Tuesday to Friday from 8 a.m. to 6 p.m. Saturdays and Sundays from 9:30 a.m. to 5:30 p.m. — *Art Centre*, 28-February Road. — Library, bookshop and *Archeological Museum* of the University of Legon.

BANKS : See chapter on Ghana for Business Travelers.

SPORTS : *Achimota Golf Club*. — *Kaneshie Sports Complex*. — *Labadi Pleasure Beach*. — *Polo Grounds*. — *Tesano Sports Club*. — *Sports Stadium*. — *El-Wak Stadium*. — *Nicholson Stadium*.

Aburi

LOCATION AND ACCESS : Eastern Region. Botanical Gardens and model village, 38 km north of Accra via an excellent paved road ; 45 km south of Koforidua ; 66 km southwest of Akosombo Dam.

HOTELS : *May Lodge* (plus bar and restaurant), near Aburi Botanical Gardens, P.O. Box 25, Aburi. *Peduase Lodge* (government-managed guest house).

Overleaf:
*Nearly all of Ghana's coastal fortresses
are inhabited by local families who go about
their daily household chores seemingly oblivious
to the presence of passing visitors.*

RESTAURANTS : Botanical Gardens Restaurants ; *May Lodge.*

HANDICRAFTS : Botanical Gardens handicrafts shop. Woodcarvers and shops at the entrance to Aburi.

coach service between Sekondi, Half Assini and Axim.

HOTELS AND RESTAURANTS : None.

Post office.

Ada

LOCATION AND ACCESS : On the Gulf of Guinea in the Volta Region, 114 km (paved) from Accra ; 78 km (paved) west of Afao ; 38 km (paved) from the Sogakofe Bridge. « Mammy trucks » and coach service to and from Accra.

HOTELS : *Ada Hotel*, tel : 22.66.93 and 22.23.01. — « *No Problem's Guest House.* »

Akosombo

LOCATION AND ACCESS : Eastern Region, south of Lake Volta and 104 km (paved) north of Accra ; 80 km (paved) west of Ho ; 82 km (paved) east of Koforidua. Coach service to and from each of these cities. On Mondays, round-trip boat service on Lake Volta to Kete-Krachi. Weekly one-way service to Buipe on the northern end of the lake.

HOTELS AND RESTAURANTS : *Volta Hotel*, P.O. Box 25, tel : 731. 40 rooms with bath, air-conditioning, private telephone, restaurant and bar. *Lakeside Motel* (between Atimpoku and Kpong), tel : 310.

Bank, post office and gas station.

Amedzofe

LOCATION AND ACCESS : Between Lake Volta and the Togo border in the Volta Region ; 60 km (unpaved) north of Ho. Round-trip « mammy truck » service between Amezdofe and Ho.

HOTELS : *Rest-House*, 5 rooms in 3 bungalows with double beds and private bath, kitchens and living rooms ; no restaurant.

Axim

LOCATION AND ACCESS : On the Gulf of Guinea in the Western Region ; 296 km (paved) west of Accra, via Takoradi-Sekondi and Cape Coast ; 75 km from Sekondi and 131 km from Cape Coast. State Transport

Bawku

LOCATION AND ACCESS : A village in the Upper East Region, 56 km (all-vehicle unpaved track) north of Nakpanduri ; 83 km (two-thirds unpaved) east of Bolgatanga. Served by State Transport coaches from Tamale, Gambaga, Bakwu, Bolgatanga ; return trips to Tamale via Wa and Damongo.

HOTELS AND RESTAURANTS : None. The nearest restaurant is at Bolgatanga. *Rest houses* in Nakpanduri and Gambaga.

Post office and gas station.

Bolgatanga

LOCATION AND ACCESS : Provincial capital of the Upper East Region ; 810 km (paved) north of Accra and 170 km (paved) north of Tamale ; 83 km (two-thirds unpaved) west of Bawku ; 384 km (good unpaved road) west of Wa, via Tumu and Hamile. State Transport coach service to Tamale, Accra, Bawku, Navrongo, Tumu, Wa and Damongo, plus « mammy trucks. »

HOTELS AND RESTAURANTS : *Black Star Hotel*, P.O. Box 18, tel : 346, 11 rooms, dance-floor, tennis courts, restaurant and bar. *Catering Rest House*, P.O. Box 50, tel : 209 ; 40 rooms, restaurant, bar and night-club. *Sandgardens* (22 rooms), *Royal Hotel* (22 rooms), *Oasis* (11 rooms), *Bolco Hotel, Bazar Hotel, Central Hotel, Saint Joseph Hotel.*

Post office, gas station and market.

(Lake) Bosumtwi

NAME : local divinity ; *Twi.*

LOCATION AND ACCESS : In the heart of the Ashanti Region, 29 km (paved and unpaved) southeast of Kumasi ; approximately 60 km (paved and unpaved) northeast of Obuasi. Bush taxi rental at Kumasi, plus « mammy trucks ».

HOTELS AND RESTAURANTS : *Rest House* above the lake with 4 comfortable rooms but no cooking facilities. Guests must bring their own food. Hotel near lake is currently closed. At

Kokofu, the small *Kyekyeku Hotel*, 15-20 km from Lake Bosumtwi on the road to Bekwai.

Busua

LOCATION AND ACCESS : On the Gulf of Guinea in the Western Region, 32 km (well-paved) west of Takoradi ; 50 km (paved) east of Axim ; 259 km (well-paved) west of Accra. State Transport coach service to Axim, Half-Assini and Takoradi.

HOTELS AND RESTAURANTS : *Busua Pleasure Beach*, 8 rooms with double beds, plus 23 bungalows (2 rooms) with bath and kitchenette. *Rest House* in Dixcove Castle, 4 rooms with separate bath, use of kitchen facilities upon request.

Gas station : post office at Dixcove.

Cape Coast

LOCATION AND ACCESS : Provincial capital of the Central Region, located on the coast, 144 km west of Accra ; 13 km east of Elmina, 74 km east of Sekondi ; 221 km (paved) south of Kumasi. State Transport coach service to and from Accra, Elmina, Sekondi, Takoradi, Busua, Axim, Half Assini and Kumasi. Taxi rental for excursions to outlying villages such as Elmina.

HOTELS AND RESTAURANTS : *Savoy Hotel*, Accra Road near State Transport coach terminal, P.O. Box 646, tel : 28.05. 20 rooms, bar, discotheque, currency exchange ; *Greenhill Motel*, outskirts of Cape Coast on the Accra road and offering beautiful view of the countryside, P.O. Box 359, tel : 25.85. 5 bungalows with bath and air-conditioning, room service, restaurant. *Catering Rest House* on the outskirts of the city, P.O. Box 305, tel : 25.94. 10 rooms with ceiling fans and bath plus a restaurant on premises. Also : *the Beach Hotel, the Elmina Motel, Sunan Lodge, Oyster Bay Hotel, the Palace Hotel, Modek Hotel* and *the Paramount Hotel*.

Banks, post office, gas station, food shops, castle museum, university, restaurants.

Elmina

LOCATION AND ACCESS : On the coast in the Central Region, 157 km (paved) west of Accra ; 13 km west of Cape Coast ; 136 km east of Axim and 61 km east of Sekondi-Takoradi. State Transport coaches to Accra and Cape Coast, plus « mammy trucks. »

HOTELS AND RESTAURANTS : *Elmina Motel*, 16 rooms in bungalows. — *Oyster Bay Hotel*, 10 bungalows, bar, swimming pool, restaurant and beach, P.O. Box 227, tel : 26.87. — *Rest House* in San Iago Castle, 6 rooms.

Gambaga

LOCATION AND ACCESS : Northeast Ghana between the Northern Region and the Upper East Region. The escarpment comprises two major cities : Gambaga and Nakpanduri. Gambaga is 93 km southeast of Bolgatanga, via Walewale and 82 km south of Bakwu. Nakpanduri is 32 km east of Gambaga, 266 km northeast of Tamale, via Yendi and 56 km south of Bakwu by an unpaved road. State Transport coach service to all of the above.

HOTELS AND RESTAURANTS : Modest *Rest House* at Gambaga. — *Rest House* at Nakpanduri, 4 rooms with double beds.

Ho

LOCATION AND ACCESS : Capital of the Volta Region, 165 km (paved) northeast of Akosombo ; 80 km northwest of Aflao (paved) ; 106 km northwest of Aflao on the Togo border ; 70 km south of Kpandu. State Transport coach service to Accra, Aflao, Hohoe, Kpandu and Jasikan, plus « mammy trucks » between these destinations and taxis to Akosombo.

HOTELS AND RESTAURANTS : Many hotels. For complete list, see end of volume.

Bank, post office, gas station.

Keta

LOCATION AND ACCESS : Volta Region, on the Gulf of Guinea, 213 km east of Accra, via Sogakofe ; 38 km west of Aflao ; 40 km east of Ada. State Transport coach service from Accra and Ho.

HOTELS AND RESTAURANTS : Small hotels at Denu and Aflao on the Togo border. (See hotel list at the end of volume).

Post office and gas station.

Kibi

LOCATION AND ACCESS : Eastern Region, 93 km north of Accra ; 86 km southeast of

Mpraeso and 59 km west of Koforidua. State Transport coach service to Accra.

HOTELS AND RESTAURANTS : Basic *Rest House*, no bath or kitchen. Many hotels in Koforidua and Nkawkaw (see list at end of volume).

Post office, gas station.

Kintampo

LOCATION AND ACCESS : In the centre of the Brong-Ahafo Region, 475 km northwest of Accra ; 208 km (well-paved) north of Kumasi ; 180 km (new paved road) southwest of Tamale. State Transport coaches from Kumasi to Techiman and « mammy trucks. »

HOTELS AND RESTAURANTS : No hotels in Kintampo. Small hotels in Techiman, 60 km south of Kintampo.

Post office and gas station.

Koforidua

LOCATION AND ACCESS : Capital of the Eastern Region, 85 km (paved, but currently being repaired) north of Accra ; 194 km (paved) east of Kumasi ; 82 km west of Akosombo ; 19 km (paved and unpaved) from Boti Falls. State Transport coaches to Accra and Kumasi, plus « mammy trucks. » Railway to Accra and Kumasi.

HOTELS AND RESTAURANTS : *Catering Rest House*, 38 air-conditioned rooms, restaurant and bar. — *Koforidua Motel*, P.O. Box 133, tel : 32.34. 10 rooms, restaurant and nightclub. Also : *Eastland Hotel*, Old Estates. — *Hotel Eredec, Residency* and *Partner's May*, Link Road.

Post office, banks and gas station.

Kumasi

LOCATION AND ACCESS : Provincial capital of the Ashanti Region, 270 km (paved) northwest of Accra ; 194 km (paved) northwest of Koforidua ; 370 km (paved) south of Tamale, via Techiman and Kintampo ; 130 km (paved) southeast of Sunyani. State Transport coaches to Accra, Tamale, Bolgatanga and the north, Wa, Wenchi, Sunyani, Berekum, Min and Cape Coast. « Mammy trucks » to all the outlying villages and smaller localities. Airline service to Accra, Tamale and Sunyani. Trains to Accra and Sekondi, via Obuasi and Tarkwa.

HOTELS AND RESTAURANTS : Numerous hotels of all categories (see list at end of volume). *Restaurants* : *Add*, tel : 61.78. — *Kwality*, tel : 40.26. — *Family*, tel : 24.41. — *Chopsticks*, tel : 322. — *Copacabana*. — *Equator*. — *Joffels*. — *Topaz*, etc.
Night-clubs : *Dimlight, Nsadwase* (City Hotel), *Hedonist, The Sphinx, Star Nite*.

LOCAL ATTRACTIONS : Fortress museum, cultural Centre and zoo.

SPORTS : University swimming pool, riding club, sports fields, ping-pong ; Ghana Social Club golfcourse. Tennis, squash, ping-pong and billiards at the Officers' Mess.

Banks, shops, post office, gas stations.

Larabanga

LOCATION AND ACCESS : Northern Region, near mole National Park and 140 km west of Tamale, 174 km southeast of Wa and 450 km (paved and unpaved) north of Kumasi.

HOTELS AND RESTAURANTS : *Camping and guest accommodations* in Mole National Park.

Mole National Park

LOCATION AND ACCESS : Northern Region, 380 km (paved and unpaved) north of Kumasi, via Techiman and Kintampo ; 174 km south of Wa and 130 km west of Tamale. State Transport coaches to Damongo. Land Rover rental at the motel located inside the park.

HOTELS AND RESTAURANTS : *Mole Motel*, tel : 071-25.63. (Reservations in Accra from the Department of Game and Wildlife or at the Kumasi Zoo.), 35 rooms with double beds, private bath and optional air-conditioning. Restaurant and bar. Guides for excursions through the park.

Mpraeso

LOCATION AND ACCESS : Eastern Region, 180 km north of Accra, 112 km (well-paved) east of Kumasi and 98 km west of Koforidua. State Transport coaches from Accra and Kumasi to Nkawkaw (8 km). « Mammy trucks » and taxi service from Nkawkaw. Coach service from Accra to Begoro.

HOTELS AND RESTAURANTS : *Rest House*, 4 rooms. — *Begoro Rest House*, 2 rooms. — *Bunso Rest House*, 2 rooms. Plus a half-dozen small hotels at Nkawkaw (see the list at the end of the volume).

Post office, fuel available at Nkawkaw and Begoro.

Navrongo

LOCATION AND ACCESS : Upper East Region, near the Burkina-Faso border, 30 km west of Bolgatanga ; 16 km south of Paga and 109 km east of Tumu. State Transport coaches to Bolgatanga and the northern villages, including Paga.

HOTELS AND RESTAURANTS : None : see Bolgatanga. *Paga Motel*, air-conditioned rooms with private bath ; restaurant.

Bank, post office, gas station, market, bus terminal and hospital.

Obuasi

LOCATION AND ACCESS : Ashanti Region, 85 km (paved) south of Kumasi ; 160 km north of Cape Coast, via Foso and Saltpond and 225 km north of Basua. Train service to Kumasi, Dunkwa, Tarkwa and Sekondi.

HOTELS AND RESTAURANTS : 9 hotels located in the city (see list at end of volume).

Bank, post office and gas station.

Paga

LOCATION AND ACCESS : Border town between Ghana and Burkina-Faso in the Upper East Region, 10 km (paved) north of Navrongo ; 50 km northwest of Bolgatanga.

HOTELS AND RESTAURANTS : Small *motel* at Paga.

Sekondi-Takoradi

LOCATION AND ACCESS : Capital of the Western Region, Sekondi is situated on the west coast of Ghana, ajacent to its sister-city, Takoradi. Sekondi is 218 km (paved) west of Accra ; Takoradi is 242 km (road under construction) south of Kumasi ; 32 km east of Basua and 75 km east of Axim. Sekondi is 61 km west of Elmina and 74 km (paved) from Cape Coast. State Transport coach service to Accra, Cape Coast and along the west coast. Trains from Sekondi to Kumasi and Accra.

HOTELS AND RESTAURANTS : 20 hotels of all categories, listed at the end of volume. *Restaurants : Harbour View. — Effies Restaurant. — Twin City* (Chinese).

NIGHT-CLUBS : *Princess Hall. — Ahenfie. — The Pelican. — Zenith.*

TRAVEL AGENT : *Ghana Airways*, at the southern limit of Liberation Road.

BANKS : All of Ghana's major banks have offices in Takoradi.

Shai Hills Reserve

LOCATION AND ACCESS : 64 km (paved) north of Accra, via Tema and 54 km (paved) east of Aburi, via Larteh. « Mammy trucks » from Aburi or Tema.

HOTELS AND RESTAURANTS : None.

Sunyani

NAME : The origin of the name is believed to be derived from *asono nwae*, « the place where elephants are slaughtered. »

LOCATION AND ACCESS : Sunyani is 400 km (paved) west of Accra ; 130 km (paved) northwest of Kumasi ; 34 km east of Berekum ; 134 km (unpaved) from Mim, and 60 km south of Wenchi. State Transport coach express service to Kumasi and Berekum. « Mammy trucks » to Wenchi and Techiman. Taxis can be hired by the day for a flat fee. Sunyani's local airport is served by Ghana Airways' domestic flights.

HOTELS AND RESTAURANTS : *Catering Rest House*, P.O. Box 104, tel : 109, 8 rooms with double beds, plus bar and restaurant. Also : *the Ebenezer Hotel, Nimpong Hotel, Tata Hotel* and *Tropical Hotel.*

Tamale

LOCATION AND ACCESS : Capital of the Northern Region, 640 km (paved) north of Accra ; 170 km (paved) south of Bolgatanga ; 130 km east of Mole National Park ; 266 km (unpaved) south of Nakpanduri, via Yendi ; 370 km (paved) north of Kumasi. State Transport coach service to all of the above. Local flights to Accra and Kumasi.

HOTELS AND RESTAURANTS : *Catering Rest House*, P.O. Box 247 ; tel : 29.78. 36 bungalows, garden, restaurant, bar, meeting room. *Marcos Hotel*, tel : 26.78. *Sparkles*, an excellent restaurant located in the Cultural Centre.

Banks, post office, gas stations, market and Ghana Airways office.

Tema

LOCATION AND ACCESS : Port and new-town on the Gulf of Guinea in the Greater Accra area. 29 km (freeway) east of Accra ; 35 km from Shai Hills and 89 km south of Aburi. State Transport coaches to Accra, Aflao, Keta and Kumasi, plus « mammy trucks » to Larteh, via Shai Hills. Train service to Accra.

HOTELS AND RESTAURANTS : Many hotels (see list at end of volume).

SPORTS : *Tema Golf Club.*

Cinema house, gas station, garage, bank and post office.

Tumu

LOCATION AND ACCESS : Upper West Region, near the Burkina-Faso border, 229 km (unpaved) northeast of Wa, via Hamile ; 139 km (unpaved) west of Bolgatanga. State Transport coaches to and from both destinations.

HOTELS AND RESTAURANTS : *Catering Rest House*, 24 rooms, bar ; meals upon request.

Wa

LOCATION AND ACCESS : Capital of the Upper West Region, 229 km (unpaved) south of Tumo ; 368 km (unpaved) southwest of Bogatanga ; 174 km northwest of Mole National Park and 318 km north of Wenchi (paved and unpaved). State Transport coaches for the northern cities and Kumasi, plus « Mammy trucks » for the neighboring villages.

HOTELS AND RESTAURANTS : Many hotels (see list at end of volume).

Gas station, post office, market.

Wenchi

LOCATION AND ACCESS : Brong-Ahafo Region, 152 km (paved) northwest ; 60 km (paved) north of Sunyani and 318 km south of Wa. State Transport coach service to Kumasi and Wa. « Mammy trucks » to Sunyani.

HOTELS : *Baah Hotel*, P.O. Box 43, 23 rooms. — *Kaff Guest House*, P.O. Box 14, 4 rooms.

Gas station, post office.

Yeji

LOCATION AND ACCESS : On Lake Volta, east of the Brong-Ahafo Region, 226 km northeast of Kumasi (Ashanti Region) and 144 km south of Tamale (Northern Region) by road and ferry. Weekly sailings to Buipe in the northwest, as well as weekly return in opposite direction to Kete-Krachi, Kpandu and Akosombo. State Transport coach service to Kumasi, Accra and Tamale. Local ferry service (approximately every two-and-a-half hours) from 6:00 a.m. to 6:00 p.m.

HOTELS : *Volta Lake Hotel*, 12 rooms, double beds, bar. P.O. Box 17. Also, smaller hotels in Sampa (*Sangeson Hotel*, P.O. Box 46) and Goaso (*Friendship Inn*, P.O. Box 22).

Yendi

LOCATION AND ACCESS : East of the Northern Region, 96 km (unpaved) east of Tamale and 170 km south of Nakpanduri. « Mammy trucks » to Tamale and Nakpanduri. State Transport coach terminal at Nakpanduri.

HOTELS AND RESTAURANTS : None.

Zebilla

LOCATION AND ACCESS : Upper East Region near the Burkina-Faso border, 45 km (paved and unpaved) east of Bolgatanga and 30 km (unpaved) west of Bawku.

HOTELS AND RESTAURANTS : None. Small hotels at Bolgatanga.

the ghanaian journey

before you go

■ Ghana's immense beaches, lively traditions and rich historical vestiges are more than enough to qualify the country as one of Africa's leading tourist destinations. Unfortunately, the unfavourable economic environment of the preceding years has seriously hampered the development of tourism.

At present, there are neither charter flights to Ghana nor the reasonably-priced travel packages that exist for the numerous destinations offered by international tour companies. If the relatively limited number of scheduled flights to Accra are generally frequented by business travellers, everything suggests that this situation will change in the very near future, as tourists progressively become aware of the attractions that Ghana offers.

A number of major airlines not currently offering service to Ghana are planning to offer scheduled flights, while France's UTA airlines will soon be providing direct service to Accra from Paris.

Ghana's recent economic boom has stimulated the renovation of many of its existing hotels and the construction of modern world-class accommodations such as the Accra Novotel. Other types of visitor accommodations are going up throughout the country at an accelerated pace, including coastal resort complexes and motels located in central and northern Ghana.

An accent on tourism

Ghana is currently marshalling its resources to prepare for the arrival of increasing numbers of visitors from abroad.

The country's road and rail networks are constantly being upgraded, and new bridges and highways are providing rapid access to regions which were previously often inaccessible during the rainy season. Even Ghana's obsolete system of river ferry-boats is being modernized to offer around-the-clock service to passengers and motorists.

But aside from all that is being done to improve tourist facilities, Ghana's most important asset remains the Ghanaian people themselves, a people whose legendary sense of hospitality and kindness constitute an immense pleasure for any visitor to the country.

Choosing the season

The best time to visit Ghana is year-round, since its geographical location between the Tropic of Cancer and the Equator make for a particularly mild and temperate climate. Ghana's rainy season arrives roughly at the same period as the European summer vacations, but since rainfall is generally intermittent and scattered, this presents no particular inconvenience.

Visitors travelling through Ghana during the rainy season (in June, for example), will encounter heavy downpours for an hour or so, followed by sunshine and nearly cloudless skies. The Ghanaian landscapes become particularly photogenic under the play of clouds and sunlight, and the ancient coastal fortresses are quite romantic when battered by foaming surf under a stormy sky.

Although tourists cannot always choose their departure period, it is possible to plan an itinerary through Ghana in terms of regional weather, since the rainfall is not equally heavy in all parts of the country at exactly the same time, and local climates are largely influenced by the prevailing winds.

Ghana is a crossroads for the dry, burning winds that whip in from the Sahara Desert and the fresh sea-breezes from the Gulf of Guinea that caress its southwestern coasts. The wind fronts move either north or south, bringing either rain or hot, clear skies. The rainy season begins earlier in the south, but the season is divided into two periods, culminating either in May or June, with intermittent dry spells in July and August. In northern Ghana, the rainy season lasts from June to October, or at least that is how it's supposed to be. In reality, the increasingly frequent impression that there are no more seasons, now a familiar fact of life for Westerners, has spread to the rest of the world. Endemic drought is a menace that hovers over many African regions, and in Ghana, the northern regions and coastal plains surrounding Accra are often hit by extended dry spells. It is thus becoming increasingly difficult to predict with any certainty the duration and amount of rainfall between May and September. All regions, however, experience significant drops in temperature during this period, whereas the hottest season remains the months of February through April.

Overleaf :
Paradoxically, even though the fishermen of Cape Coast often navigate in rough seas that drench them to the bone, they also open their umbrellas during the lightest of showers!

Even when the rains aren't heavy, the north acquires a pristine verdant hue as the first drops fall, and is transformed into a veritable garden. The beauty of this Ghanaian spring largely compensates for the inconveniences caused by the violence of the succeeding downpours. Although the nights can be fairly cool during this period, the merest ray of sunshine quickly warms up the daytime temperatures.

The rainy season, with its riot of vegetation and washed-out dirt roads, is not the ideal moment for viewing animal reserves such as Mole National Park. However, in many regions the thin topsoil supports only low ground cover, with wildlife fully visible through the short grass.

Dirt roads may pose a problem for motorists in July and November, but again, road conditions often depends on local soil conditions and the violence and frequency of rainfall.

Average daytime temperatures

In the southwest, humid conditions prevail nearly all year round, making this area the most difficult of all of Ghana's regions to visit during the rainy season. Visitors planning to practise water sports or those who prefer simply relaxing under the sun are advised to avoid the southwest from June to September. Rather than encountering the hot summer weather expected, Western travellers may be unpleasantly surprised by average daytime temperatures of 22 degrees Centigrade (72 degrees Fahrenheit) — practically Siberia!

If this may discourage sun-seekers, it should reassure prospective travellers worried about problems of adaptation to the African climate. The former can choose the warmer northern regions or the months from January to April, both of which should be avoided by the latter.

Health regulations

All the countries of sub-Saharan Africa, and particularly Ghana, require arriving visitors to be in possession of an international vaccination card as well as having previously been immunized against yellow fever in Europe prior to departure. It is recommended to do this at least ten days in advance, since some people may suffer from headaches or fever during the immediate period following vaccination. Once vaccinated, immunity lasts for ten years, but remember that it is always necessary to present your vaccination card to the health officials at Accra-Kotoka airport upon arrival.

Vaccination for yellow fever is available throughout Europe at a number of specially authorized centres. Here are some useful addresses in Great Britain where vaccinations are available: *Hospital for Tropical Diseases*, 4 ST. Pancras Way, London, NWI, Tel: (071) 387.44.11. *West London Designated Vaccination Centre*, 53 Great Cumberland Place, London WI, Tel: (071) 262.64.56. *British Airways Immunisation Centre*, Victoria Terminal, Buckingham Palace Road, London SWI, Tel: (071) 834.23.23. *British Airways Medical Centre*, Speedbird House, Heathrow Airport, Hounslow, Middlesex, Tel: (01) 759.55.11.

Since some tropical viruses have long incubation periods, visitors returning from a voyage to Africa should contact their doctor in the event of fever, infection or stomach problems. The doctor should also be informed of the regions or countries visited, as well as the possible causes (polluted drinking water or bathing sites, insect bites, etc.).

Upon leaving for, and during your stay in Ghana, visitors are also advised to follow a Nivaquine anti-malaria treatment, and to continue the treatment for six weeks after returning to your home coun-

Temperatures and rains : averages by month

	J	F	M	A	M	J	J	A	S	O	N	D
Accra	27	28	28	28	27	26	25	24	25	26	27	28

Average temperatures (in centigrade C)

☐ scattered showers   ▨ heavy rain

▨ light rains   ☐ sunny skies

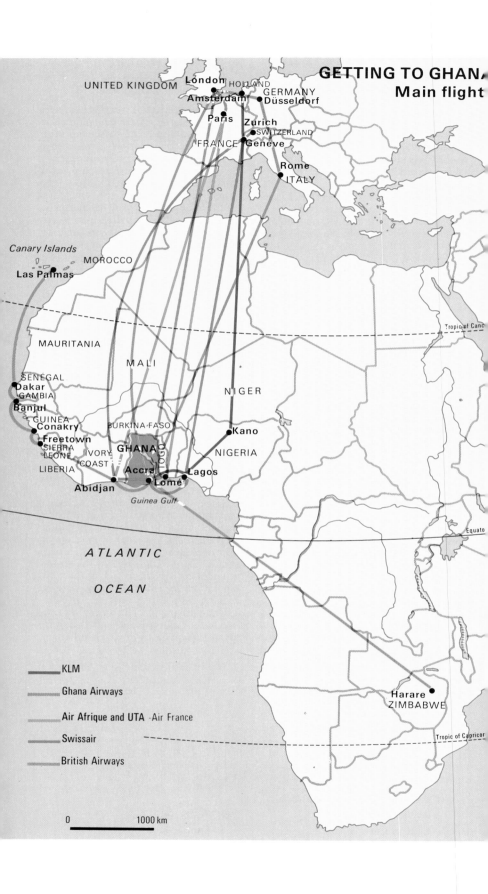

GETTING TO GHANA
Main flight

UNITED KINGDOM London
HOLLAND
GERMANY
Amsterdam Düsseldorf
Paris
Zurich
FRANCE Genève SWITZERLAND
Rome
ITALY

Canary Islands
MOROCCO

Las Palmas

Tropic of Canc

MAURITANIA
MALI
NIGER

SENEGAL
Dakar
GAMBIA
Banjul
GUINEA
Conakry
BURKINA-FASO
Kano
Freetown
SIERRA
LEONE
IVORY
GHANA
NIGERIA
COAST
Accra
LIBERIA
Lagos
Abidjan
Lomé
Guinea Gulf

ATLANTIC

OCEAN

Equato

Harare
ZIMBABWE

Tropic of Capricor

KLM
Ghana Airways
Air Afrique and UTA -Air France
Swissair
British Airways

0   1000 km

try. Any abnormal symptoms should be systematically reported to your doctor, along with the locations or countries visited.

Entry formalities

Visitors to Ghana are required to obtain an entry visa. In Great Britain, visas are delivered within 48 hours by the Ghanaian Embassy, 104 High Gate Hill, London N 65 HE, Tel: (081) 342.86.86. Be sure to bring two passport size photos and enough cash to cover the cost of the type of visa required. Fees vary in function of the type of visa demanded, i.e., tourist, business or professional.

Game hunters are required to obtain a special authorization from the Ghanaian Department of Game and Wildlife.

What to pack

For the city: light summer clothing, preferably cotton (avoid synthetic fabrics in all seasons). For women, the wearing of slacks or shorts can create problems, especially in the heavily-Islamic north, and it is therefore advised to bring fairly long dresses or skirts. Don't forget an umbrella (or buy one locally), a heavy sweater and sunglasses.

For the trekking safaris in Mole National Park: Heavy walking shoes, short-sleeved shirts, shorts (for men) or light cotton trousers, all in neutral colours for reducing the visitor's visibility to the wildlife. A hat will also be needed for long hikes under the strong sun.

Useful accessories include binoculars, a camera with a telephoto lens (see below) and two basic reference-works: *Le Guide des grands mammifères d'Afrique*, by J. Dorst and P. Dandelot, published by Delachaux and Niestlé; and *Les Oiseaux de l'Ouest africain*, by W. Serle and G.J. Morel, also published by Delachaux and Niestlé.

Game hunting: Heavy hiking boots and camouflaged hunting-wear.

For the beach: Swim-wear and sunglasses.

Everywhere else: Solid clothing, jeans and sturdy walking shoes.

Amateur photographers will find Ghana a paradise for photo-taking. The subjects range from the ancient Portuguese coastal fortresses to the picturesque mosques and splendid vestiges of the former Ashanti kingdoms. Also particularly photogenic are the innumerable ceremonies, colourful markets, breathtaking landscapes and the wildlife of Ghana's national parks. Visitors should also be aware that many Ghanaians are particularly sensitive about having their photo taken. Before doing so, it is a wise idea to ask their permission to avoid misunderstandings. Photographers must also obtain a special permit, issued by the Ministry of Information.

Before arriving in Ghana, stock up on film (generally 100 Asa, Kodachrome or Ektachrome), and often less expensive to buy in an airport duty-free shop just before boarding. Once in Ghana, make sure to protect your rolls of film from the heat and humidity by resealing them in their original packaging after exposure, while your camera itself should also be well-protected from the sun and humidity. Specially waterproofed and airtight camera bags are also a good idea.

Ghana's bright skies show up best when shot through appropriate cloud filters. Bring a 50 mm lens for wide-angle shots of landscapes, markets, beaches, lakes, etc., and a 500 mm telephoto lens (or zoom) for photographing the wildlife in the national parks.

Sports and camping

The campsites in Ghana's interior generally offer fairly basic levels of comfort. For extended travel outside the main cities, it is therefore recommended that visitors bring sleeping bags, cooking utensils and a stock of food provisions.

A lightweight sleeping bag will get you through the nights, but don't forget a can or two of standard aerosol insecticide (on sale everywhere in Ghana) to discourage the mosquitoes. Tap or well water is acceptable for washing, but should not be drunk unless filtered, boiled or disinfected by water purification tablets. The best idea is to purchase several cases of bottled water before leaving Accra, while additional stocks can be purchased in larger cities such as Kumasi. Soft drinks such as Coca-Cola, fruit juice and local beer are available at roadside stands throughout the country, and can be kept cool in a thermos or an insulated container.

Obtaining groceries can sometimes be a problem in the bush or more remote regions. Visitors should bring canned goods (sardines, corned beef, cheese, etc.), and purchase fresh fruit and bread locally. Don't forget to bring spoons and forks, a camping knife, and a can-opener. Other necessary items include a good flashlight and a travel clock.

Tennis players should pack their tennis-wear, rackets and balls; for golfers, it is recommended to bring your bag and clubs.

Hunters will want to bring their guns and ammunition, on the condition of having obtained a hunting license from the Ghanaian authorities.

Communicating

Since English is the official language of Ghana, it's a good idea to take a few lessons before leaving if you are not already more or less fluent. And whatever your mother-tongue, don't forget to bring along a good bilingual English dictionary...

Information and documentation

Although a network of Ghanaian tourist information offices do not as yet exist in Europe, a certain amount of visitor information can be obtained from your local Ghanaian embassy. In Great Britain, the embassy is located at 104 High Gate Hill, London N 65 HE, tel: (081) 342.86.86. A number of informative guides and books on Ghana can be found in any good bookshop. Additional reading material can be found in the bibliography appearing at the end of this work.

Lastly, don't forget to purchase road maps of Ghana and Western and Northern Africa if you are driving overland from Europe.

For information in other countries

The following is a brief list of international Ghanaian consulates:

Algeria: 62 rue Parmentier-Hydra, Algiers.
Angola: Rua Vereador Castelo Branco 5, 10 caixa postal 1012, Luanda.
Belgium: 44 rue Gachard, 1050 Brussels.
Benin: P.O. Box 488, Cotonou.

THE LANGUAGE BARRIER

■ *Since English is the official language of Ghana, visitors having a sufficient command will be able to make themselves understood nearly wherever they go. In some localities, a relatively basic form of "pigeon English" comprising a mixture of local dialects and English vocabulary may be encountered. Akan, the second most commonly spoken language in Ghana, is derived from the ethnic group of the same name. It is recommended that visitors to Ghana learn at least a few basic phrases, perhaps less out of the need to communicate, than by simple courtesy towards the inhabitants whose guest you are, and as a means of expressing your friendship and interest in who they are. The visitor who employs any of the following Akan expressions during his encounters with Ghanaians either in the cities or the countryside will be amply rewarded by the added dimension of contact that will result. A brief phonetic list appears below.*

yes: myew
No: day-bee
Thank you: mida-asi
Good morning: maa-chi

Good afternoon: maa-aha
Good evening: maa-djuu
Welcome: akwaba
Goodbye: naanti-yeeh, or yea-koh

Brazil: Shis Q1, 10 conjunto 08 Casa 02 Box 07-0456, Brasilia.
Bulgaria: 9 Pierre Degueyter Street BLK3, apt. 37038, P.O. Box 38, 113 Sofia.
Burkina-Faso: Route de Po, P.O. Box 212 Ouagadougou.
Canada: Ghana High Commission 810, 85 Range Road, Ottawa, Ontario, KIN 8J6.
China: 8 San Li Tunn Road, Bejing.
Cuba: 5A Avenida No. 1808, Havana.
Czechoslovakia: V Tisine 4, Prague 6.
Denmark: 13 Egeberg Alle, 2900 Hellerup, Copenhagen.
Egypt: 24 Ahmed Abdel Aziz Street, Dokki, Cairo.
Ethiopia: P.O. Box 3173, Addis Ababa.
France: 8 Villa Saïd, 75116 Paris.
Germany: Rhein Allee 58, 53 Bonn-Bad Godesberg, and Niederschenhausen Waldstrasse 10, 1110 Berlin.
Great Britain: Office of the High Commission for Ghana, 13 Belgrave Square, London SWLX 8 PR.
Guinea: Building ex-Urbaine, P.O. Box 734, Conakry.
India: Ghana High Commission A-42, Vasant Marg, Vasant Vihar, New Delhi, 110 057.

Ivory Coast: 01 P.O. Box 1871 Abidjan 01.
Italy: 4 Via Ostriana, 00199, Rome.
Japan: Azaba, P.O. Box 16, Tokyo.
Liberia: P.O. Box 4471, Monrovia.
Libya: P.O. Box 4167, Tripoli.
Nigeria: Ghana High Commission, 21323 King George V Road, Onikan, P.O. Box 889, Lagos.
Saudi Arabia: P.O. Box 94339, Riyad.
Sierra Leone: Ghana High Commission, 16 Percival Street, Freetown.
Switzerland: 11 Belpstrasse, Post Fach 3001, Berne.
Togo: P.O. Box 92, Lome.
U.S.S.R.: 14 Skatertny Pereulok, Moscow.
U.S.A.: 3512 International Drive, NW Washington DC, 20008, and the Permanent Mission of Ghana to the United Nations, 19 East 47th Street, New York, N.Y. 10017.
Yugoslavia: Ogujena Price 50, 11000, Belgrade.
Zimbabwe: Ghana High Commission, 11 Downie Avenue, Begraviaa P.O. Box 4445, Harare.

Where is the hotel?: hotel wo hin?
I'd like (to eat) some: me zi bi
Chicken: akuko
I'd like to drink: me-peh bribi anon
Beer: beer
Water: insu
In front of: enim
In back of: echir
Yesterday: enn'rra
Tomorrow: otchin-aah
I want to sleep: me-ko-da
How much does this cost?: ahin?
It's too expensive: ni bu ye zin
I'm looking for: me-pay
one: baako
two: me-nou
three: miensa
four: inann
five: inoum
six: n'sia
seven: n'son

eight: nwot'chi
nine: n'kron
ten: eidou
twenty: eduonu
one hundred: oha
one thousand: apim
Monday: d'zoada
Tuesday: binada
Wednesday: woukouada
Thursday: ya'wada
Friday: feeada
Saturday: mimi'nida
Sunday: kwassiada

TRANSPORTATION NETWORK

BURKINA FASO

Ouagadougou

Hamale
Han
Tumu
Paga
Navrongo
Bolgatanga
Bawku
Zebila
Nakpanduri
Gambaga

Wa

Mole

Black Volta

Sawla
Larabanga
Damongo
Buipe

Tamale
Yendi
Zan
Zabzugu
Bimbila

IVORY
COAST

Bamboi
Kintampo
Yeji
Salaga
Ktare
Dumbai
Kete Krachi

Daka

Oti

Hani
Boabeng
Atebubu
Kokua
Wenchi
Techiman
Berekum
Sunyani

Lake Volta

Jasikan
Hohoe
Kpandu
Amedzofe
Vane
Ho
Kpetoe

Kumasi
Konongo
Mpraeso
Nkawkaw
Bekwai
Awaso
Begoro
Akosombo
Obuasi
Bosuso
Kibi
Koforidua
Aflac
Kade
Akuse
Sogakofe
Dunkwa
Oda
Nsawan
Larteh
Shai
Hills
Ada
Anyan
Aburi
Asamankese
Tema
Samreboi
Swedru
ACCRA
Prestea
Huni Valley
Senya Beraku
Winneba

Pra

Tano

Bia

Abidjan

Half Assini
Saltpond
Cape Coast
Tarkwe
Shama
Takoradi
Sekondi
Axim
Busua
Prince's Town
Dixcove

TOG

Express way	
Tarred road (or under construction)	
Track	
Ferry crossing ★	Railroad
	Air service
International airport	Boat service
Local airport	

0   50   100 km

ADMINISTRATIVE REGIONS, ETHNIC GROUPS

UPPER EAST REGION

Lobi
Dagati
Dagati
Sissala

Kasena
Nankansi
Gurense
Frafra
Bolgatanga

Busanga
Namnam
Kusasi
Talensi

UPPER WEST REGION

Wa

Buílsa

Bimawba

Grusi

Mamprusi

Chokosi

NORTHERN REGION

Wala

Lobi
Dagati

Dagomba

Tamale

Konkomba

Vagala
Gonja

Nakumba

Lobi
Gonja
Gonja

Konkomba

Banda
Mo

Atwode

Brong

Adele

Krachi

BRONG AHAFO REGION

Nchumuru

VOLTA

Ntrubu

Ahafo
Sunyani

Nchumuru

ASHANTI REGION

Kwahu

Ewe

Avatime

Kumasi

Ho

Ashanti

EASTERN REGION

Asin

Juaben
Krobo

Ewe

Denkyira
Akim
Koforidua

REGION

Sefwi

WESTERN

Wasaw

Adangbe

Ga
ACCRA

GREATER ACCRA

Aowin
REGION

CENTRAL REGION

Fanti

Nzima
Ahanta
Cape Coast

Sekondi

Ethnic group *Fanti*
National park
Departemental town ●
Administrative region limit ——

0   100 km

getting there

By air

Ghana is only a five to six-hour direct flight from Europe on modern jets such as DC-10s or Boeing 747s. About a dozen major airlines schedule flights to Accra-Kotoka, Ghana's international airport, which is located to the northeast of the capital and 12 kilometres from the city centre.

FROM EUROPE TO AFRICA:
— *France:* Since Air Afrique and UTA/Air France no longer schedule direct flights to Accra, stopovers are necessary. At present, UTA/Air France is considering the possibility of a direct flight to Accra in 1992. Both airlines offer flights from Paris-Roissy to Abidjan in the Ivory Coast or Lome in Togo, with an interconnecting flight to Accra on Ghana Airways. Another possibility is Paris-Roissy to London-Heathrow on Air France or British Airways, followed by a Ghana Airways or British Airways flight from London-Gatwick to Accra.
— *England:* London-Gatwick is the gateway for near-daily direct flights to Accra by Ghana Airways or British Airways.
— *Netherlands:* Depending on the time of the year, KLM schedules one or two flights per week from Amsterdam-Schiphol to Accra, via Kano or Lagos, Nigeria.
— *Switzerland:* Swissair offers several weekly flights from Geneva and Zurich to Accra, via Abidjan (Ivory Coast) or Lagos.
— *Scandinavia:* SAS.
— *Germany:* Ghana Airways schedules two flights per week from Dusseldorf to Accra.
— *Italy*: Ghana Airways flies from Rome to Accra twice a week.
Other compagnies offering international flights to Accra-Kotoka include Ethiopian Airlines, Egyptair, MEA (Lebanon) and Nigeria Airways.

INTER-AFRICAN AIR TRAVEL:
For travellers already in Ghana and desiring to visit the neighbouring countries, Ghana Airways offers a number of flights from Accra to the Ivory Coast (five flights per week to Abidjan), Sierra Leone (five flights per week to Freetown), Guinea (three flights per week to Conakry), Gambia (four flights per week to Banjul), Senegal (three flights per week to Dakar) and two flights per week to Las Palmas in the Canary Islands. Eastern destinations include Accra-Togo (two flights per week to Lome) and Nigeria (seven weekly flights to Lagos). Ghana Airways also schedules a weekly flight from Accra to Harare, Zimbabwe.

By using the system of interconnecting flights available in major international airports such as London, Paris or Rome, Ghana is just a hop away from any point on the globe. It is possible, for instance, to fly from New York to London on any one of a number of regularly scheduled flights. Once in London, change for Accra via Ghana Airways or British Airways. For visitors leaving Ghana and continuing their voyage south, the West African travel hub of Harare in Zimbabwe, serviced once a week by Ghana Airways from Accra, permits travels to connect with flights to southern Africa and Australia.

AIRLINES SERVING GHANA:
Ghana Airways: Accra headquarters: Ghana House, P.O. Box 1636, Tel: 66.48.56. Cocoa House offices: P.O. Box 1636, Tel: 22.19.01 or 22.11.50. White Avenue, airport residential area: Tel: 77.33.21, 77.33.41 or 77.60.61. Kotoka International Airport, P.O. Box 1636, Tel: 77.61.71 or 77.74.06. Abidjan, Ivory Coast: the General Building, Avenue du Général-de-Gaulle, 01 P.O. Box 1605, Tel: 32.27.83 or 32.42.21. Dusseldorf, Germany: 43 Graf Adolf Strasse, 4000, Tel: 0211/37.03.37. Lome, Togo: 1 Rue du Commerce, P.O. Box 3456, Tel: 21.56.92. London, England: 3 Princes Street, London W1, Tel: 071-499-0201. Rome, Italy: 116 Via Veneto, 00187 Rome, Tel: 488.51.40, 481.76.50, 474.45.01 or 601.11.79.
British Airways: In Accra, Kojo Thompson Road at the corner of N. Liberia Road, P.O. Box 2087, Tel: 22.83.73, 66.78.00 or 66.79.00. Paris: 12 Rue de Castiglione, 75008, Tel: 47.78.14.14. London: P.O. Box 10, Heathrow Airport, Hounslow, Middx. TW6 2JA. (Telephone reservations taken from 7 a.m. to 10:30 p.m. at 01-897-4000).
Air Afrique. In Paris, at 104 Avenue des Champs-Elysées, 75008, Tel: 44.21.33.33 (reservations: 44.21.32.32). Abidjan: headquarters on Rue Joseph Anoma, Le Plateau, Tel: 32.05.00. Lome: Tel: 21.20.42.
UTA. In Paris, at 3 Boulevard Malesherbes, 75008, Tel: 40.17.46.46. Abidjan: SMGL Building, 11 Rue Joseph Anoma, Le Plateau, Tel: 33.22.31 or

32.90.93. Lome, Togo: Taha Building,
P.O. Box 2990, Tel: 21.69.10 or
21.69.10. or 21.23.87.
KLM. In Amsterdam, at 1 Leidseplein,
Tel: 020/649.36.33. Accra: Republic
House, Kwame Nkrumah Avenue, Tel:
22.40.30/20/50 or 22.43.70.
Swissair. Geneva: reservations at (022)
799.59.99. Zurich: reservations at (01)
251.34.34. Accra: 47 Independence
Avenue, Pegasus House, 1st floor, Tel:
22.81.50 or 22.81.90. Accra-Kotoka Airport: Tel: 77.56.34.

In addition to the basic first class, business and economy fares, most of the
above airlines offer youth fares and
reductions for families, the elderly and
groups, subject to certain conditions. Excursion tickets are also available, but
generally cannot be cancelled without
loss of the initial deposit. Off-season
reductions are also granted, except during school and year-end holidays. For
further information concerning fares, see
your travel agent or the airline company
of your choice.

By sea

Since the disappearance of many of the
steamship lines which formerly served
colonial Africa, few people ever consider
travelling to the African continent by sea.
There nevertheless still exist a few merchant ships offering passenger accommodations, but despite the near-absence of
demand and the length of the voyage (12
days), it is often difficult to negotiate a
passage, no matter how motivated one
may be.

Among the last of the remaining
steamship companies serving West Africa, Ghana's *Black Star Line* regularly
sails from most of the major ports of
northern Europe and Italy. For further
information, prospective passengers
should contact the Line's representatives
in London, Rotterdam or Hamburg.

Overland

Driving from Europe to Accra is an
authentic adventure, possible on the condition of being able to navigate on African roads, and above all, of having a
certain experience in driving under desert
conditions. Traversing a desert as immense as the Sahara requires adequate
preparation, specialized equipment and
driving skills very different from those
applying to normal "off-the-road"
jaunts. Il is not unusual for even experienced drivers to bog down in the sand
the first day out, and despite the inconvenience occasioned by digging a vehicle
out, leaving the main route for secondary
tracks can often mean leaving forever.

After crossing the Mediterranean sea
by car-ferry, the classic itinerary begins
in Algiers. Driving due south from
Tamanrasset, you eventually reach the
northern border of Niger. Although used
by a fair number of trans-Saharan truck
convoys, the route is far from being a
freeway, as a number of non-local
motorists have learned from bitter experience. Drivers are strongly advised to
avoid any other itinerary, and particularly that of Tanesrouft in northern Mali
which is extremely rough, poorly-
marked, and traverses a semi-militarized
zone regularly the theatre of Touareg up-
risings.

A well-paved road runs from Niger to
Arlit. The route, nicknamed "Uranium
Road," continues to Agadez, gateway to
the Aïr Mountains, the Tenere Desert,
Tahoua and Niamey. From Niamey, after heading southwest and crossing the
Niger River, the road continues to the
border of Burkina-Faso and thence to the
capital city of Ouagadougou. From here,
it's child's play to reach northern Ghana
by heading south on the Po Highway.
The Ghanaian border village of Paga
offers a major north-south highway running from Bolgatanga to Accra, via Tamale, Kintampo and Kumasi.

Coastal
roads

Visitors driving from neighbouring
countries such as the Ivory Coast and
Togo can take advantage of the excellent
coastal roads leading to Ghana, such as
the Abidjan-Accra route via Grand-
Bassam or Lome-Accra, via Aflao.

The following recommendations are
imperative for drivers making the overland voyage from Europe to Africa via
the Sahara: *Don't travel alone.* Also,
never go off the road, especially at night
or during a sandstorm, under risk of becoming hopelessly lost. Notify the local
authorities of your departure and estimated time of arrival on each leg of your
voyage to permit rescue teams to be alert-
ed in the event of abnormal delays.

Spare parts
and food

Your vehicle should be one of the current four-wheel drive models manufactured by Land-Rover, Toyota, Nissan, etc., and in perfect mechanical condition. After a major tune-up before departure, the vehicle should be equipped with a full set of spare tires, essential spare parts, a tool-set, spade and metal wheel ramps for providing traction in sandy bottoms. A several-day supply of gasoline and drinking water is a must, as is sufficient food for the driver and passengers. A good compass and precise roadmaps are an obvious necessity, with the newly-revised Michelin maps of North and Western Africa particularly recommended.

Seasonal factors are also of the utmost importance. From October to April, the Sahara is hot but bearable in the day but icy cold at night, calling for extremely warm clothing and heavy sleeping bags. Although the day/night temperature extremes decrease as you head south, they nevertheless remain extreme, particularly in northern Ghana.

A real
adventure

During the summer months the Sahara becomes a veritable furnace, and some drivers may discover that confronting its scorching heat, blinding glare and apocalyptic sandstorms is somewhat more than they originally bargained for. The nearer one gets to the Gulf of Guinea, the rainier it gets, while in the mountainous regions — and particularly the Aïr, the road can become impassable, or at the best, an unnerving moment for even experienced drivers.

Despite the considerable amount of precautions and preparations involved, an overland voyage to Ghana represents real adventure in the best sense of the word. Like all adventures, the voyage is best undertaken with a sense of realism and without undue over-confidence. Motorists possessing the skill and determination to sucessfully overcome the challenge will amply be repaid for their efforts.

Since Ghana is also a camper's paradise, it's recommended to bring the necessary equipment. Given the stringent 20-kilo baggage allowances imposed by most airlines, visitors planning to tour the country by automobile but not eager to cross the Sahara in it, should consider shipping both their vehicle and camping equipment before embarking for Ghana by air.

Packaged
tours

At the present time, no major international tour company offers packaged tours to Ghana. Nevertheless, many of the Accran agencies can offer help in organizing your voyage.

Insurance and
travel assistance

For all of the inherent risks and inconveniences that international travel often comprises, there now exists a simple solution in the form of travel assistance/insurance policies. In the event of sickness, the policy refunds more or less all of the expenses incurred for treatment or hospitalization, and also guarantees repatriation in case of serious illness, injury or death. In case of a road accident or other litigation in Ghana, lawyers' fees, bonds and bail are also paid by the insurer. And if your vehicle breaks down, towing and repair charges are also covered. In certain cases, the insurer will even air-freight a necessary automobile part which is unavailable locally, or in extreme cases, repatriate both the vehicle and the passengers. Check with your local insurance company for more details.

*The rainy season: this kind
of scene is becoming increasingly rare
as Ghana progressively constructs
an excellent system of paved roads
throughout the country.*

daily life

■ The majority of visitors to Ghana arrive by airplane at Accra-Kotoka International Airport, approximately 12 kilometres distant from the city centre.

Entry formalities and return flights

Visas: Visitors must be in possession of a valid passport and an entry visa (see "Entry Formalities"). Upon landing at the airport, the Ghanaian immigration officials will give you a questionnaire to be filled in (you'll also need two identity photos) and deposited with the District Immigration Office of Accra *within 48 hours of your arrival.*

Vaccinations: visitors must also show their international vaccination card and proof of innoculation against yellow fever at an authorized centre. The validity of this vaccination is ten years (see "Health Regulations"). In case of an emergency, all airports have their own vaccination services.

Anti-malaria treatment should begin two weeks before leaving, be continued during your entire stay and followed up six weeks after your return. For those with a tendency to forget taking medication, daily doses of quinine tablets are preferable to weekly.

Customs duty: The following items are exempt from customs duty: up to one pound of cigarettes, cigars or tobacco; one quart each of wines or spirits; up to one-half pint of perfume or toilet water; personal effects such as clothing, cameras, toilet articles, sports equipment, portable typewriters, etc. Guns and ammunition are subject to authorization, while objects such as bicycles, radios, record-players and musical instruments are taxed, except in the case of repatriation within a period of three months. Food products are also subjected to duty. Since the customs agents who search incoming vehicles at the border can be quite strict on this point, avoid bringing in anything more than light snacks, since larger stocks of food will be either taxed or confiscated, if not both.

Finally, visitors entering Ghana by automobile should be aware that insurance is compulsory for all vehicles, as is an international driver's license and the necessary clearance papers for customs.

Airport arrival/taxis: Upon arrival, visitors should convert a small amount of currency into Ghanaian cedis to cover porters' tips and taxi fares. As you will sooner or later discover (and it's best to be aware of this sooner rather than later), Ghanaian taxis are not equipped with metres, so make sure that the driver states the fare *before* you start out, since once on the road it will be difficult to pay anything other than the outrageous fare that will be demanded upon arrival.

It is recommended that visitors leaving Ghana confirm their outgoing flight a minimum of 72 hours beforehand in Accra or Kumasi. Passing through customs and clearing the other administrative formalities can often take longer than expected, so be sure to arrive at the airport at least three hours ahead of departure time.

Also be sure to have your passport handy for presentation to the immigration officials, and be prepared to pay a small *departure tax* in dollars. Since the Ghanaian cedi is not convertible into foreign currency outside the country, it's a good idea to spend nearly everything before leaving. Nevertheless, keep a few cedis to cover the airport taxi, porters' tips and refreshments in the airport lounge.

The duty-free shops of Accra-Kotoka airport offer spirits, perfume, Ghanaian handicrafts and a fairly limited selection of electronics goods. Again, it is important to know that these shops only accept foreign currency, and that they generally close well before the last flights out of the country have departed. Since many airlines offer tax-free goods during the flight, you can stock up on last-minute purchases as you wing your way back home. Passengers transiting through London's Heathrow Airport will have the pleasure of discovering a veritable gold mine of bargain-priced duty-free merchandise.

Information, please?

A number of official agencies offer infomation to visitors either planning a voyage to Ghana, or those who have already arrived there.

In Accra, the Ghana Tourist Board (P.O. Box 3106, Tel: 233-21 or 22.89.33, Telex: 2143) provides helpful tips and colourful leaflets to foreign visitors.

Although certain other official or semi-official agencies are theoretically supposed to do the same, the quality of the service provided is not always of the highest. As elsewhere in the world, obtaining specific information and contacts often involve professional affinities or shared interests, as in the case of the University of Legon professors specialized in botany, zoology or African studies who are often delighted to meet with overseas colleagues or individuals having a particular interest in their field of study.

In the majority of Ghana's cities and larger towns, visitor information centres provide valuable tips concerning local or regional attractions, curiosities and traditional festivals, as well as help in reserving hotel rooms, rest houses and other amenities. Given the Ghanaian's legendary sense of hospitality, paying a visit to the chief or the elders of the village in which you've elected to stay is not merely a matter of courtesy, but also a rare opportunity to make a rewarding personal contact with individuals who are delighted to explain the deeper aspects of their culture and traditions.

Currency and exchange rates

Ghana's currency is the *cedi*, which exists in 50, 100, 200, 500 and soon-to-be-issued 1,000-cedi denominations. Coins known as *pesewas* also exist, but recent inflation has reduced their value to negligeable levels. One notable advantage of Ghana's high level of inflation is that the exchange rate for foreign currency is particularly advantageous, and for the equivalent of approximately one hundred dollars or 60 pounds sterling, visitors will have the pleasant surprise of receiving enough cedis to fill a small suitcase!

Visitors should pay special attention to exchange rates, since these may vary widely from one day and one currency-exchange to another. The best method is to change a small amount of money upon arriving at the airport to cover porters' tips and taxi fares, and once in Accra, to compare the going rates which are posted in front of the main currency exchanges. Hotels often offer somewhat better rates, but this can also pose certain logistical difficulties when large sums of money are involved. In any case, before setting off for the interior of Ghana, be sure that you have a sufficient amount of cedis to cover your travel expenses, including gasoline, hotel and restaurant charges. If a large sum of currency is needed at the outset of your trip, inform the exchange office beforehand, since they may need a day or two to obtain the corresponding amount in local currency. It should also be remembered that in Ghana, as elsewhere in the world, American dollars are preferred over anything else, and are thus always accorded the highest exchange rates.

Since at the moment of writing, Ghana's economy is in a particularly critical phase of reactivation, necessitating the imposition of a somewhat severe series of austerity and anti-inflationary measures, visitors should not count on using international credit cards such as Visa, American Express, Diners Club or Master Card other than in an extremely limited number of shops, hotels and restaurants in Accra. And although traveler's checks are generally accepted in Accra or Kumasi, the hotel and shop-keepers in Ghana's smaller localities are not yet familiar with the system and prefer to be paid in local currency.

With the exception of Accra's international hotels, best restaurants and car rental agencies, the cost of living is extremely low in Ghana. From Mole National Park or Tamale in the north to Bolgatanga on the Atlantic coast, a number of simple but charming hotels offer inexpensive room and board. In addition, the small rest houses which have been created in many of Ghana's historic coastal fortresses offer visitor accommodation for less than the price of one night at a European youth hostel.

For visitors interested in sampling the local cooking, a multitude of small local restaurants offer an unvarying but delicious fixed-price menu consisting of chicken and rice or beef-stew, plus a beverage, at rock-bottom prices.

Handicrafts also represent excellent value-for-money, but only on the condition of bargaining like Saudi camel-trader. In Ghana, as in most African countries, the customer is expected to bargain, and the rule applies to everything from hiring a taxi to purchasing a banana at the food market. In general, the initial asking-price can be knocked back three or four times, so visitors are advised to suggest a ridiculously low counter-proposition. After that, it's up to you to accept or refuse the final price. A bit of good-humoured theatrics can go a long way here, and in the event of your flat-out refusal of the "last price," the merchant will often drop it a notch lower, even if this means button-holing you in the street after your have left the shop.

Unfortunately, the system doesn't apply to car rentals. Both in Ghana and throughout all of Africa, local and international car-rental agencies are hard-nosed and inflexible, and charge exorbitant prices (particularly for four-wheel drive vehicles), when not imposing the services of a driver or the payment of a colossal security deposit. For visitors on a limited travel budget, local buses,

RELIEF, HYDROGRAPHY AND TOURISTIC ACCOMODATIO

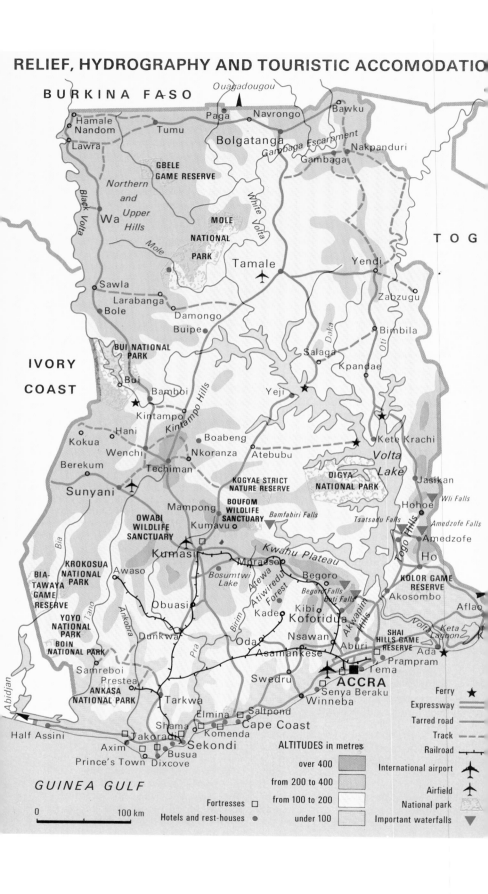

BURKINA FASO

Ouagadougou

TOG

IVORY

COAST

Hamale
Nandom
Lawra
Tumu
Paga
Navrongo
Bawku
Bolgatanga
Gambaga Escarpment
Nakpanduri
Gambaga
Gambaga

GBELE
GAME RESERVE

Northern
and
Upper
Hills

Wa

Black Volta

White Volta

MOLE
NATIONAL
PARK

Mole

Tamale

Yendi

Zabzugu

Sawla
Larabanga
Bole
Damongo
Buipe

Bimbila

Daka

Oti

BUI NATIONAL
PARK

Bui
Bamboi

Salaga

Kpandae

Kintampo

Yeji

Kete Krachi

Volta

Lake

Hani
Kokua
Wenchi
Berekum
Kintampo Hills

Boabeng
Nkoranza
Atebubu

DIGYA
NATIONAL PARK

Jasikan

Techiman

KOGYAE STRICT
NATURE RESERVE

BOUFOM
WILDLIFE
SANCTUARY

Bamfabiri Falls

Hohoe
Wli Falls

Tsatsadu Falls
Amedzofe Falls

Sunyani

Mampong

OWABI
WILDLIFE
SANCTUARY

Kumavu

Logo Hills

Amedzofe

Ho

Bia

Kumasi
Bosumtwi
Lake
Mpraeso
Kwahu Plateau
Atewa
Atiwiredu
Forest
Begoro
Begoro Falls
Boti Falls

KOLOR GAME
RESERVE
Akosombo

Aflao

KROKOSUA
NATIONAL
PARK

Awaso

Tano

BIA-
TAWAYA
GAME
RESERVE

YOYO
NATIONAL
PARK

BOIN
NATIONAL
PARK

Obuasi

Ankobra

Dunkwa

Brim

Kade
Kibi
Koforidua

Akwapim Hills

Oda
Nsawan
Aburi

Volta

Keta
Lagoon

Samreboi
Prestea

ANKASA
NATIONAL PARK

Tarkwa

Pra

Asamankese

SHAI
HILLS GAME
RESERVE
Ada

Swedru

ACCRA
Senya Beraku
Winneba

Prampram
Tema

Abidjan

Elmina
Shama
Axim
Busua
Prince's Town Dixcove

Saltpond
Komenda
Cape Coast

Half Assini

Takoradi
Sekondi

GUINEA GULF

ALTITUDES in metres

over 400	
from 200 to 400	
from 100 to 200	
under 100	

Fortresses □
Hotels and rest-houses ●

0   100 km

Ferry ★
Expressway
Tarred road
Track
Railroad
International airport ✈
Airfield ✈
National park
Important waterfalls ▼

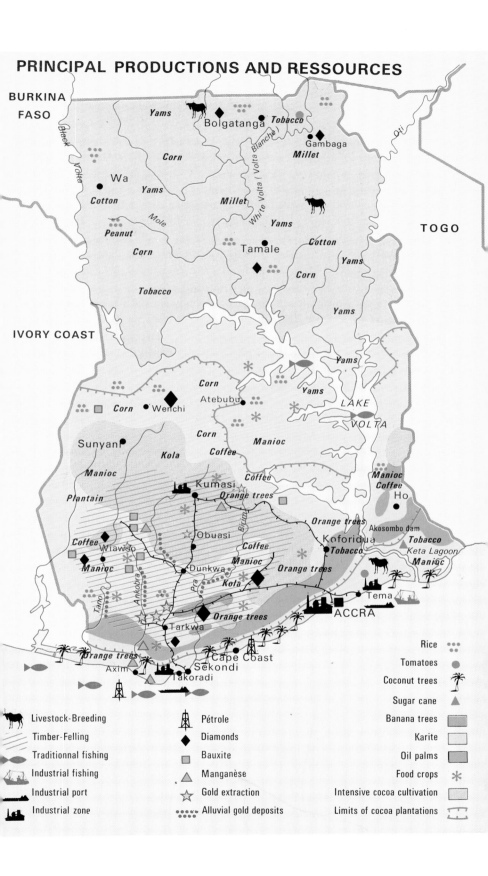

PRINCIPAL PRODUCTIONS AND RESSOURCES

BURKINA FASO

Black Volta

TOGO

Oti

Yams

Bolgatanga *Tobacco*

Corn

Gambaga

Millet

Wa

Yams

Cotton

Millet

White Volta (Volta Blanche)

Mole

Yams

Peanut

Corn

Tamale

Cotton

Corn

IVORY COAST

Yams

Tobacco

Yams

Yams

Corn

Yams

Atebubu

LAKE VOLTA

Corn

Wenchi

Corn

Manioc

Sunyani

Kola

Coffee

Manioc
Coffee
Ho

Manioc

Coffee

Kumasi

Plantain

Orange trees

Orange trees

Akosombo dam

Tobacco

Coffee

Obuasi

Wiawso

Coffee

Koforidua

Keta Lagoon

Tobacco

Manioc

Manioc

Dunkwa

Manioc

Orange trees

Kola

Pra

Tano

Ankobra

Tema

Brim

Orange trees

Tarkwa

ACCRA

Orange trees

Cape Coast

Orange trees

Sekondi

Axim

Takoradi

Livestock-Breeding	Pétrole
Timber-Felling	Diamonds
Traditionnal fishing	Bauxite
Industrial fishing	Manganèse
Industrial port	Gold extraction
Industrial zone	Alluvial gold deposits

Rice

Tomatoes

Coconut trees

Sugar cane

Banana trees

Karité

Oil palms

Food crops

Intensive cocoa cultivation

Limits of cocoa plantations

colourful "tro-tros" or the train represent an inexpensive way of getting about, if you are not particular about overcrowding, flat suspension and fixed itineraries.

Local time

Ghana officially runs on Greenwich Mean Time, which means that it is either several hours ahead or behind your home-country, depending upon the number of time-zones separating them.

The principal business hours in Ghana are as follows:

Banks are open from 8 a.m. to 4 p.m. daily, except on Fridays, when they close at 3 p.m. The banks are also closed all day Saturday and Sunday, but if necessary, money can be changed at one of the larger hotels.

Government offices are open from 8 a.m. to 12:30, and reopen from 1:30 to 5 p.m. Closed Saturdays and Sundays.

Shop hours can be variable, often in function of the day of the week. In general, however, most shops open from 8 a.m. to noon, and from 2 to 5:30 p.m. Department stores and supermarkets are closed on Saturday afternoons, and in certain cases, Wednesday afternoons as well.

There are, of course, many exceptions to all of the above. Some provincial supermarkets close well after 7 p.m., while the business hours of Ghana's innumerable small shops and open-air stalls often depend on factors ranging from the vagaries of supply-side economics to the phases of the moon. For visitors seeking local night-time colour or merely looking for a snack, Accra's Osu fisherwives sell the daily catch by the light of oil lamps, while in practically every quarter of the major cities, merchants sell roasted or boiled ears of corn, fresh fruit, fried delicacies and whole meals far into the evening — or in any case, until the movie houses let out at 10:30 p.m.

In the villages, it's advisable to try to arrive on the main market day, which occurs only once a week in some localities, but nevertheless provides an overview of everything that can be either bought or sold in the region. Street vendors can always be found plying their trade on any day of the week, and if you are simply overcome by the urge to look or buy, another major market can usually be found open in a neighbouring town. Purchasing anything at all can be a problem in the afternoons, except in the bus terminals where local "mammies" can always be found selling fruit, vegetables and freshly-cooked delicacies.

In the mornings, English or Continental-style breakfasts are served in hotel dining rooms from 6:30 or 7 a.m. on. If you enjoy having your breakfast in bed (and who doesn't?), be sure that you've chosen to stay in one of the larger hotels, since these are the only establishments offering this small but infinitely pleasurable luxury. When you start thinking about lunch, remember that restaurants serve it from noon to 2 p.m., while dinner-hours are from 7 p.m. to whenever, depending on the location and category of the establishment chosen. Thirsty visitors soon realize that at practically any hour of the day or night in Ghana, it is possible to obtain a marvellous bottle of cold beer.

In the streets of Ghana's major cities, the time of the day determines who's doing what, as well as where they're doing it. Automobile traffic is particularly heavy between noon and 2 p.m., and just like back home, from 5 to 7 p.m. The problem of finding an available taxi during these hours has been solved by the system of shared taxis, an ingenious local form of mass-transport in which each passenger descends at his or her given destination.

In the early evening, beginning at 7 or 8 p.m., the administrative and residential quarters either empty out or seemingly go to sleep, while in the popular neighbourhoods and around the movie houses, life often continues merrily into the night. Conversely, the provincial towns of Ghana are generally very calm in the evenings — an exception to the general rule prevailing in many African countries and a somewhat deceptive impression — since in reality, the inhabitants have only deserted the streets for the intimacy of the inner courtyards of their homes. One major exception to all this serenity periodically occurs in Accra during night-time soccer matches, when the reflection of the stadium floodlights illuminate half of the city and the roar of the crowd can be heard throughout the other half.

Weekends, especially in the larger and heavily-Christianized southern towns of Ghana, follow a special and invariable pattern: Saturday afternoons are reserved for weddings, while Sundays are given over to all-day religious services.

For Ghana's large Muslim population, weekly worship is conducted on Friday afternoons, while the rhythm of daily life is played out against the muezzin's call and the five prayers that are recited —

after ritual ablution — upon a rug facing the holy city of Mecca.

Ghana's Muslim and Christian populations have remained extremely faithful to their ancestral customs and traditions, and particularly to their funeral ceremonies, which generally take place on Saturdays and are quite distinct from the actual burial rites. Sacrifices and offerings are accompanied by special prayers, while much of the ceremony is conducted in the privacy of the deceased's home. The purpose of these rites is to create the optimum conditions for the journey to the afterlife and to appease the deceased's spirit in the event that it still might be wandering the limits between the visible and invisible worlds. When the deceased's family and friends finally proceed through the streets, joy rather than grief is manifested, since all has now entered into the immutable order of the cosmos. The participants, moving to the beat of ceremonial drums and brandishing garlands of ritual leaves, march through the entire city before gathering on a main square.

Quite apart from such ceremonies, but also on Saturdays, the sound of often first-rate bands and dance orchestras can be heard coming from the hotels of the bigger cities, as the population gets set for an afternoon and evening of music and relaxation. The atmosphere of these get-togethers is often curiously restrained, evidence of the continuing influence of Protestant pastors.

Legal holidays

Ghana has eight legal holidays per year:
— New Year's Day (January 1),
— Independence Day (March 6),
— Good Friday,
— Holy Saturday,
— Easter Monday,
— Republic Day (July 1),
— Christmas,
— Boxing Day (the day after Christmas).

Postal services and telecommunications

The Ghanaian postal system and telecommunications services have recently been automated. Modern and efficient mail, telephone, fax and telex facilities are available in all of the larger cities, and are linked both to the interior of the country and the rest of the world.

Personal mail can be stamped and mailed at your hotel, which will generally possess its own mail-box. Air mail letters from Ghana take from two to three days to arrive in Europe, but somewhat longer to reach destinations elsewhere in the world.

Many of the larger hotels such as the Accra Novotel offer direct dialing to overseas numbers, but be sure to check for time differences before calling. Since long-distance calls are fairly expensive, il's a good idea to reverse charges or use an international telephone credit card.

Fax and telex can also be sent from the High Street annex of the main post office in Accra. For calling within the country, visitors may find it handy to purchase a local "telecard," accepted by an increasing number of public telephones in Ghana. The telephones in the main post office are equipped with a counter which indicates the number of call-units consumed during your conversation, but as overseas calls are expensive, it's best to be as brief as possible.

Overseas dialing from Accra: International routing is obtained by dialing 00, followed by your country and city codes and the number of the party you want to reach. To get New York from Accra, for example, dial 00, wait for the buzz-tone, then dial 1 (for the United States), followed by 212 (for New York city) and the local number desired.

The principal country-codes of Europe and North America are as follows:
Belgium: 32
Canada: 1
France: 33
Germany: 49
Great Britain: 44
Italy: 39
Netherlands: 31
Switzerland: 41
United States: 1

Receiving international calls in Accra: To dial direct, your caller should compose the appropriate international-access code, followed by 233 (for Ghana), 21 (Accra area code) and your number in Accra. Person-to-person calls should be made through your caller's local operator.

Useful numbers

The following is a short list of useful numbers in Accra for handy reference:
British Airways: 22.83.73 and 66.78.00.
Ghana Airways: 66.48.56/22.19.01.
Kotoka-Accra Airport: 77.61.71.
Ambulance Service: 999.

Eternal femininity:
this young woman is having
her hair braided in her shop,
where she sells a great choice of
traditional ''wax'' garments.

Hospitals: 66.54.01 and 22.83.82.
Main Post Office: 22.10.01.

Road traffic and metric system

As in many other countries having a British colonial heritage, Ghana's automobilists used to drive on the left, calculate their speed in terms of miles rather than kilometres-per-hour and purchase their gasoline in gallons instead of litres. Since 1974, however, the nation has joined the international metric mainstream, and now, as in the neighbouring countries of Togo, Burkina-Faso, the Ivory Coast and practically everywhere else in the world, traffic moves on the right and the language of metres, litres and centimetres is spoken by one and all. There nevertheless remain certain vestiges of the glory days when tomatoes were sold by the pound rather than the kilo, and if you should be tempted by the purchase of Ghanaian fabrics, know that cloth merchants, ever-faithful to tradition, calculate in feet (30.4 centimetres) and yards (0.914 metres).

Electrification

The Akosombo Dam and hydro-electric complex provides nearly all of Ghana with standard 222-volt current. Particularly isolated villages and regions (such as Mole National Park) generate their own current, and are perhaps wise to do so, since during the rainy season, storms have the habit of knocking out much of Ghana's national power grid. During moments such as these, be sure to disconnect your lap-top computer or portable CD player, since when the current comes on again, they may be blown out by the power-surge!

Health hints

Overall, the health and medical infrastructure in Ghana is quite adequate. Most cities and towns have their pharmacies, clinics, hospitals and well-trained medical personnel, and one need not be overly preoccupied by the question of one's general well-being.

As for tropical diseases, the only real risk for most visitors is contracting malaria, after having been bitten by an infected mosquito. Since the Ghanaian mosquitoes do bite, the solution lies either in avoiding them totally (impossi-ble) or more reasonably, to begin a daily treatment of quinine tablets before leaving to build up your resistance, continue the treatment on a daily basis once you're in Ghana, and to follow through for six weeks after you've returned home. Although this implies quite a bit of tablet-taking, your malaria-free body will thank you for the effort invested , even as your unworried spirit will be free to pursue the pleasures of the Ghanaian voyage. To further protect yourself, and for your general comfort as well, anti-mosquito lotions and insect sprays can be effective, as is turning up the air-conditioning in your hotel room if it is so equipped.

One other common inconvenience familiar to travellers in tropical countries the world over is a form of intestinal malfunction called, not without a certain sense of irony, "Montezuma's Revenge," or more prosaically, diarrhea. General rules which aid in either avoiding or limiting its effects include the consumption of fresh fruit such as pineapples and mangoes in reasonable quantities, drinking bottled and not-too-chilled water, avoiding temperature extremes and if it's already too late for any of the above, a bland rice diet, specialized medication and plenty of rest until things calm down.

Health-wise, it's also a good idea to avoid trekking through mud during the rainy season, and to provide yourself with a good umbrella, since colds can come on quickly in the alternating heat, cool and damp of the season.

And when the sun comes back out again, watch out for over-exposure, particularly on the beach, pool-side or lakefronts. Treat yourself to a total-protection sun cream, and for the first few days, limit your exposure time if you don't want to turn out terminally over-developed.

For trekking safaris in one of the national parks, in addition to a water canteen or bottle, be sure to bring along a hat and sun cream, since the savannas that you'll be traversing offer little in the way of shade or protection from the elements.

Tipping and social conduct

To tip or not to tip: in Ghana, this is often the question. In many restaurants the service charge is included in the check along with local taxes, and comes to about 20 percent of the bill. In other cases, only the taxes are included. However, even when the tip is included, some waiters will do their best to make you feel that it is not, or that at least a further effort to secure their ultimate financial independence would be highly appreciated if not absolutely imperative. Paradoxically, in the cases where the tip is not included, some waiters — perhaps out of compassion for people whose home-countries are so uninteresting that they must pay large sums of money to go elsewhere — may express a high degree of astonishment at the sight of any amount in excess of that already appearing on the bill. In still other situations, a trifling few hundred cedis will be received with effusive gratitude, while in others, the recipient will suggest that the situation calls for a least several thousand more, even if in both cases, the service rendered was exactly the same.

In fact, the question of the service to be renumerated or of the gift to be given is an extremely delicate one, and should be approached on a case-by-case basis. If it's perfectly normal to tip a park attendant or a local youngster who's guided you for an afternoon, the same gesture may be misinterpreted by someone who has taken the time to direct you to a village curiosity or point of interest, particularly if he happens to be a local dignitary, schoolteacher or merely a particularly hospitable passerby. In this case, the appropriate gesture will be your sincere thanks, perhaps followed by an invitation to become better-acquainted over a few bottles of cold beer.

When visiting certain *kraals*, you may be made to feel that a financial contribution would be appreciated. Elsewhere, even in the poorest villages, your spontaneous gift of money to the village chief may result in his reciprocating with the gift of a live chicken, leaving you with the impression that despite your well-meaning sincerity, somehow things have gone wrong. If the world over money talks (when it is not shouting its head off), many Ghanaians are not particularly interested in hearing what it has to say, having not yet forgotten that basic human sentiments carry an even more powerful message. In this sense, your friendliness and concern might be better expressed through more personalized gifts — medicine for the sick, a lighter or cigarettes for a smoker, or items of food unavailable in the local markets.

By and large, the Ghanaians enjoy being photographed and may even nonchalantly go out of their way to appear in the frame of your camera or camescope. For others, the mere sight of a camera of any type is enough to send them into a blind fury that can occasionally develop into real violence. The only way to intelligently navigate between these two extremes is to systematically ask the permission of the people you want to photograph or film. An even surer approach is to wait until they ask you, as they often will. In remote villages where English may not even be spoken, it's a good idea to keep your photo equipment slung unobtrusively over your shoulder, while trying not to give the impression that your unique objective in being there is to to capture the entire population on film. There'll usually be at least one child who will eventually come over to see what you're up to, and timidly let you know that he or she is willing to be ulteriorly projected upon your living room wall in living Kodacolor. Once the ice has been broken, you can expect the rest of the village to good - naturedly follow suit, with the merriment lasting right through your last roll of film or videotape cartridge.

Visitors should also remember that an authorization to photograph is obligatory, and is obtainable from the Ministry of Information in Accra. In addition, a certain number of buildings and areas are off-limits to photographers; these include airports and government agencies in and around Accra.

The etiquette here is simplicity itself: whatever the age and sex of two persons who meet, the one who arrives first offers the initial greeting, whether indoors or on the street. By extension, visitors arriving in a new village should acknowledge the presence — even if only by a perfunctory nod of the head — of the people encountered along the way, since as a newcomer, it is expected that you make the initial overture. Try it and see: the slightest sign of polite recognition produces volumes of affability in even the most impassive of Ghanaians.

When entering or leaving a house, it is also customary to shake hands with everyone present, proceeding from right to left, and regardless of the social rank or one's degree of friendship with the individuals present.

In Ghana, when two friends meet, they express their pleasure by bringing their respective palms together with a resounding smack. Upon taking leave, they shake hands by gripping each other's middle fingers in such a way that the latter make a snapping sound when their hands separate. Visitors not accustomed to such auditory phenomena may be somewhat

The fortress of Cape Coast, Ghana's largest,
was long occupied by European colonists from many nations.
Under the British, the fortress was the home of
the poetess Elizabeth Landon, whose tomb can still
be seen in the middle of the main courtyard.

getting around ghana

taken aback at first, but one rapidly becomes used to this convivial little gesture, which can signify both the pleasure of seeing an old friend, or even a particularly pleasurable first encounter with a total stranger.

As in all Muslim countries, the use of the right hand always takes precedence over the left. Visitors should therefore avoid giving or receiving anything, pointing to or even greeting someone with the left hand. As strange as it may seem to Westerners, another act of blatant rudeness is to cross one's legs in such a way that the end of your shoe points towards the person facing you.

As you will undoubtedly have the pleasure of discovering for yourself, Ghanaian hospitality is legendary, and is perhaps exceeded only by their sensitivity towards others, be they family, friends or total strangers. To the same extent that a Ghanaian will generously offer gifts of friendship, it is also customary for the receiver to reciprocate by enthusiastic and repeated expressions of gratitude for what has been so sincerely given. Proud of their country, Ghanaians enjoy hearing fulsome praise of its merits; and if your compliments aren't offered quickly enough, don't be astonished if your interlocutor begins "fishing" for them.

Like all Africans worthy of the name, Ghanaians want to be liked. Convivial and naturally outgoing themselves, it is of vital importance to their own sense of well-being that others show an interest in all that makes up their life: their customs, their art and even, in some cases, their very souls. Above all, they want you to recognize their essential uniqueness, and on a more general level, to distinguish them from their neighbours.

Given this context, the key to a Ghanaian's heart lies in any visitor's reach, providing that he is sincerely interested in using it. Throughout the Ghanaian countryside, people of all social stations and walks of life will be eager to explain whatever the visitor doesn't understand or simply wants to know more about. In exchange, visitors will find themselves deluged by an endless series of questions aimed at gaining an insight into what is perceived as the exotic and often perplexing mysteries of Western life. These impromptu sessions of cross-cultural interrogation can be as revealing for the visitor as they are to his Ghanaian counterpart, and are an essential part of getting to know the country and its people.

By air

Ghana Airways is not only an international carrier serving Africa and a number of European capitals, but also schedules local flights on Fokker 28s to several towns and cities located in Ghana's interior. It is thus possible, if one so desires, to fly from Accra to Kumasi once a week, and from Accra to the northern city of Tamale twice a week.

The main and regional offices of Ghana Airways are as follows: Accra: Ghana House, P.O. Box 1636, tel: 66.48.56; Cocoa House, P.O. Box 1636, tel: 22.19.01 or 22.11.50; White Avenue Offices, Airport Residential Area, tel: 77.31.21, 77.33.41 or 77.60.61; Accra-Kotoka Airport: P.O. Box 1636, tel: 77.61.71 or 77.74.06. Bolgatanga: Ghana Commercial Bank Building, tel: 23.48. Kumasi: Adum Street, P.O. Box 299, tel: 38.33, 37.81 or 63.21. Sunyani: P.O. Box 368, tel: 271 or 272. Tamale: Dagomba Road Junction, P.O. Box 10, tel: 20.85 or 27.86. Takoradi: Prince of Wales Road, P.O. Box 64, tel: 22.85.

By rail

Ghana's rail network, constructed to facilitate the transport of the country's ore and timber, is particularly scenic. The line connecting Accra to Kumasi via Koforidua, Asuboni, Nkawkaw and Kononga runs parallel to the Kwahu foothills, offering travellers spectacular views of its lovely landscapes. However, since this line was not created with tourism in mind, the train stops are mainly located in semi-industralized centres such as the gold-mining town of Konongo.

From Kumasi, located in central Ghana, a second line descends to the west coast in the direction of Sekondi, via Obuasi, Dunkwa (with a branch line to Awaso, the centre of the lumber industry), Huni Valley and Tarkwa, all of which are mining towns.

At Huni Valley, a third line runs to Accra and Tema, with branch lines to other mining towns such as Oda and Kade.

Two major projects are being undertaken to extend the line from Awaso to Sunyani through the timberland and timber-processing regions, and to build a branch line from Bosuso to Kibi and its neighbouring bauxite deposits.

In reality, there is no particular reason for visitors to choose the train over other forms of transport, except between

Dunkwa and Sekondi (on the Sekondi-Kumasi line to the west) pending completion of the repair and paving of the Dunkwa-Tarkwa highway. On the other hand, the extension of the line from Awaso to Sunyani will constitute an excellent stimulus for the development of the region, which is blessed with Ghana's finest forests but practically without roads. The project should consequently bring tourism to a fascinating semi-virgin territory that fully merits discovery by visitors.

As elsewhere throughout Africa, the drawback to train travel is that the rail system was originally designed principally for the transport of merchandise rather than passengers. Visitors should therefore not expect the same level of organization and service as in Europe or North America. Timetables and train schedules simply do not exist, nor is it possible to reserve so much as a seat in an Accra or Kumasi travel agency. For a visitor determined to experience rail travel in Ghana, the only solution is to make one's way to Accra's central station (located on Kwame Nkrumah Avenue), get in line, find out the departure-time of the next train out, buy a ticket (non-refundable and valuable only on the same day that it has been issued), and try to find a seat.

Fortunately for those who wouldn't think of travelling any other way, rail transport is gaining increasing attention in the higher spheres of Ghanaian decision-making circles, where the creation of a modern rail system is currently under consideration. The current availability of blue and white Express trains (with first and second-class compartments) has already improved the overall level of Ghanaian rail travel. It can only be hoped that the government will continue in this direction; the creation of a computerized reservation system would also be a most welcome initiative.

By boat

A boat trip on Lake Volta constitutes one of the choicest moments of any voyage to Ghana. Entirely man-made and one of the largest artificial bodies of water in the world, Lake Volta stretches from Akosombo Dam in the south to the

DISTANCES BY ROAD (IN KM)

	Accra	Bolgatanga	Cape Coast	Ho	Kintampo	Koforidua	Kumasi	Sekondi	Sunyani	Tamale	Tema	Wa	Yendi
Accra	0	810	144	165	478	85	270	218	400	658	29	740	754
Bolgatanga	810	0	779	914	350	752	558	853	470	170	839	368	266
Cape Coast	144	779	0	309	429	229	221	74	351	609	173	691	705
Ho	165	914	309	0	564	162	356	362	486	476	135	790	380
Kintampo	478	350	429	564	0	402	208	503	120	180	507	280	276
Koforidua	85	752	229	162	402	0	194	303	324	582	114	664	678
Kumasi	270	558	221	356	208	194	0	242	130	388	299	470	484
Sekondi	218	853	74	362	503	303	242	0	372	683	247	765	779
Sunyani	400	470	351	486	120	324	130	372	0	300	429	378	396
Tamale	658	170	609	476	180	582	388	683	300	0	687	314	96
Tema	29	839	173	135	507	114	299	247	429	687	0	769	515
Wa	740	368	691	790	280	664	470	765	378	314	769	0	410
Yendi	754	266	705	380	276	678	484	779	396	96	515	410	0
	Accra	Bolgatanga	Cape Coast	Ho	Kintampo	Koforidua	Kumasi	Sekondi	Sunyani	Tamale	Tema	Wa	Yendi

*Even when full-up, there's always room
for one more on the roof! Whatever the season,
bush taxis, "mammy trucks" and "tro-tros" can be counted
on to arrive at their destination after
epic voyages through the Ghanaian countryside.*

outskirts of Tamale in the north. Three days are necessary to traverse the lake from Akosombo Marina to the newly-created port of Buipe, some 418 kilometres distant.

The landscapes are magnificent, ranging from the heavily-forested mountains in the south to the rolling savannas of the north. Sunsets over the lake are among the most breathtaking in the world, and largely compensate for the notable absence of creature comforts encountered during the voyage. The boats that ply the lake are principally merchandise transports; there are no restaurant facilities aboard, nor cabins, and since passengers sleep on the deck, visitors are therefore advised to make the voyage other than during the rainy season. The government is contemplating the creation of a modern car-ferry complete with the last word in passenger comfort.

The main route over the lake runs from Akosombo to Buipe, via Kpandu and Keta-Krachi (Eastern Region). A second route serves the lake's western reaches (Akosombo-Adowso) and still a third attains the shores of Dambai and Oti-Domanko in the east.

Sailings from Akosombo to Buipe theoretically occur every Monday morning, with information on arrival and departure times as well as specially-organized excursions available from the *Volta Lake Company*, P.O. Box 75, Akosombo.

Visitors planning a crossing on Lake Volta should remember to bring a sleeping bag, a three-day supply of food and a plentiful reserve of water or soft drinks.

By highway (and byway)

In many regions, Ghana's highway network holds only pleasant surprises for motorists. In the south, the southeast and along the coast to the west, even secondary roads are paved.

A modern highway also runs from Accra to Kumasi in the Ashanti Region, and continues north via Techiman and Kintampo (Brong-Ahafo Region), Tamale (Northern Region) to Bolgatanga (Upper Region).

Public transportation is also well organized. The State Transport Corporation's highly comfortable green coaches cover practically the entire country, are regularly scheduled and, most importantly, take on no more passengers than can realistically fit inside. On any given voyage, travellers can therefore be certain of not being obliged to find seating accommodations on the roof. Offering the possibility of travelling comfortably from Accra to any number of major cities and small towns, the coaches also represent a source of considerable savings for visitors on a limited budget, even if other means of transport must eventually be employed to reach some of the more remote villages or points of interest.

As may be expected, two such means exist. The first are the local taxis, which can be hired (by a group of three or four persons) at a reasonable price for half and full-day excursions. Many of the points of interest in the greater-Kumasi area can be visited in this manner. As ever, remember to bargain as if your life depended on it, and never even put your foot through the door without having first agreed on a fixed price for the distance to be covered as well as the exact rental period. But before doing any of the above, try and get an idea of the going rate for your projected excursion by inquiring at your hotel. And as for the second...

Whatever you do, don't leave Ghana without having a go at the incomparable "mammy trucks" and "tro-tros." Purists establish a clear distinction between the two, since theoretically the former are bigger than the latter, and perhaps slightly less bizarre in appearance. If to the casual observer the difference is minimal, what is certain is that both types of vehicles regularly defy all the known laws of Newtonian physics. As for their mechanical condition and upkeep, most look as if they haven't seen a wrench or screwdriver since leaving the factory, years before most visitors were even born. And yet, they *do* run...

As the first waves of culture-shock subside, the visitor, much like an explorer discovering the hieroglyphics of some unknown civilization, will begin to notice a series of messages, each one stranger and more incomprehensible than the next, adorning the front or rear of the vehicles.

These messages can range from religious themes such as "With God's aid, all is possible" to the more esoteric "Confidence," "Truth," or "The times are changing, my friend", and although the wry humour of some of the inscriptions will immediately be apparent to even the uninitiated, others can only be appreciated after their true savour and subtility has been revealed by someone familiar with their deeper, more cosmic implications, in this case, usually one of the crew-members or even the driver himself.

To be perfectly frank, you'll need a healthy amount of cosmic humour yourself to endure a voyage in which you'll find your knees squeezed up against a conspicuously unpadded seat-back, while all about you, an inextricable mass of humanity, merchandise and domestic animals struggle to maintain themselves more or less right-side-up as the hours and kilometres joltingly unwind.

"Mammy trucks" are so called because of their predominantly female clientele, who generally never travel other than in the company of bundles of fish, yams, assorted fruit, palm wine or what-have-you. The advantage for visitors is that here, the already-rich visual possibilities afforded by the presence of fellow passengers and the passing countryside is enhanced by the deeper, and perhaps for some, more satisfying encounter with its olfactory characteristics.

It would be wishful thinking to expect these vehicles to comply with anything resembling a schedule or timetable.

Since false modesty is not a characteristic of the "tro-tros" and "mammy trucks", they can often be found proudly plying their trade even within the capital city of Accra itself. And this despite the presence, as in all of Ghana's major towns, of a doughty fleet of red and yellow buses. With their extremely low fares, buses are an unbeatably economical means of getting about, as well as constituting a particularly efficient way of seeing the city. But like public transportation elsewhere in the world, we don't recommend taking them during rush hours.

Taxis and car rental

As mentioned earlier, Ghanaian taxi drivers, perhaps because they believe it beneath so noble a calling, have thus far disdained the use of the taxi-meter. To avoid being held for ransom at the end of the trip, visitors are therefore advised to negotiate a price well before starting out. It's also wise to avoid hailing one near the entrance of the larger hotels, to avoid the informal but invariable "luxury tax" that drivers feel justified in applying to what they consider to be well-off clients.

The majority of Ghanaian taxis are also profoundly democratic, which is to say collective. This means that after innumerable detours to collect and drop off other passengers, visitors will be asked to pay a fare corresponding to the hypothetical point-to-point distance co-vered had they been the only occupant. It's a fair enough system and offers the opportunity of making the acquaintance of local inhabitants and often obtaining valuable bits of local and regional information.

Despite these obvious charms, it is undeniably more practical to rent one's own car for any extended trip through the country. Ghanaian car rental agencies offer daily, weekly and monthly rates, but these unfortunately do not include unlimited mileage. All types of vehicles are nevertheless available, and with or without a driver. Once again, all of the agencies are located in Accra, and all are expensive, particularly for the rental of four-wheel drive vehicles. Accra's leading rental companies include Hertz, Avis, Budget and Europcar.

Road hazards

Visitors conducting their own vehicle or a rental car should remember that African roads can present special conditions for which European or American motorists are not always prepared. All tropical countries experience torrential rainfalls during several months out of every year. These rains often wash away roads to a greater or lesser extent, depending on the relief and nature of the soil. It is therefore wise not to plan covering long distances if you are not absolutely sure of the road conditions, particularly during or after the rainy season. Visitors taking to the roads during the rainy season should check with the local bus terminals for information concerning the condition of highways and secondary roads, which may be impracticable even in four-wheel drive vehicles.

Fuel is widely available in most of the country. However, since both the Eastern Region between Yendi and Jasikan and the Western Region are sparsely populated, fueling your vehicle may be difficult if not impossible. Motorists are therefore advised to take along ample reserves of both fuel and drinking water, as well as several spare tires when travelling through Ghana's outlying regions.

As mentioned previously, traffic moves on the right since 1974, but motorists should be prepared to encounter wildlife in all shapes and sizes travelling on either side of the road at any moment of the day or night, and are therefore urged to drive with all the prudence and attention that this eventuality requires. Local drivers practically never dim their headlights when meeting another car at night, so if you're easily dazzled by oncoming lights or subject to night blindness, it's better to travel during the daylight hours.

Since police checks are frequent at the exits of major cities and towns, as well as in international border zones and between neighbouring regions, motorists are advised to keep their passports and car registration papers within easy reach.

With the exception of signs announcing certain larger cities and towns, the frequency of road markers varies from region to region, while the distance between two localities is almost never mentioned.

Road maps and trekking

Motorists in Ghana will imperatively need a reliable road map. We particularly recommend both Shell Petroleum's and KLM Royal Dutch Airline's road maps of Ghana, available in all of Accra's bookstores as well as at some of the larger hotels.

Ghana's unique "foot (trekking) safaris" in Mole National Park offer visitors the possibility of car-free contact with nature and close encounters with park wildlife, including antelope, monkeys, elephants, lions and leopards.

Sightseeing tours

The majority of Accra's travel agencies issue tickets for international air carriers, but few offer organized tours of Ghana. It's nevertheless a good idea to contact them once you're there, since they can offen provide excellent advice concerning your own visit to the country.

Some of the more helpful agencies are: *Akuba Tourist and Travel Agency*, Republic House Annex, Liberty Avenue, P.O. Box 2059 Accra, Tel: 233.21.80.20 or 22.40.22. *Pan African Travel and Tours, Ltd.*, Republic House Annex, Kwame Nkrumah Avenue, P.O. Box 5419, Accra, Tel: 233.21.22.68 or 22.54.05.

The following is a brief list of suggested sights and itineraries in function of the length of time available to visitors: *Half-day tour:* Rapid sightseeing in Accra and a visit to the National Museum. *Full-day tour:* Sightseeing in Accra in the morning, and a visit to Aburi Botanical Gardens in the afternoon.

A two - to five - day trip: The Atlantic coast and the old Portuguese fortifications (Elmina, Cape Coast, Axim, etc.). Or alternatively, a visit to Kumasi, capital of the Ashanti Region (cultural centre, fortifications, zoo, etc.), and the Obuasi gold mines. A tour of Lake Bosumtwi, the Kibi Forest and the Kwahu Mountains.

Third possibility: The East Coast (Tema, the littoral from Ada to Keta) and Lake Volta (Ho, Hpandu, Hohoe).

A week's tour: Boat trip on Lake Volta, from Akosombo to Buipe and return by car.

From two to three weeks: Grand tour of the Northern Region. From Accra to Mole National Park, the Larabanga Mosques, chieftainries of Wa and Zebilla, decorated houses between Navrongo and Bakwu, etc.

From Ghana to...

Situated between the Ivory Coast to the west, Burkina-Faso on the north and Togo to the east, Ghana is centrally located for travellers who desire to visit her neighbouring countries.

From Ghana to the Ivory Coast: A well-paved coastal road takes you from Accra to Abidjan, the capital of the Ivory Coast. Stop-overs at the seaside resorts of Assinie and Grand-Bassam.

From Ghana to Burkina-Faso: An excellent highway runs from northern Ghana (Navrongo, Paga) to Burkina-Faso's capital, Ouagadougou. Stop-overs at Po National Park south of Ouagadougou, celebrated for its majestic herds of elephants.

From Ghana to Togo: The Accra-Tema freeway, followed by a good highway, leads to Togo's capital city Lome, located just accross the border from the Ghanaian city of Aflao. Continuing east, a coastal road runs to Lake Togo (resort area and water sports), Benin (the beaches of Grand-Popo, the Ouidah Museum and the lakeside villages of Ganvie, just outside Benin's capital city Cotonou). From Accra, Togo can also be reached via the Akosombo Dam, the Ho country and thence to the border town of Dafo. Stop-overs in the Klouto Hills (hotel and camping facilities), and the charming Togolese village of Kpalime, located in the centre of a region of cocoa plantations, streams and waterfalls.

traditional festivals

■ Even more than its picture-postcard beaches, visitors to Ghana will appreciate the country's fascinating heritage of rituals and ancestral traditions. In addition to her many festivals, Ghana also offers the possibility of practising sports such as swimming, tennis, golf, fishing and sailing, as well as activities such as trekking safaris and game hunts.

Traditional celebrations

Among Ghana's many traditional celebrations, some of the most interesting are those that accompany the bestowing of a name upon an infant shortly after its birth, the initiation rites that symbolize the passage from adolescence to adulthood, and marriage and funeral ceremonies.

Each ethnic group and every town or village also has its own annual festival, serving to strengthen inter-personal bonds. These may include inter-tribal reconciliations, or the renewal of pledges of fidelity to chiefs and ancestors who are considered as forming an invisible link to the world of their present-day subjects and descendants. Such festivals may vary considerably in their form, the period in which they occur and their underlying significance, but by their sheer diversity they testify to the richness of Ghana's cultural heritage while constituting an ongoing source of fascination for visitors.

In a general manner, these celebrations also commemorate historical events endowed with a special significance for the inhabitants of a given locality, or the members of an ethnic group or clan. In many cases, festivals also mark the beginning or end of harvest seasons, the purification of ancestor' stools or the pacification of a divinity. But whatever their form or purpose, all are based on the belief in an invisible universe peopled by supernatural beings whose thoughts and actions influence the events and inhabitants of the material world.

During the *Kuntum* festival, celebrated by the Nzima and the Ahanta on the west coast, participants are granted the right to insult their neighbours and ridiculize their superiors. Faults and shortcomings are mercilessly exposed, while the "victims" are obliged to listen to a long litany of complaints and criticisms without being able to respond.

A similar ritual takes place during the *Gologo* festival in the north of Ghana, during which villagers mock the physical and moral imperfections of their neighbours.

Other ceremonies exist for the ritual exorcism of collectively-feared catastrophies and natural calamities. During the Ga's *Homowo* celebration held near Accra, the spectre of famine is mocked in the hope of humiliating it so badly as to usher in a period of abundance.

Ritual ceremonies may also involve the testing of the courage and skills of adolescents. In the *Ayerye* festival, the sons of Fanti warriors demonstrate their military prowess in mock battles between opposing clans.

Another ritual, known as the *Winneba Deer Hunt*, formerly involved capturing a leopard barehanded. The toll on human life eventually became so prohibitive that the divinity to whom the leopard was sacrificed was beseeched to accept a less dangerous substitute, and the leopard was replaced by an antelope.

Among the festivals based on historical themes, the *Papa* celebration of the village of Kumawu serves to exorcise the negative connotations stemming from the name of the locality, which literally signifies "dead branch." The underlying story concerns a decision made by the celebrated King Osei Tutu. At the moment when the king was choosing the location of his future capital, he planted two twigs from a Kum tree, one of which symbolized Kumawu and the other Kumasi. The twig symbolizing Kumasi flowered, and both Kumawu and its inhabitants were left behind as the court relocated to the new city. The inhabitants of Kumawu were ultimately able to save face in 1699, when one of their chiefs offered himself in sacrifice to obtain victory over the oppressor Dankyira.

In many instances, festivals are also occasions for renewing the bonds between one's ancestors and tribal divinities. The *Adae* festival celebrated by the Ashantis is based on their annual calendar, divided into nine cycles of forty days. Each cycle is the occasion of a celebration held either on a Sunday (*Akwasidae*) or a Wednesday (*Awukudae*), the purpose of which is to render hommage to the Ashanti ancestors while soliciting the ongoing protection of their descendants.

Offerings and "Durbars"

In general, most ritual offerings are divided into two phases: the rites which are observed in private, including sacrifices to divinities and ancestors, ritual libations and incantational magic.

Once this is accomplished, the public celebration commences, during which the village chief dons his finest regalia and displays all the symbols of his power and prestige. Enthroned upon on a palanquin and protected by a splendid canopy, the local chieftain is paraded through the village by retainers and members of his court dressed in their best ceremonial finery. These rituals or *Durbars* draw huge crowds which gather to renew their pledge of fidelity and allegiance to their leader. As the Durbar festivities spread to every street of the village, the inhabitants joyfully sing and dance, accompanied by ritual drums often used solely on these occasions. There is nothing religious about these festivities, and the same type of celebration may take place in honor of the arrival of an illustrious guest or important visitor.

The annual cycle

JANUARY: In the Northern Region, the town of Walewale holds the *Bugum* festival to commemorate the finding of a lost son by an ancient king. *Ramadan* is the occasion for the Muslim community of Bole (Northern Region) to celebrate the arrival of the New Year. January also marks the holding of the Rice Festival of Akpafu (Volta Region), as well as the *Kpini-Kyiu* and *Tenghana* festivals of Wa and Tongu (Upper Region), and the *Denso Abaim* and *Ntoa Fukokuese* festivals of Techimentia and Nkoranza (Brong-Ahafo Region).

MARCH: In Walewale, the *Damba* festival commemorates the birth of Mohammed. There is also *Asikloe*, held in Anfoega in the Volta Region, while in the Region of Akuse, *Volo* commemorates the end of the exodus of the Volo people from Togo, forced to flee the tyranny of an impious ruler. Other festivals taking place in March include *Lekoyi*, held in at Likpe (Volta Region), *Kotokyikyi* and *Ogyapa* at Senya Beraku (Central Region), the *Kurubie* at Namase (Brong-Ahafo Region), the *Lalue Kpledo* at Prampram, *Dipo* at Manya and Yiko Krobo (Eastern Region).

APRIL: The *Damba* festival of Bole marks the end of the year and the beginning of a new annual cycle. The *Bugum, Serpeemi* and *Wodomi* festivals are occasions for the Krobo people of the Eastern Region to assemble. In the Northern Region, *Bugum* and *Dam* are celebrated by the Dagombas.

MAY: In addition to the "Deer Hunt" mentioned above, May is also the month of the *Beng* festival, honouring the great fetish of the Gonja people and held at Sonyo Kipo, near Bole (Northern Region). The *Osudoku* festival, held near Asutsuare (Eastern Region), marks the beginning of the New Year. Other festivals include *Donkyi*, at Namase (Brong-Ahafo Region) and *Don*, held at Bolga in the Upper Region.

The blessing of the ancestors

JUNE: An important month, since it includes the purification of the divinity *Assafua* by the inhabitants of Sekondi; *Ahumkan* of the Akim of Kibi, a celebration in which the local population reaffirm their loyalty to their chieftains; *Gyenprem*, held at Fafo, marked by a Durbar of thanksgiving for an abundant harvest and a year of peace; *Ahobaa*, in Enyan-Kakraba near Saltpond, for obtaining the benediction of the ancestors; *Kete*, in honour of the Kete-Kyen fetish at Sekondi; *Ebisa*, in honour of the fetish of the same name, also in the Sekondi Region; *Kli-Adzim*, in honour of the local divinity of Agbozume; *Ahoba Kuma* in Abura, and *Apiba* at Senya Beraku, both in the Central Region.

JULY: The inhabitants of Elmina celebrate *Bakatue* to commemorate the founding of their city, while in Sekondi — certainly Ghana's city of festivals — the population celebrates *Bombei*, as well as the *Ekyen Kofie*, the "Yam Harvest" festival and *Kuntum*. For visitors particularly fascinated by this vegetable, still another "Yam Festival" takes place at Enyam-Maim in the Central Region, while those simply interested by festivals of any sort will surely want to take in *Wodomi* at Manya Krobo in the Eastern Region.

AUGUST: Another month rich in festivals, which include *Asafotu-Fiam* in the Ada country, commemorating the conquest of the territory during the seventeenth century by the ancestors of the inhabitants; *Ahoba Kese*, held in Abura (Central Region); *Edim Kese* — once again in Sekondi and marked by a Durbar; *Equadoto* at Ayeldu near Cape Coast, in honour of the ancestors, and *Homowo*, in the Accra Region, to com-

outdoor activities

memorate the hardships endured during the fourteenth century migrations to the territory. For visitors possessing the time and stamina, *Apatwa*, held at Dixcove, lasts almost a month; for those interested in the afterlife, *Awubia* held in Awutu to the west of Accra celebrates the memory of the dead, while for the living, *Fetu Afahye* is the occasion for the inhabitants of Cape Coast to don their finest regalia at the moment of the renewal of their pledge of loyalty to their chief.

SEPTEMBER: Festivals include *Akwambo* and *Ayerye* in Enyam-Maim; the "Yam Harvest" festival of Ho; *Abaadze-Dominase* near Saltpond, and in the same region, *Akwambo* and *Abangye*. *Akyempem* is held in Agona in the Ashanti Region, and the *Fetu* at Cape Coast (Central Region).

OCTOBER: The time of the *Kundum* festival of the Nzima and the *Ohumkyire*, identical to the *Ohumkam*, and also celebrated in Kibi.

NOVEMBER: The *Fao*, a harvest festival, is given by the inhabitants of Paga, near Bolgatanga in honour of their gods. Other celebrations in November include *Bohyenhuo* and *Atweaba*, both of which take place in the Ashanti Region.

DECEMBER: The ubiquitous yams are once again honoured, but this time in Anfoega; *Odwira*, the main festival for the purification of the sacred stools is held by the Akim; *Tutu*, in Assin-Manso (Central Region) lasts two weeks and celebrates the memory of the ancestors represented on the totem-stool of the head chief; *Eeok*, held in Sandema (Upper Region), honours the victory of the inhabitants' ancestors over slave raiders, while *Afahye* in Assin-Manso is a new year's celebration featuring a lavish Durbar.

Water and land sports

On most of Ghana's beaches, ocean swimming requires the utmost prudence due to the violence of the surf and undertow. Localities offering calmer waters can nevertheless be found along the west coast, whose beaches are protected by innumerable promontories and capes.

Among the principal beaches and resorts from west to east are Axim and Busua; the littoral between Sekondi and Takoradi; the region from Elmina to Cape Coast; Biriwa and Winneba; Accra (Riviera Beach and New Labadi Beach); the Acapulco Club, 16 kilometres to the east of Accra; Paradise Beach (30 kilometres east); Prampram (50 kilometres east); and Ada and Keta Beaches.

River swimming is also practised near the mouth of the Volta, at Ada. It's also theoretically possible in the estuaries of the rivers on the west coast, such as Ankobra and Pra, but bathers run the risk of contracting bilharziosis and are therefore advised to check with the local health authorities before entering the water.

Opinions differ as to the risk of contracting bilharziosis in Lake Volta and Lake Bosumtwi. Since the disease is caused by a micro-organism favoring stagnant waters of rivers and lakes, it's a safer idea for swimmers to proceed by boat into the deeper offshore waters.

Although at the present time, swimming pools are a fairly rare phenomenon outside of Accra, a number of new pools are being constructed throughout the country. Accra itself boasts an Olympic-sized pool, while the localities of Teshie, Tema, Takoradi, Akosombo, Kumasi and Mole also offer pool facilities. A new swimming pool is currently under construction at Bolgatanga.

Swimming as an official national sport has existed only since 1971, which explains why so much remains to be done to develop the necessary infrastructures.

Ghana possesses several yacht clubs, notably in the region of Accra and Takoradi-Sekondi.

Fishing — a particularly popular pastime in the delta of the Volta River — can be practised on an individual basis, with visitors making their own arrangements with local boat owners.

Like all the other former possessions of the British Empire, Ghana has inherited its share of *golf* courses and *tennis* courts. Beautiful fairways can be found

handicrafts and souvenirs

in Accra (Achimota and Sakumo) and near the Port of Tema, as well as at Kumasi, Akwatia, Obuasi (Ashanti Region), Tafo (Eastern Region) and Takoradi (Western Region). Tennis can be practised on the courts of many of the larger Accra hotels (Novotel and Shangri-La), as well as in cities such as Tema, Kumasi, Cape Coast, Bolgatanga, etc. Other pastimes include *polo*, but exclusively in Accra.

Trekking safaris

Outside the capital, Ghana's numerous wildlife reserves offer the *trekking safaris* first developed in Ghana's Mole National Park. *Game hunting* is possible throughout the country, on the condition of obtaining a hunting permit from the Ghanaian authorities.

Horseback-riding is possible in Accra as well as Takoradi and Kumasi, with riding facilities planned for the Shai Hills Wildlife Reserve.

Leisure activities

The cinema rates high among the Ghanaians' leisure activities, with numerous movie houses found in Accra and the major cities. Other forms of entertainment are regularly presented at Accra's Art Centre and Drama Studio, and the Kumasi Cultural Centre, all of which host amateur and professional theatrical productions featuring traditional and contemporary music and dance.

Live rock music can be heard both in Accra and the outlying provinces, while the country's best bands compete for a national award once a year.

"Ghana by night" can be a richly-rewarding experience, since as in most other African countries, dancing is one of the most popular activities of the entire population, from taxi drivers to high-ranking government officials. Accra's best nightclubs include the Apollo Theatre, Holly Gardens, Piccadilly Circle, the Moon, the Cave du Roi, the Tip-Toe, Blow Up and Black Caesar's Palace, while in Kumasi serious night-lifers will want to check out the Dimelite.

■ The fact that Ghana was formerly called the Gold Coast has not gone unnoticed by many of her visitors, who often arrive in the country harbouring secret dreams of acquiring priceless jewelery and heirloom handicrafts at bargain-basement prices. An abundance of gold can certainly. be found in the form of nuggets, necklaces, earrings and rings.

But such items are most often of recent manufacture and always behind the counters of Accra's jewellers, who, had it been left up to them, would have never traded Manhattan for a handful of glass beads. Stated more succinctly, we can affirm that visitors should abandon all hope of bringing back a diamond-studded royal diadem or two, and often of even seeing such objects other than upon a well-guarded royal head.

Despite this discouraging fact, a number of contemporary examples of traditional ceremonial jewellery are available from the former royal goldsmiths' shops located near Kumasi. In addition to the above, the goldsmiths' shops also turn out a wide range of traditional regalia in gilded and sculptured wood rings, royal sceptres, bracelets and diverse insignia, as well as magnificent woven *kente* and *adinkra*.

Prior to the purchase of a kente, whether in one of the shops of the capital or at the main production centre in Bonwire (near Kumasi), the visitor may want to learn more about its history. This can be done by paying a visit to the excellent and informative presentation of traditional Ghanaian clothing on display at the National Museum in Accra.

Traditionally worn by the *Asantehene* — the legendary emperors of the Ashanti — and their court dignitaries, the kente is also an attribute of several other of Ghana's ethnic groups, and notably of the Ewe, who claim to have invented it long ago in the Volta Region.

Fairly expensive, since entirely hand-made and requiring several months to complete, the kente is a sumptuous souvenir that any visitor will be proud to acquire. It is traditionally woven strip by yard-long strip upon small looms, and then sewn together to form a complete garment. Commercial pressures and limited tourist budgets have resulted in the manufacture of much smaller articles woven in the same material, which although presented as kente, are about as similar to the traditional garment as a toy piano to a Steinway concert grand. Sold as bedspreads, tablecloths and even

*Traditional Ghanaian
garments:
handwoven "kente"
and boldly-printed "adinkra"
are worn by kings and
commoners alike.*

belts, shorts and shirts, they are nevertheless handsome examples of traditional weaving techniques. For visitors planning an extended visit of Ghana, it is possible to order a kente which will be custom-woven to the size, colour and pattern of one's choice.

Printed fabrics

Traditional *adrinka* are produced by the Baffour Gyimah Enterprise (Tel: 3), located in Tewobaabi, near Bonwire and east of Kumasi. This veritable fabric design studio, owned by Chief Nana Kwaku Dua II, also offers a large assortment of chieftain's insignia in sculptured wood. Unlike the hand-woven kente, adrinkas are brightly-coloured cotton fabrics (generally yellow, blue, red, green or even black, when worn for a funeral service) printed in a multitude of geometric patterns. Each of the designs is highly symbolic and often illustrative of a proverb. The principal motifs include spirals, the moon and stars, the sun, stripes and triangles.

Visitors to Chief Kwaku Dua's workshop will be fascinated by the gourds filled with vegetable dyes as thick as tar and the carved wooden templates which the workers ink and hand-press upon the cloth to impart the designs. Relatively compact and less expensive than a kente, the extremely decorative adinkra is always a highly-appreciated gift for one's friends and a beautiful souvenir of the Ghanaian voyage.

Antiques and souvenirs

Employing cast bronze rather than sculptured wood, traditional Ghanaian artisans have left few examples of the mask-maker's and sculptor's art other than the celebrated *akuaba* or "Ashanti doll," replicated by the Kumasi Cultural Centre and sold in the stalls of the Makola flea-market in Accra. The chances of finding an original are extremely rare, since collectors and antique dealers from all over the world bought every example they could find decades ago. And even if by great good luck, one should manage to discover one, a special export permit would be needed to take it out of the country.

The same holds true for highly-prized antique bronze weights sculptured in figurative or abstract designs that were formerly used on the gold-weighing scales. Local craftsmen nevertheless continue to turn out excellent imitations which are often nearly indistinguishable from the originals, and which can be found on sale at the handicraft shop of the Kumasi Cultural Centre and the Makola Market in Accra.

In the stands that line Accra's 28th February Avenue, the visitor is likely to make some interesting finds, such as metal - or cowrie-shell covered masks, cast-bronze horsemen from Benin or Cameroon and sculptured bronze Ashanti receptacles of various sizes.

The wood and ivory carvings on sale in numerous souvenir shops are nearly all of recent manufacture, while the traditional chieftain's stools found in Accra and Kumasi are of variable quality and workmanship, with the finest examples produced at Ahwiaa, near Kumasi.

In an entirely different register, Ghanaian rag dolls representing characters taken from daily life are available in two basic sizes and are often fairly striking, as well as having the additional advantage of being easy to fit into an already-overflowing suitcase.

Traditional garments

Northern Ghana offers the choice of three specialities: the striped cotton men's shirts, whose generous volumes, flat pleats and wide armholes are generally unbecoming on Westerners but handsomely worn by Ghanaians. Curiously enough, they often look just fine when worn by women, but wait until you get back home before doing so. Similarly, the men of the north wear two types of conical straw hats, the first being an unruly affair with wildly-flying wisps of multicoloured straw, and the other pointed at the top and circled with a leather band. Women being women, these exclusively masculine items are snapped up by the fair sex as fast as they are found. Once again, we don't recommend your wearing them until you get home (after which you may want to change your mind anyway), and good luck in trying to get them to fit into a suitcase or flight bag. To-date, the only known solution to getting them out of the country is to sling them over your shoulder like a surrealistic sombrero as you mount the ramp to your waiting Jumbo Jet.

Another northern specialty are the fringe-trimmed soft leather pouches, some of which are large enough to serve as shoulder bags and others small enough to be worn about the neck. There are also rigid black and red tooled-leather boxes which can be used as change purses.

Ceramics and pottery

Just about everywhere in Ghana, and particularly in the northern markets, visitors can find ochre or red or black terracotta plates, pitchers and jars, often decorated in geometrical patterns. These receptacles serve a wide variety of uses in Ghana, ranging from cooking pots to plates or water jugs. The largest examples are used for brewing millet beer, but before you purchase one for use as a flower vase, remember that you'll also have to practically purchase its own air ticket just to get it back home with you.

Basket-ware

Ghanaian villagers will often be seen carrying a wide variety of baskets upon their heads. Some of these will be round with handles on either side, and others conical or even triangular, but often quite lovely despite their lack of decoration and rustic appearance. Once again, the problem is getting them back, since they rarely fit into a suitcase, are cumbersome to bring aboard as hand-held baggage and generally are crushed to bits when placed in the plane's luggage compartment. So once again, good luck!

Philately

If you have to ask what this is, then just go on to the next paragraph... If not, you will be pleased to learn that Ghanaian stamps are often beautiful. The pity is that no facilities for stamp collectors exist at the Accra central post office, and admirers will have to content themselves by purchasing the most current specimens over the counter just as if they were destined to adorn a simple ''wish you were here'' postcard.

Tropical fruit

Before leaving the country, visitors should dash off for a quick visit to the Accra food market for a last-minute purchase of the incredibly delicious locally-grown pineapples, mangoes and papayas generally unavailable in Europe.

recommended reading

■ Since Ghana was formerly a British colony, it is in London that the visitor will find the greatest number of books on the country. A few tourist guides and historical studies are available in Accra's larger hotels, the museum shops of Accra, Elmina and Cape Coast and at local bookstores. For visitors who read French, the following list includes a number of untranslated but interesting books on Ghana.

General interest

Ghana, in volume XI of *La Grande Encyclopédie du Monde* (éditions Atlas).
Le Ghana, published in Larousse's illustrated *Beautés du Monde* series, and also comprising an article on Togo and Benin.
Le Ghana, Atlas des Civilisations Africaines, published by Nathan Beaux Livres.

Ghanaian history and ethnology

Most of the following works are only available in Ghana:
Forts and Castles of Ghana, by Albert van Dantzig, Sedco Publishing Ltd.
Christiansborg Castle-Osu, published by the Ghana Museums and Monuments Board.
The Castles of Elmina, a Brief History and Guide, by Tony Hyland, published by the Ghana Museums and Monuments Board, series 3.
Clay Figures Used in Funeral Ceremonies, published by the Ghana Museums and Monuments Board.
Festivals of Ghana, by A.A. Opoku, Ghana Publishing Corpotation.
The Apoo Festival, by E.V. Asihene, Ghana Publishing Corporation.
Traditional Rule in Ghana, Past and Present, by Kwame Arhin, Sedco Publishing Ltd.
Adinkra Poems, by A. Kayper-Mensah, Ghana Publishing Corporation.
Ancient Ashanti Chieftaincy, by Ernest E. Obeng, Ghana Publishing Corporation.
The Ashanti of Ghana: People with a Soul, by J.W. Tufuo and C.E. Donkor, Anowuo Educational Publications.
Naissance d'un État africain, le Ghana, by J. Boyon, Paris, 1958.
Le Ghana de Nkrumah, by S.G. Ikoku, Paris, 1971.
Histoire de l'Afrique, by R. and M. Cornevin, Payot.
Histoire de l'Afrique Occidentale, by Djibril Tamsir Niane and J. Suret-Canale, Éditions Présence Africaine.
Histoire générale de l'Afrique, by Ibrahima Baba Kaké and Elikia M'Bokolo, Éditions ABC.
L'Univers Akan des Poids à Peser l'Or, by G. Niangoran-Bouah, 3 volumes, Éditions NEA-MLB.

Zoology

The following list contains recommended reading for visitors to the Ghanaian national parks, and in particular Mole National Park.
Guide des Grands Mammifères d'Afrique, by Jean Dorst and Pierre Dandelot, Éditions Delachaux et Niestlé.
Les Oiseaux de l'Ouest africain, by W. Serle and G.J. Morel, Éditions Delachaux et Niestlé.

Economics

Le Ghana, an article on the country's economy in *l'Atlaséco*, a world economic atlas, published annually by les Éditions SGB, 9 rue d'Aboukir, 75002 Paris.

Miscellaneous

Ghana, the Land, the People and the Culture, Ghana Tourist Development Company Ltd.
Ghana, a Traveller's Guide, by Jojo Cobbinah, Books on African Studies, Jerry Bedu Addo.
Guide l'Afrique Occidentale, published by the French airline company UTA, and containing an extensive chapter on Ghana and updated visitor information.

Literature

Anthologie Negro-Africaine, by Lilyan Kesteloot, Marabout-Université.

Periodicals

Jeune Afrique, a weekly magazine often featuring in-depth articles and special supplements on Ghana.
L'Empire de l'Or: les Ashanti, by Claude Tardits, appearing in the November-December 1986 issue of *Balafon*, published by Air Afrique.

The education of children is one of Ghana's most important priorities as well as an immense challenge given the country's spiralling birth-rate.

ghanaian cuisine

Maps

The indispensable companion of visitors motoring through Ghana will be Shell's Ghana Road Map. Netherlands' KLM airline also publishes an excellent road map of Ghana, featuring an extremely detailed street map of Accra.

In France, the Institut Géographique National publishes good maps of western Africa, including a map of the coast and the littoral of Togo and Benin, entitled *Accra-Lome-Porto-Novo*, as well as a map of northern Ghana entitled *Tamale*. The ever-dependable Michelin tire company also publishes an updated road map of western Africa.

■ A principally agricultural country, Ghana offers a wide variety of vegetables and tropical fruit, including kassava (manioc), yams, sweet potatoes, rice, plantain bananas, pineapples and mangoes. A number of these items are used as the basic ingredients for stews and, according to the common African usage, "sauces", by which is meant a meat dish accompanied by vegetables and an infinite variety of seasoned gravies. Pigs, cows, sheep and poultry are raised on small farms throughout the country, while the northern savannas are the home to large cattle ranches. This may explain the generally excellent quality of the meat used in the delicious Ghanaian stews, often prepared with cabbage-palm oil.

Ghana's 550 kilometres of coast is dotted with fishing villages. The quality of the seafood is excellent, with sole, crayfish and red mullet available on the menus of the better restaurants in the south. Unfortunately, Ghana does not as yet possess refrigerated freight transport for bringing these delicacies out of the littoral and into the capital. In the north, however, the rivers and lakes provide tasty fresh-water alternatives.

TOILET ARTICLES AND FIRST-AID-KIT

■ *There is no problem if you have left your toilet accessories behind before leaving, since a toothbrush or a bottle of shampoo are as easy to find in Accra as in Paris or London.*
The same holds true for most pharmaceutical products. With the exception of certain specialized prescription drugs, Ghanaian pharmacies stock a wide range of current products.
Nevertheless, a small first-aid kit is always useful, and should include the following:
— *Nivaquine (anti-malaria treatment);*
— *Alka-Seltzer;*
— *Milk of magnesium;*
— *An anti-diarrheatic (Intetrix, Immodium or Diarsed).*
Also useful are:
— *Antibiotics;*
— *Pharmaceutical alcohol, a skin disinfectant (or Dakin), and bandages, cotton and adhesive tape;*
— *Talcum powder;*
— *Anti-mosquito lotions and creams for insect bites;*
— *Tanning lotion;*
— *Aspirin.*

Another aspect of Ghanaian cuisine is wild game. Like all sub-Saharan Africans, the Ghanaians are particulary fond (of eating) the small antelope (cephalopes) that inhabit the forests and savannas. Another animal that invariably ends up on Ghanaian tables is the agouty, a rodent-like animal the size of a beaver, which is served grilled or stewed and is reputed to taste much like rabbit, although it would be difficult for us to personally confirm this fact.

If first-time visitors to Africa are often somewhat hesitant about the idea of sitting down to a meal of monkey or agouty stew, their reticence will nevertheless constitute a source of boundless hilarity in the local restaurants where such dishes are served.

"Fufu" and "peanut soup"

Other typically Ghanaian dishes include the delicious "peanut soup," consisting of beef or chicken stew served with a sauce of onions, tomatoes, spices and roasted peanut puree. "Fufu" consists of a puree of plantain bananas, yams or manioc accompanied by chunks of cooked meat, crab or fish braised in cabbage-palm oil and spices. "Cabbage-palm soup" is made with boiled and ground cabbage-palm nuts mixed with tomatoes, onions and hot peppers. "Kenkey" consists of fermented corn flour puree rolled in a banana leaf which is boiled until tender, and served with a variety of sauces.

The tempting dishes described above may give the impression that Ghana is a gastronomic paradise, but it should not be forgotten that the long series of economic crises endured by the country has left a number of after-effects. In general, Ghanaians observe a certain frugality in their meals. In most of the local restaurants, the menu consists of a single main dish, without starters or deserts. This situation is of course different in the larger hotels, where diners may chose from a full array of standardized "international" cuisine.

Different beverages

Beer is Ghana's national beverage. Everywhere in the country, from the largest supermarkets in Accra to the smallest open-air soft drink counter in the most remote villages, one finds Ghana's light and excellent domestically-brewed beer.

Ranking second in popularity — and first place among the Muslim population — are carbonated soft drinks and Coca-Cola.

The Ghanaian breweries have recently launched "Malta", a non-alcoholic malt-based soft drink. Accompanied by multi-media advertising blitz "Mama, don't forget the Malta"! the dark, sirupy beverage is immensely popular with Ghanaian families.

All the markets in the southern and central regions sell "nsafu" (or "nsa fufu"), a fermented palm wine with widely varying degrees of alcohol-content. The popular custom is to drink it from small gourds, and when well-chilled, it's a first-rate thirst quencher. When highly fermented, it turns into "African gin," a powerful alcoholic drink that should be consumed moderately by visitors subject to severe hangovers and totally avoided by drivers who want to get where they're going.

In northern Ghana, "pito" is brewed from an extract of millet, and is similar in taste to both cider and beer. Visitors to any of Ghana's traditional taverns will discover that the custom is to chug down an entire gourd of pito at one go. The unanimous applause and admiration of the onlookers is guaranteed for those remaining upright after this exercise.

In every region traversed during your voyage, you'll have the opportunity to sample the local gin or schnaps. It occupies a special place in the hearts and minds of the Ghanaians, since it is used in the ritual libations offered during the ceremonies honoring ancestors or divinities. By extension, visits to native juju priests automatically entail the gift of a bottle, or even more, if the visit includes the consultation of an oracle.

After pouring some of the liquor on the ground, the priest passes the bottle around to his attendants and visitors, after which everyone begins to commune with other, and perhaps higher planes of existence. In the interest of sobriety, visitors desirous of participating in such rituals are therefore advised to limit their attendance to one ceremony per day.

Total abstainers may find coffee and tea difficult to find other than in Ghana's larger restaurants and hotels.

*Like an inland sea created by
the Akosombo and Kpong Dams, gigantic Lake Volta
is criss-crossed by ferryboats destined
to play an increasingly important role
in the development of Ghanaian tourism.*

accommodation

■ The revival of Ghana's economy, coupled with the government's recent determination to develop tourism, is resulting in the construction or renovation of much of the country's hotel infrastructure. A number of well-appointed guest accommodations have been constructed throughout Ghana's provinces, in a welcome departure from the habitual concentration of visitor accommodations in the larger cities practised in other developing countries as they open up to tourism.

Ghana has chosen a diametrically opposed policy. Its innumerable camping facilities, guest houses, fully-catered resthouses, motels and hotels have been or are in the process of being constructed in the country's most attractive sites, and often in unique settings such as the ancient coastal fortresses.

Unfortunately, Ghana's former economic crises resulted in the almost total interruption of tourism for decades, as well as the closure or semi-abandon of most of the nation's best hotels.

New smaller hotels

Least too dark an image be given of the results of Ghana's former economic problems, it should also be remembered that the successive crises ultimately led to the privatization of the nation's hotels. And now that the country's economic comeback is in full swing, local investors are creating an entirely new infrastructure of smaller hotels and visitor accommodations throughout the country. Visitors on a limited travel budget or simply seeking a change from the impersonal atmosphere of international hotels will appreciate the human scale and friendly atmosphere of these new establishments, examples of which currently exist in Bolgatanga and Wa in northern Ghana, as well as Kumasi and Obuasi in the centre of the country, and Ada, Cape Coast, Takoradi and Elmina on the Atlantic coast. Existing hotels are being progressively renovated, while many of the half-completed construction projects have been reactivated following years of abandon. At the same time, luxurious establishments for the upscale tourist and business traveller market have recently opened in Accra, such as the marvellous Novotel with its adjoining restaurant, swimming pool, tennis courts, shops and business centre.

selected hotels

ACCRA
Novotel***, Barnes Road (centre), P.O. Box 12720, tel: 66.78.46, fax: 66.75.33. 200 rooms, restaurant, swimming pool, tennis courts, conference facilities, business services.
Shangri-La***, Airport, P.O. Box 9201, tel: 77.75.00, fax: 77.48.73. 44 rooms, restaurant, swimming pool, sauna, horseback riding, business services.
Sharita Lodge***, Akosombo Street (next to the Shangri-La), P.O. Box C45, tel: 77.34.45, fax: 77.26.19. 10 rooms, restaurant.
Fissure Lodge***, Roman Ridge, P.O. Box 2665, tel: 77.21.90. 8 suites, restaurant.
Granada**, Airport Area, P.O. Box 6250, tel: 77.75.43. 35 rooms, restaurant and swimming pool.
King David**, Kokomlenle, P.O. Box 10323, tel: 22.98.32. 15 rooms, restaurant.
Kingsby**, New Achimota, P.O. Box 5496, tel: 22.37.42. 22 rooms, restaurant.
North Ridge**, North Ridge, P.O. Box 1365, tel: 22.58.09. 28 rooms.
Sunspot**, Airport Area, P.O. Box 0165, Osu, tel: 77.33.22. 14 rooms, restaurant, swimming pool.
Sunrise**, North Ridge, P.O. Box 2287, tel: 22.45.75, fax: 22.76.56. 19 rooms, restaurant.
Sanaa Lodge**, Tesano, P.O. Box 6461, tel: 22.04.43. 13 rooms, restaurant, swimming pool.
Penta**, Osu, P.O. Box 7354, tel: 77.45.29, fax: 77.43.18. 31 rooms, restaurant.
Maple Leaf**, New Achimota, P.O. Box 3787, tel: 22.51.85. 22 rooms, restaurant.
Marriset**, Airport Area, P.O. Box 0608, tel: 77.59.22, fax: 77.20.85. 16 rooms, restaurant.
Parker House**, Darlau Man, P.O. Box 2067, tel: 22.03.75. 14 rooms, restaurant.
Blue Angels Guest House**, Dzorwulu, P.O. Box 0427, tel: 77.23.52. 10 rooms, restaurant.
Sunlodge**, Tesano, P.O. Box 6909. 12 rooms, restaurant.
Martins Guest House*, Tesano Police, P.O. Box 6730, tel: 22.17.92. 4 rooms.
Dimples Inn*, Dzorwulu, P.O. Box 354, tel: 77.21.53. 10 rooms, restaurant.

NOTE : The following four-star hotels are scheduled to open in early 1992: *Golden Tulip* (formerly the Continental), Liberation Avenue, 150 rooms. — *Ambassador Hotel* (next to the Novotel), 120 rooms. — *Star Hotel*, Cantonments, 60 rooms, . — *Labadi Beach Hotel*, 100 rooms and 4 luxury suites.

Grisfarm*, Osu, P.O. Box 1070, tel: 77.46.02. 11 rooms, restaurant.
Johnson's Guest House, New Achimota, P.O. Box 40. 4 rooms.
Esi Executive Lodge, Labone, P.O. Box 15068, tel: 77.69.72. 3 rooms.
Cocobeach Resort, Teshie Nungua, in Osu, P.O. Box 0738, tel: 71.28.87. 9 rooms, restaurant, swimming pool.
Flair Guest House, Cantonments, P.O. Box 2220, tel: 77.55.99. 4 rooms, restaurant.
Aama, Kokrobite Beach Resort, P.O. Box 2923 (Reservations at Accra Novotel). 30 rooms, restaurant, conference room.
In addition to the above, many other, smaller hotels can be found in the Greater Accra area.

ABURI (Eastern Region)
May Lodge, near Botanical Gardens, P.O. Box 25. 4 rooms, restaurant.
Aburi Botanical Gardens, tel: 22. 30 rooms, bar and restaurant.

ADA (Greater Accra Region)
Ada Hotel, tel: 22.66.93 and 22.23.01. 13 rooms.
Cisneros**, Sogakofe, P.O. Box 96. 35 rooms.
Volta View, Sogakofe, P.O. Box 77. 22 rooms.

AKOSOMBO (Eastern Region)
Volta, P.O. Box 25, tel: 731. 40 rooms, bar and restaurant.
Lakeside Motel*, Senchi, P.O. Box 84. 11 rooms.

AMEDZOFE (Volta Region)
Rest House, 5 rooms.

AXIM (Western Region)
Monte-Carlo, P.O. Box 86. 11 rooms.

BEGORO (Eastern Region)
Rest House

BOLGATANGA (Upper East Region)
Catering Rest House, P.O. Box 50, tel: 23.99. 24 rooms, bar and restaurant.
Black Star, P.O. Box 40, tel:23.46, 11 rooms, bar and restaurant.
There are also many smaller hotels, including: *Sandgardens* (22 rooms), *Oasis* (11 rooms), *Central* (11 rooms), *Saint-Joseph* (10 rooms), *Bazar, Royal* (12 rooms).

BOSUMTWI (LAKE) (Ashanti Region)
Rest House, 4 rooms.

BUNSO (Eastern Region)
Rest House.

BUSUA (Western Region)
Busua Pleasure Beach, P.O. Box 7.
32 rooms.

CAPE COAST (Central Region)
Savoy Hotel, Sam Road, P.O. Box 646,
tel: 28.05 and 28.68. 22 rooms.
Saana Lodge, P.O. Box 504, tel: 23.91
and 25.70, 4 rooms.
Catering Rest House*, P.O. Box 305, tel:
25.94. 13 rooms.
Dan's Paradise, Ayikoo, P.O. Box 989,
tel: 29.42. 17 rooms.
Mudek, Pedu, P.O. Box A9, tel: 27.87.
35 rooms.
Pedu Holiday Inn, Pedu, P.O. Box 1214,
6 rooms.
Also, smaller hotels at Anomabo
(*Adaaho Hotel*, 24 rooms); *Biriwa*
(*Biriwa Beach*, 6 rooms) and Mankessim
(*Greenwood*, 12 rooms; *Royal Palace*,
16 rooms).

DUNKWA (Central Region)
Grandee, P.O. Box 121, tel: 420.
12 rooms.
Subin Valley, P.O. Box 277, tel: 305.
11 rooms.
Super Melody, P.O. Box 269, tel: 415.
12 rooms.

ELMINA (Central Region)
Elmina Motel, P.O. Box 100, tel: 20.
67 rooms.
Hollywood, P.O. Box 41, tel: 23.
13 rooms.
Oyster Bay, P.O. Box 277, 20 rooms.

ENCHI (Western Region)
Akwaaba, P.O. Box 33. 11 rooms.
Aowinman, P.O. Box 79. 10 rooms.

GAMBAGA (Northern Region)
Rest House.

HALF ASSINI (Western Region)
Victory, P.O. Box 88. 20 rooms.

HO (Volta Region)
Wdezor, P.O. Box 339. 38 rooms.
Alinda, P.O. Box 484. 10 rooms.
E.P. Social Ho Centre, P.O. Box 224.
12 rooms.
Emmanuel Guest House, P.O. Box 423.
4 rooms.
Fiave Lodge, P.O. Box 352. 5 rooms.
Hek Lodge, P.O. Box 355. 8 rooms.
Hotel de Tarso. 22 rooms.
Majestic, P.O. Box 248. 5 rooms.

HOHOE (Volta Region)
Matvin, P.O. Box 197. 25 rooms.
Africa Unity, P.O. Box 98. 4 rooms.
Grand Hotel, P.O. Box 38. 10 rooms.
Pacific Rest House, P.O. Box 361.
7 rooms.

KETE-KRACHI (Volta Region)
Simon, P.O. Box 122. 15 rooms.

KETA
Vilcabamba*, Hedzaanawo-Denu, P.O.
Box 73. 22 rooms.
Makavo*, Aflao, P.O. Box 123.
20 rooms.
Bwotsige, Aflao, P.O. Box 221.
14 rooms.
Klom Dedie, Aflao, P.O. Box 5.
12 rooms.
Sansa, Aflao, P.O. Box 37. 12 rooms.

KOFORIDUA (Eastern Region)
Saint James**, P.O. Box 187, tel: 31.65.
23 rooms.
Eredee*, P.O. Box 979, tel: 32.34 and
32.96. 44 rooms.
Parters May*, P.O. Box 688, tel: 31.38.
11 rooms.
Eastland, P.O. Box 564, tel: 22.16.
10 rooms.
Kes, P.O. Box 824, tel: 33.26. 15 rooms.
Kobs, P.O. Box 158. 18 rooms.
Motel, P.O. Box 158, tel: 25.14.
9 rooms.
Oywuka Guest House, P.O. Box 221, tel:
26.75. 6 rooms.
Passo Lodge, P.O. Box 232, tel: 26.15.
4 rooms.
Serwa Guest Inn, P.O. Box 257, tel:
30.43. 4 rooms.
There are also smaller hotels at Akim-
Oda (GME, 13 rooms; *Madarena*,
11 rooms; *Morning Star*, 10 rooms;
O Right Guest House, 7 rooms;
Top View Lodge, 4 rooms) and Somanya
(*Palm Lodge*, 8 rooms; *Paradisco*,
10 rooms ; *99 Westend Lane*, 8 rooms).

KPANDU (Volta Region)
Lucky, P.O. Box 145, 12 rooms.
Refco Guest House, P.O. Box 89.
10 rooms.
Slyka Lodge, P.O. Box 161. 5 rooms.

KUMASI (Ashanti Region)
City Hotel**, P.O. Box 1980, tel: 23.93.
and 23.97. 150 rooms, bar and restaurant.
Cicero Guest House**, West Nhyiaeso
Extension, P.O. Box 1178, tel: 44.73.
13 rooms.

There is an extensive network of hotels
which are suitable for tourists
and business people through the country.
Above : Accra Novotel.
Below : the Labadi Beach, on Tema road.

*Other places where you can stay :
Above, the Golden Tulip
in Accra on the airport road.
Below, the Kokrobite Beach resorts
on Winneba road, 30 km from Accra.*

Georgia**, Adiebeba, P.O. Box 2240, tel: 41.54. 30 rooms.
Roses Guest House, Nhyaeso, P.O. Box 4176, tel: 40.72. 12 rooms.
Catering Rest House*, Ridge-Kumasi, P.O. Box 3179, tel: 65.06 and 36.56. 28 rooms.
Amissah*, Asokwa, P.O. Box 343, tel: 30.46. 18 rooms.
La Sab*, Atwima-Amanfrom, P.O. Box 1937. 16 rooms.
Noks*, Asokwa, P.O. Box 8556, tel: 41.62 and 44.38. 18 rooms.
Nurom*, Suame, P.O. Box 1400, tel: 40.00. 24 rooms.
Airport. New Tafo, P.O. Box 138, tel: 46.22. 15 rooms.
Justice, Amakom, P.O. Box 3583, tel: 25.24. 39 rooms.
De Kingsway, Adum, P.O. Box 178, tel: 62.28. 21 rooms.
De 77, Dichemso, P.O. Box 3590, tel: 42.02. 25 rooms.
St. Patrick, Akrom, P.O. Box 195, tel: 61.91. 39 rooms.
Stadium, Asokwa, P.O. Box 3340, tel: 36.47 or 63.74. 19 rooms.
Texas, Asokwa, P.O. Box 1124, tel: 32.39. 15 rooms.
Kesewaa Memorial, New Tafo, P.O. Box 4582, tel: 27.05. 24 rooms.
Plaza, Dichemso, P.O. Box 8442, tel: 49.07. 63 rooms.
Pollux, New Tafo, P.O. Box 4464, tel: 63.55. 24 rooms.
Gyaskoff, Tafo, P.O. Box 2452, tel: 35.28. 25 rooms.
Gulder, Dichemso, P.O. Box 7. 18 rooms.
De Cote d'Ivoire, Dichemso, P.O. Box 3776, tel: 60.42. 17 rooms.
Ayigya, Ayigya, P.O. Box 3515. 21 rooms.
Christian Village Guest House, Santasi, P.O. Box 99. 19 rooms.
Ducor Palace, New Suame Extension, P.O. Box 4606, tel: 55.76. 17 rooms.
Abena Donkor Memorial, Amakom, P.O. Box 1888, tel: 256. 20 rooms.
Abidjan, Dichemso, P.O. Box 3053, tel: 55.39. 16 rooms.
Ebiniebinie, Dichemso, P.O. Box 1269. 14 rooms.
Ash Food Court, Bantama, P.O. Box 952, tel: 29.17. 21 rooms.

And many other smaller hotels: *Agoro, Confidence, Aresa, Ask, Boahemaa, Corner, Fabulous, Hafia, Ekuona, Family, Farmyard, Freeman, de Candolfo, La Belle, Jatakrom, Kings, Montana, Pase One, Sarfo, Transport, Timber, University*, etc.

MOLE NATIONAL PARK (Northern Region)
Mole Motel, located at the entrance to the park, P.O. Box 8, tel. : 25.63. 35 rooms (bungalows), bar and restaurant.

NAKPANDURI (Northern Region)
Rest House.

NKAWKAW (Eastern Region)
Afoanima, Atibie, Nkawkaw Road, P.O. Box 76, tel: 33. 15 rooms.
Betrams, P.O. Box 41, 13 rooms.
De Ship, P.O. Box 279, tel: 128. 14 rooms.
Okoman, P.O. Box 400, tel: 163. 8 rooms.
Starlight, Akyiaso, P.O. Box 174. 16 rooms.
Top Way, P.O. Box 285. 11 rooms.

OBUASI (Ashanti Region)
Adansiman, P.O. Box 515, tel: 90. 18 rooms.
Black Star, P.O. Box 201, tel: 323. 10 rooms.
Cecis, P.O. Box 156, tel: 419. 8 rooms.
Dapps Guest House, Tutuka, P.O. Box 1. 5 rooms.
Falizar Guest House, P.O. Box 48. 4 rooms.
Georgina Guest Inn, P.O. Box 204, 8 rooms.
De Sennet, P.O. Box 21, tel. : 12.63. 22 rooms.
De Silence, P.O. Box 253, tel. : 280. 12 rooms.
Super Mambo, P.O. Box 251, tel: 222. 30 rooms.

SALTPOND (Central Region)
Nkubem, P.O. Box 286, tel: 108. 21 rooms.
Palm Beach, 15 rooms.

SEKONDI-TAKORADI (Western Region)
Atlantic**, Takoradi, P.O. Box 273, tel: 300/9. 70 rooms.
Animens**, Takoradi, P.O. Box 0475, tel: 16.76/7. 18 rooms.
Westline Guest House**, Takoradi, P.O. Box 0408, tel: 46.79. 5 rooms.
Ahenfie*, Takoradi, P.O. Box 0684. 39 rooms.
Devon*, Apremdo-Takoradi, P.O. Box 903, tel: 21.94. 8 rooms.
Lagoonside*, Sekondi, P.O. Box 192. 24 rooms.
Midwood*, Takoradi, P.O. Box 65. 20 rooms.
Palme*, Apremdo-Takoradi, P.O. Box 874, tel: 45.96. 12 rooms.

Western Palace*, Takoradi, P.O. Box 62, tel: 36.01. 25 rooms.
Arvo, Takoradi, P.O. Box 0269, tel: 36.31. 32 rooms.
Amenla, Takoradi, P.O. Box 0208, tel: 25.43. 20 rooms.
Apollo II, Apremdo-Takoradi, P.O. Box 0242, tel: 37.71. 11 rooms.
Beachway, Takoradi, P.O. Box 741. 16 rooms.
Brotherhood, Takoradi, P.O. Box 0470. 7 rooms.
Emcham, Ngyeresia-Sekondi, P.O. Box 274. 5 rooms.
De Star, Takoradi, P.O. Box 757, tel: 36.15. 15 rooms.
Majestic, Takoradi, P.O. Box 841, tel: 31.74. 14 rooms.
Manukof, Takoradi, P.O. Box 0591. 4 rooms.
Western Home, Takoradi, P.O. Box 322. 16 rooms.
Kwakwaduam, Takoradi, P.O. Box 0368, tel: 32.96. 18 rooms.
New Mexico, Takoradi, P.O. Box 0511, tel: 21.06. 9 rooms.
Peace Guest House, Takoradi, P.O. Box 239. 4 rooms.
Super Gardens, Kojokrom-Sekondi, P.O. Box 638. 10 rooms.
Valley, Sekondi, P.O. Box 812. 18 rooms.
Whin River, Apremdo-Takoradi, P.O. Box 1093, tel: 40.74. 5 rooms.
Dick Farm, Takoradi, P.O. Box 0676, tel: 35.29. 9 rooms.
katelove, Sekondi, P.O. Box 801. 12 rooms.

SUNYANI (Brong-Ahafo Region)
Tropical*, P.O. Box 180. 28 rooms.
Catering Rest House, P.O. Box 180. 8 rooms.
Ebenezer, P.O. Box 878, tel: 619. 12 rooms.
De Nimpone, P.O. Box 73. 17 rooms.
De Petra, P.O. Box 1262. 16 rooms.
Point Four, P.O. Box 586. 19 rooms.
South Ridge, P.O. Box 1707. 9 rooms.
Tata, P.O. Box 487, tel: 511. 16 rooms.
Many other smaller hotels can be found in Berekum including : *Adjei, Asie du Memorial, Damoah, Do Good, Nyame* and *Inn*.

TAMALE (Northern Region)
Catering Rest House*, P.O. Box 7247, tel: 29.78. 35 rooms, bar and restaurant.
Al Hassan, P.O. Box 73, tel: 28.34. 24 rooms.
Atta Essibi, P.O. Box 223, tel: 25.69. 17 rooms.
Inter Royal, P.O. Box 308, tel: 24.27. 11 rooms.

Las, P.O. Box 121, tel: 22.17. 21 rooms.
Maalos, P.O. Box 900, tel: 26.78. 10 rooms.
Miricha, P.O. Box 739, tel: 29.35. 7 rooms.

TARKWA (Western Region)
Railview, P.O. Box 73. 8 rooms.
Golden Home, P.O. Box 274. 12 rooms.

TECHIMAN (Brong-Ahafo Region)
Agyeiwaa, P.O. Box 35, tel: 16. 28 rooms.
Ananwoma Lodge, P.O. Box 286. 5 rooms.
Atomic Paradise, P.O. Box 97. 24 rooms.
Ebenezer, P.O. Box 7. 7 rooms.
Emmanuel Inn, P.O. Box 142. 12 rooms.
Farlako Inn, P.O. Box 73. 10 rooms.
Khakito, P.O. Box 245, tel: 63. 9 rooms.
Nyame Nnae, P.O. Box 89. 6 rooms.
St Michael's Lodge, P.O. Box 117. 8 rooms.

TEMA (Greater Accra Region)
Meridian Hotel, P.O. Box 33, tel: 28.78. 40 rooms, bar and restaurant.
Page Hotel, Community 8, P.O. Box 1182, tel: 60.98. 10 rooms.
And many other smaller hotels, including : *Mac Barm, Palace, Ahomka, Oceana Lodge, Friends Club, Oak Royal, Apple, Coco Beach* (Nungua), etc.

TUMU (Upper West Region)
Lims, P.O. Box 16. 13 rooms.

WA (Upper West Region)
Upland**, P.O. Box 308, tel: 180. 30 rooms, bar and restaurant.
Dupond, 15 rooms.
Kunateh Lodge, P.O. Box 11, tel: 102. 14 rooms.
Sawaba Rest House, P.O. Box 143. 29 rooms.
Seinu, P.O. Box 144, tel: 57. 17 rooms.
Last Penny, 27 rooms.

WENCHI (Brong-Ahafo Region)
Baah, P.O. Box 43. 28 rooms.
Kaff Guest House, P.O. Box 14. 4 rooms.

WINNEBA (Central Region)
Sir Charles Beach Resort, P.O. Box 107, tel: 189. 62 rooms.
Yeenuah, P.O. Box 197, tel: 161. 18 rooms.
Hatampa Guest House, Swedru, P.O. Box 388. 13 rooms.

special business travel section

BEFORE LEAVING...

Visitors travelling to Ghana on business should accomplish several formalities prior to leaving their home-country. These include obtaining a business visa from their local Ghanaian embassy, and if desired, information on markets and business conditions, financial arrangements, transportation infrastructures and the rules governing foreign investment.

Useful addresses for the business traveler :

Ghanaian Embassy: 104 High Gate Hill, London N65HE, Tel. (0) 81.342.86.86.

Foreign and Commonwealth Office, Downing Street, London SW1A 2AL, Tel. (01) 270.30.00, Telex 297.711.

Department of Trade & Industry, 1 Victoria Street, London SW1H OET, Tel. (01) 215.78.77, Telex 881.1074.

British Overseas Trade Board, Department of Trade and Industry, 1 Victoria Street, London SW1H OET, Tel. (01) 215.78.77, Telex 881.1074.

Technical Help to Exporters, Linford Wood, Milton Keynes, MK 14 6LE, Tel. (0908) 32.00.33, Telex 825.777.

Export Credits Guarantee Department, P.O. Box 272, Aldermanbury, London EC2P 2EL, Tel. (01) 383.70.00, Telex 883.601.

International Airlines:

All of the international airlines serving Ghana offer particularly comfortable business-class flights whose service and quality is similar to first-class. These airlines also offer air-freight services making it possible to rapidly transport merchandise in or out of Ghana.

Ghana Airways, Cocoa House, POB 1808, Accra. Tel. 66.64.88. Airport: 77.56.34. (London, Dusseldorf, Rome, Abidjan, Lagos, Monrovia-Robertsfield, Dakar, Cotonou, Banjul, Freetown, Conakry, Harare.)

Ethiopian Airlines, Cocoa House, Kwame Nkrumah Avenue, POB 3600, Accra. Tel. 22.23.56. Airport, 77.51.68. (Abidjan, Addis Abada, Nairobi, Brazzaville, Lagos, Douala, Monrovia-Robertsfield).

Nigerian Airways, Danawi Building, Kojo Thompson Road, POB 9068, Accra. Tel. 22.37.49. Airport: 77.61.71 Ext. 460 (Lagos, Abidjan, Monrovia-Robertsfield, Freetown, Banjul).

KLM, Republic House, Kwame Nkrumah Avenue, POB 223 Accra. Tel. 22.40.20. 22.43.70. Airport, 77.65.09, 77.57.29. (Amsterdam).

Aeroflot Soviet Airlines, Caledonia House, Kojo Thompson Road, POB 9449, Accra. Tel. 22.56.04. (Moscow, Tripoli, Vienna, Malta).

British Airways, Caledonia House, Kojo Thompson Road, POB 2087, Accra. Tel. 66.62.22. (London, Abidjan, Lagos).

Air Africa, Cocoa House, Kwame Nkrumah Avenue, POB 539, Accra. Tel. 22.83.51. Airport: 77.74.14. (Abidjan, Cotonou, Lome).

Balkan Airlines, 37/1C Kwame Nkrumah Avenue, POB 14910, Accra. Tel. 22.20.97/22.20.49. (Sofia, Tripoli).

Egypt Air, Kwame Nkrumah Avenue, POB 2943, Accra. Tel. 66.46.03/4. (Cairo).

Swissair, Regabos House, 47, Independence Avenue, POB 1808 Accra. Tel. 22.81.50; 22.81.65; 22.81.90. (Zurich, Geneva, Abidjan, Lagos).

Gemini Air Cargo, America House, Kojo Thompson Road. (Gatwick, Frankfort, Heathrow, Amsterdam, Basel, France, Lagos).

Rainbow Cargo, Luxemburg. (Ostende, Amsterdam).

LOCAL INFORMATION:

Talking business:

Ghanaian businessmen and government officials speak English, the country's official language.

Opening and closing hours:

Ministries and government offices are open from 8:00 a.m. to 12 and 2:00 to 5:00 p.m. The hours of embassies and consulates vary between 7:30 a.m. and 4:00 p.m.

Banking hours are from 8:30 a.m. to 1:00 p.m. Monday through Thursday and from 8:30 a.m. to 3:00 p.m. on Friday.

Meetings and Conferences:

In addition to the *Kwame Nkrumah Conference Centre*, Accra boasts newly-constructed conference facilities located in the heart of the administrative district (next to the stadium and the ministries). With a surface area of over 15,000 m², this immense and luxurious building contains a 1,600-seat conference hall (with a stage and complete audio-visual and translation facilities, two smaller 208-seat conference rooms, three 40 to 70-seat meeting rooms and six cafeterias. (Contact: Energoproject, Tel. 66.87.17/18 in Accra).

Some of Accra's larger hotels also provide conference facilities (see hotel list).

Overleaf:
One of Accra's main thoroughfares,
February 28 Avenue runs from Independence Arch,
past ministries and government offices, to
the business district in the centre-city.

Trade fairs and exhibitions:
The international Trade Fair buildings are located to the east of Accra, in the Labadi district. A number of international exhibitions (mainly industrial) are regularly organized.

USEFUL ADDRESSES

International agencies and organizations:
The World Bank: North Ridge, Tel. 22.96.81, POB M 27 M2, R. Ndaw.
FAO. Maxwell Road, POB 1628, Tel. 66.68.51, Mr. Capoluongo.
Unicef: 2 Milne Close, off Dr. Amilcar Cabral Road, POB 1423, Tel. 77.79.72.
UNDP (United Nations Development Programme): Ring Road East, POB 1423, Tel. 22.14.16.
Central Economic Cooperation Agency:, 72 B 8th Avenue, North Ridge, POB 9592, Tel. 22.51.40, Fax: 22.96.80, Mr. Benedic.
IMF: (at the Ministry of Finance), Tel. 66.60.31.
World Health Organization: POB M 142, Tel. 66.54.21.
EEC: Kotoko International Airport, P.O. Box 9505, Tel. 77.42.01, Fax: 77.41.54. Representative: Mr. M. Lake.
United Nations Information Centre: P.O. Box 2339, Tel. 66.68.51, Ext. 148.

Embassies and consulates:
Belgium: P.O. Box 7475, Tel. 22.32.64.
Canada: Independence Avenue, P.O. Box 1639, Tel. 22.85.55.
China: 6 Agostino Neto Road, Tel. 77.46.11.
Egypt: off Cantonments Road, Tel. 77.68.54.
England and Northern Ireland: Osu Link, near Abdul Nasser Avenue, Tel. 22.16.65.
Ethiopia: 6 Adiembra Road, Tel. 77.59.28.
France: 12th Road/Liberation Avenue, P.O. Box 187, Tel. 22.85.71.
Germany: Valdmosa Lodge, 7th Avenue, Tel. 22.13.11.
Iran: 10 Agbooma Street, Tel. 77.44.74.
Italy: Jawaharlal Nehru Road, Tel. 77.55.36.
Japan: Tito Avenue, Tel. 77.56.16.
Netherlands: 83 Liberation Road, Thomas Sankara Circle, Tel. 22.16.55.
Saudi Arabia: 10 Noi Fetreke Street, Tel. 77.66.51.
Spain, Lamptey Avenue, Tel. 77.40.04.
Switzerland: North Ridge.
United States: Ring Road East, Tel. 77.53.47.

Official and semi-official government agencies:
Ministry of Finance and Economy: P.O. Box M40, Tel. 66.49.93.
Ministry of Industry, P.O. Box M39, Tel. 66.60.49.
Ministry of Trade and Tourism: P.O. Box MO 40, Tel. 66.54.21.
Ministry of Agriculture: P.O. Box M37, Tel. 66.54.21.
Ministry of Information: P.O. Box M41, Tel. 22.80.11.
PNDC Office: P.O. Box 1627, Tel. 66.54.15.
Ghana Ports and Harbours Authority: Tema, Tel. 02.21-26.01/9.
State Transport Corporation: Accra, Tel. 22.19.12.
Ghana Railways Co: Takoradi, Tel. 031-21.81.
Ghana Cocoa Board: Accra, Tel. 22.12.12.
Internal Revenue Department, Accra, Tel. 66.49.61.

Translators and language interpretors:
Translatics. Evelyne Djin, P.O. Box 10373, Tel. 22.19.56 (French), 7, Samora Machel Road.
Dr. E. OT. Prempah M & J Business Services Centre, P.O. Box 9732 KIA, Tel. 77.45.87, Fax: 77.35.93.

Law and accounting firms:
K PMG Mobil House, Liberia Road, P.O. Box 242 AC, Tel. 66.48.81, Fax: 66.79.09.
Law and accounting firm, Price Waterhouse, Opeiba House, Liberation Road.
Ghana Export Promotion Council, Republic House, P.O. Box M 146, Tel. 22.88.1, Fax: 66.82.63.

Periodicals:
The Survey Department, Tel. 77.73.31 (maps, geographical and geological surveys).
The Central Statistics Bureau, Tel. 66.65.12. Price indexes and trade information.
The Exporter (published by Ghana Export Promotion Council).
Ghana stock Market Review (published by Databank, UTC Building, 2nd floor, 41, Knutsford Avenue, P.O. Box 12043, Tel. 66.64.53, Fax: 66.64.53. Stock Exchange reports, financial and investment advice.)
Gold and Diamonds in Ghana, a brochure published by the Minerals Commission, the State House, P.O. Box M 248, Tel. 66.29.86.

Constructed in the city's administrative district, Accra's new Conference Centre is one of Africa's most striking contemporary buildings.

Principal banks:
Bank of Ghana, P.O. Box 2674, Tel. 66.29.86.
Ghana Commercial Bank, P.O. Box 2971, Tel. 66.49.11.
Barclays Bank, P.O. Box 2949, Tel. 66.49.01.
Standard Chartered Bank, P.O. Box 768, Tel. 66.15.91.
National Savings & Credit Bank, P.O. Box 5292, Tel. 22.83.22.
Merchant Bank, P.O. Box 401, Tel. 66.63.31.
National Investment Bank, P.O. Box 3726, Tel. 22.13.12.
Agricultural Development Bank, P.O. Box 4191, Tel. 22.84.53.
Bank of Credit & Commerce, P.O. Box 11011, Tel. 22.80.01.
Bank for Housing and Construction, P.O. Box M1, Tel. 66.61.43.
Social Security Bank, P.O. Box K444, Tel. 22.17.26.
Ghana Cooperative Bank, P.O. Box 5292, Tel. 22.94.38.
Ecobank, P.O. Box 16746, 19 Seventh Avenue, Ridge, Tel. 22.95.32, Fax: 77.54.06.

It is of interest to note that Ghanaian nationals possess a 42 percent stake in *Ecobank*, with the remaining 58 percent controlled by *Ecobank Transnational Incorporated*, headquartered in Lome. Ecobank is affiliated with the West African Federation of Chambers of Commerce (ECOWAS), which includes member-countries such as Togo, Nigeria, the Ivory Coast, Ghana and Benin. Ecobank is therefore particularly useful for companies projecting business or trade in any or all of these countries.

Shipping companies:
Umarco Ghana, Ltd., P.O. Box 215 Tema, Tel. 4031. President: Mr. Risse.
Scanship, CFAO Building, P.O. Box 1705 Accra, Tel. 66.67.61, or P.O. Box 587, Tema, Tel. 2651.
Delmas Agencies, 3 Fishing Harbour Road, P.O. Box B 57 Tema, Tel. 23.32, Fax: 71.29.36. President: James Pan.
Maersk Ltd., located in Tema Port, near Umarco, since March 1991.
Roro Services Ltd., P.O. Box 148 Tema, Tel. 6586.

VITAL STATISTICS

Population : 15 million inhabitants (62,9/km²)

Main towns :
Accra : 1,400,000 inhabitants
Kumasi : 500,000 inhabitants
Sekundi/Takoradi : 260,000 inhabitants
Tema : 200,000 inhabitants
Tamale : 170,000 inhabitants

Total area : 239,460 km²

Paved roads : 35,000 km

Rail system : 1,300 km

Main products :
- *Cocoa : 280,000 tons (third highest world output, 40 percent of GNP) Grain harvest : 906,000 tons*
- *Timber : 370,000 m³ roughcut logs*
- *Commercial livestock : 4 million sheep/goats 810,000 cattle 400,000 pigs*

- *Fisheries : 230,000 tons*
- *Gold production : 13,4 tons*
- *Diamond production : 280,000 carats*
- *Bauxite : 374,000 tons*
- *Manganese : 365,000 tons*
- *Electricity : 4,75 billion kw/hour*

Currency : the Cedi (100 cedi = FF 1.6/$US 0.20)

GNP : $US 6 billion

Growth rate : 5 %

Importations : $US 1.16 billion

Total exportations : $US 830 million

- *Cocoa : $US 423 million (60 % of total export revenue) Gold : $US 168 million Electricity : $US 117 million Timber : $US 80 million*

Research institutes:
I.R.H.O. c/o Ghana Oil Palm Development Corporation, P.O. Box M 428, Accra, Tel. 66.75.13. General Manager: M. Huguenot.
Rubber Research Institute, c/o the French Embassy, P.O. Box 187, Accra, Tel. 22.85.04 or c/o the Ghana Rubber Estate, P.O. Box 228, Takoradi, Tel. 25.76, Telex: 2656. Director: Mr. Labbe.
Bureau Veritas: c/o Faablin Ltd Accra, P.O. Box 7686, Tel. 22.58.21. N.K/Sena.

Office equipment and services:
ABSC (Accra Business Services Centre), 39 Cantonments Road, Osu R.E., P.O. Box 1632 Accra, Tel. 77.39.70 and 77.25.91; Fax: 77.22.95, Telex: 2586. (Fax and Telex facilities, word processing, photocopies, printing and binding, translation services, organization of conferences).

Many of the larger hotels also offer business support services, including stenographers, Fax machines and photocopiers (see section on hotels for business travellers).

Post and telecommunications:
The General Post Office, located on the corner of Pagan Road and Lutteroot Circle, handles letters and packages sent by mail. International telephone, telegram, telex and fax services are located at the High Street annex. An international call costs from 2,700 to 4,500 cedis per three minutes.

Advertising agencies:
ADS Graphics, P.O. Box 14858 Accra, located in front of Kaneshic Kings Way, offers graphics, space sales, printing, etc.
Rex Image Assoc., Ltd., P.O. Box 11924, Accra North, Toyota House Annex, Graphic Road, Tel. 22.98.74, provides a full range of advertising services, including printing, sales promotion and consulting.
Incentive Marketing Ltd., P.O. Box 11296 Accra, N° 3 Second Street, Tesano Accra, Tel. 22.70.74. Sales promotion, advertising, graphics, publishing.
Jay and Joe Asoc. Ltd., Accra North, P.O. Box 7200, Accra, Tel. 22.16.98, D 552/4 Kojo Thompson Road, facing the Avenida Hotel. Space sales, sales promotion, sponsorship consultancy.

INVESTING IN GHANA

A number of factors contributed to Ghana's economic downturn in 1990. The growth rate fell two points, sliding to 3 percent in 1990 as against 5 percent for the previous year, while inflation shot up to 37.2 percent, representing a twelve-point jump over 1989. In 1991, however, economic growth is showing signs of steady recovery, while inflation is steadily diminishing.

Even though much of the country's financial activity is still dominated by state-owned banks, the Ghanaian government is pursuing its policy of privatization on all fronts, including state-owned companies and financial institutions. Private investment is being given a boost by the easing of credit, while loans increased by 30 percent between 1984 and 1989.

Another indication of the liberalization of the economy was the reopening of the Ghana Stock Exchange in November 1990, after twenty years of inactivity. Investor information and a list of authorized brokerage houses is available from the Ghana Stock Exchange Department of Marketing, located on the second floor of the Kingsway Building, P.O. Box 1849 Accra, Tel: 22.53.53. Director: Dr. Charles Yao Asembr.

The fiscal system:
The fiscal legislation applicable to private companies was revised in 1991, with a 10 percent corporate tax deduction (from 45 percent to 35 percent) accorded to companies involved in agriculture, industry and services. The capital gains tax for private companies was also reduced to a 5 percent maximum limit, while taxes on share dividends held by private investors dropped from 30 to 15 percent. Private banking, insurance, printing and trading companies are slated for similar tax breaks, and the abolition of double taxation for foreign investors is being considered.

Foreign investment legislation:
The political and economic policies of Ghana have been completely transformed from near-total state control to the progressive creation of an open-market environment, similar to the wave of privatization and economic liberalization recently witnessed in the former Eastern-bloc countries of Europe.

*Located on the Gulf of Guinea
and endowed with a rich
historical past, both
Cape Coast and Elmina
are highly appreciated by tourists.*

Obsolete legislation and economic policies are being transformed in accordance to Ghana's Investment Code, created in 1985. At the same time, much is being done to encourage foreign investment: administrative formalities have been streamlined and foreign exchange control and import licenses abolished, while an important feature of the Investment Code provides for the repatriation of profits and the possibility of staffing by non-nationals.

Ghana is also a member of the MIGA, a multinational investment guarantee agency affiliated with the World Bank; to further attract outside capital, the government is planning the creation of overseas offices with the objective of interesting foreign investors in the business possibilities offered by Ghana.

Since certain economic sectors are considered as being particularly important to the country's development, it is natural that special incentives are being accorded to favour their growth via the legalization of wholly-owned foreign companies, or joint-ownerships with Ghanaian partners.

These priority sectors include agricultural products, animal ranches, fisheries, packaging, construction (habitations and roads), tourism — and in particular, the development of resort complexes along Ghana's 540 kilometres of seacoast — as well as world-class hotels catering to business travellers, the transportation infrastructures, restaurants and camping facilities.

Ghana's State Hotels Corporation will be dismantled as soon as its remaining hotels are sold to private investors; once again, this is indicative of the government's determination to open this sector to local or foreign development.

The trade representative : The trade representative of the Ghanaian embassy in your home-country — or in Ghana itself, the Ghana Investments Centre located on 28th February Road at the intersection of Oval Road, or the executive secretary of the Divestiture Implementations Committee, (P.O. Box C 102, Tel: 77.20.49), are all qualified to offer potential investors further information, as are the agencies mentioned above.

HOTELS FOR BUSINESS TRAVELLERS

The following is a selected list of hotels offering business support and office services, meeting rooms, a central location and international standards of comfort:

Novotel***, Barnes Road, P.O. Box 12720, Tel: 66.75.46, Fax: 66.75.33. 200 rooms with bath, air-conditioning, television, private telephone, 24-hour room service. The Novotel business centre offers Fax and telex lines, secretarial services, photocopies, translations, car rental and travel services. The hotel features a swimming pool, tennis courts and a French restaurant. A second poolside restaurant is scheduled to open soon. Two modulable conference halls can be subdivided into five smaller rooms, all with modern audio-visual equipment. Since its opening in 1988, the Accra Novotel has remained an essential address for visiting business travellers and the local business community. The hotel is well situated, and it is possible to walk to many destinations in the lower end of the city, a notable advantage in Accra, where traffic is usually extremely heavy.

Shangri-La***, P.O. Box 9201, located on Liberation Road near the airport and the Tetteh Quarshie Circle overpass, Tel. 77.69.93, Fax: 77.48.73. The hotel offers 44 rooms with bath, air-conditioning, a restaurant, a pool, tennis courts, gym with sauna, beautiful gardens, an adjoining polo ground and a horseback-riding school, a discotheque, car rental and secretarial services (word processing, translations, photocopies, Fax and telex lines) and a 100-seat conference room. The hotel is small, peaceful and well decorated, notably with African sculpture. Its location outside of the Accra city centre can be an advantage for those doing business in Tema, since the highway is just adjacent to the hotel grounds.

Sunrise Hotel**, located in North Ridge, on 7th Avenue, P.O. Box 2281, Tel. 22.33.21; 19 air-conditioned rooms with bath, restaurant, pool, tennis courts, a small shop, car rental, office services including protocopies, telex and Fax lines, and a live band in the evening. Situated in a calm and verdant residential district.

North Ridge Hotel**, North Ridge, 8th Avenue, near Ring Road, P.O. Box 1365, Tel. 22.58.09, 27 rooms with bath, restaurant, bus, secretariat services, conferences room.

Blue Angels Guest House, located in Dzorwulu in North-Accra, near the main highway. The Guest House is a small family-style boarding house offering office services and a Fax line (the same as the house telephone: 77.23.52). About a dozen rooms with shower.

A number of other Accra hotels offer acceptable levels of comfort, but lack business support services.

Conversely, a number of four-star hotels are on the point of opening, and will effectively increase the range of potential accommodations for business travelers:

Ambassador****, located next to the Novotel, and offering a pool and 120 totally renovated rooms with bath. P.O. Box 3044, Tel. 66.46.46.

Golden Tulip (formerly the Continental), P.O. Box 5252, Tel. 77.73.61; 140 rooms, pool, tennis courts and shops. Located near the airport, and also totally renovated.

Star, located in the Cantonments district and currently undergoing renovation. 4th Circular Road, P.O. Box 652, Tel. 77.77.28; 60 rooms.

Lastly, mention should be made of the *Labadi Beach Hotel*, an entirely new establishment likely to receive a four-star rating, and destined for business travellers as well as tourists. Like the hotels mentioned above, the Labadi will offer the same range of sports and leisure activities, and will also probably be equipped with full business support services given its proximity to the International Trade Centre and Accra's administrative, financial and governmental offices.

"HEAVEN HELPS THOSE WHO HELP THEMSELVES..."

Such is the philosophy of the women belonging to the December 31 Movement, headed by Ghana's dynamic first lady, Nana Konadu Agyeman-Rawlings.
The bylaws of the organization stipulate that its members "must be aware of their responsibilities and willingly contribute to the effort of national reconstruction." To this end, the women of the movement recently defined an all-important central priority: the care and education of Ghana's children. Their efforts resulted in the creation of the country's first two day-care centres for children aged from two to five. The two initial centres were followed by no less than 723 others throughout the country.
In Accra, tourists can visit the centre serving the mothers employed at the Makola Market, which like the centre adjacent to Independence Square, is filled with impeccably clean, happy children who may be occupied by the rehearsal of a play or busily at work on a drawing, when not singing.
The 178 children of the Makola centre as well as the 290 members of the Independence Square facility are taken in charge for 2,000 cedis every four months, plus 250 cedis per week to cover the cost of the two well-balanced daily meals that are served on-site.
Other notable activities of the Ghanaian Women's Movement include specialized farms entirely run by women, as well as the manufacture of a variety of products which are sold in shops created and managed by the movement's members.

*After their parents' long struggle to emerge
from colonialism, Ghana's younger generations
are preparing to continue the effort
to create a modern society and better
living conditions for the entire population.*

index

This index includes the sites, towns, parks and rivers described or mentioned in the text. Those given particular attention are in **bold type**.

GHANAIAN CUISINE

■ *Peanut soup : Use prepared peanut butter, or hulled, crushed roasted peanuts with a little water added. In a heavy frying pan, cook onions, tomatoes and beef or chicken, diced, with a smaller amount of water. When the meat is tender add tomato concentrate, spices, peppers, and the peanuts or peanut butter, and simmer for one hour.*

Fufu : This is made with yams or plantain and manioc, used together or separately. The vegetable is cut into small pieces, cooked, and pureed, with no liquid added, and is shaped into a ball. It is served with a sauce made with meat, fish or crah and containing tomatoes, eggplant, hot peppers and onions, or can be served with palmetto-nut soup.

Palmetto-nut soup : The palmetto nuts are stewed in water, powdered, mixed with cold water, and passed through a sieve to remove the skins. They are then boiled with hot peppers, tomatoes and onions. This soup can be blended with peanut soup.

Kenkey : Corn meal is blended with enough water to form a paste which is allowed to ferment for a day or two. This paste is rolled up in banana leaves that are then tied and cooked in boiling water for two or three hours. Kenkey can be eaten with all kinds of sauces.

The vast beaches of Greater
Accra's coastline are
dotted with the canoes
of the region's
traditional fishermen.

ghana today

translated by j.s. kundra
series editor: jean hureau
photographs: olivier blaise except D.R : pp. 2-3,
p. 59, p. 70 (bottom and left), p. 218 (bottom),
p. 219 (top and bottom) ; guy philippart de foy :
p. 34 (top and bottom left — collection of m. joe appiah), p. 207 (bottom)
layout : laurence moussel

in the same series

countries-regions

- l'algérie (*6th ed.*)
- les antilles (*4th ed.*)
- l'argentine
- l'australie (*4th ed.*)
- le brésil (*4th ed.*)
- la californie
- le cameroun (*5th ed.*)
- le canada (*3rd ed.*)
- capri, naples et pompéi
- le cher en berry (*2nd ed.*)
- la chine (*4th ed.*)
- les comores (*2nd ed.*)
- le congo (*2nd ed.*)
- la corée du sud
- la corse (*7th ed.*)
- la côte d'ivoire (*6th ed.*)
- la crète (*3rd ed.*)
- l'égypte (*7th ed.*)
- l'espagne, les baléares, les canaries (*4th ed.*)
- la finlande
- le gabon (*4th ed.*)
- le ghana (*2nd ed.*)
- la grande-bretagne (*2nd ed.*)
- la grèce (*6th ed.*)
- la guinée-bissau
- la guyane
- la hollande
- l'île de la réunion (*6th ed.*)
- l'île maurice (*4th ed.*)
- l'inde (*2nd ed.*)
- l'indonésie (*4th ed.*)
- l'irlande (*3rd ed.*)
- l'islande, le groenland et les féroé
- le japon (*2nd ed.*)
- le kenya (*4th ed.*)
- la louisiane (*4th ed.*)
- madagascar (*5th ed.*)
- la malaisie
- le mali (*2nd ed.*)
- le maroc (*8th ed.*)
- la mauritanie
- le mexique (*4th ed.*)
- le népal
- le niger (*4th ed.*)
- le portugal, les açores et madère (*5th ed.*)
- rhodes
- la scandinavie, l'islande et le groenland (*4th ed.*)

- le sénégal (*2nd ed.*)
- les seychelles (*3rd ed.*)
- la sicile (*5th ed.*)
- sri lanka (ceylan) (*2nd ed.*)
- la suisse et le liechtenstein (*2nd ed.*)
- la syrie (*3rd ed.*)
- tahiti et toutes ses îles (*2nd ed.*)
- la thaïlande (*2nd ed.*)
- le togo (*3rd ed.*)
- la tunisie (*8th ed.*)
- la yougoslavie (*4th ed.*)
- le zaïre (*3rd ed.*)

cities

- barcelone et la catalogne
- bruxelles, flandres et wallonie
- budapest et la hongrie
- chicago
- florence et la toscane (*2nd ed.*)
- hong kong et singapour
- istanbul et la turquie égéenne (*3rd ed.*)
- jérusalem
- la mecque et médine (*3rd ed.*)
- londres
- lisbonne
- madrid et tolède
- moscou et léningrad (*3rd ed.*)
- new york (*3th ed.*)
- prague
- rome et le vatican (*2nd ed.*)
- séville et l'andalousie
- venise (*4rd ed.*)

in preparation

- amsterdam et la hollande
- copenhague et le danemark
- l'écosse
- la floride
- la guinée équatoriale
- le pakistan
- les philippines
- strasbourg et l'alsace
- prague
- tokyo

LES ÉDITIONS DU
JAGUAR
63, rue d'Auteuil - 75016 Paris
© 1977 - 1st edition - all rights reserved
© **1992 - 2nd édition - all rights reserved**
Printing completed Ist quarter 1992
by Tardy-Quercy - S.A. - Bourges - France - N° 16984
Legal copy deposited Ist quarter 1992
Publisher's n° 1144/2 - ISBN-2-86950-208-7
ISSN 0240-8058